THE
MAGAZINE
WRITER'S
HANDBOOK

Franklynn Peterson and
Judi Kesselman-Turkel

A SPECTRUM BOOK

PRENTICE-HALL, Inc., Englewood Cliffs, N.J. 07632

Library of Congress Cataloging in Publication Data
Peterson, Franklynn.
    The magazine writer's handbook.
    (A Spectrum Book)
    Includes index.
    1. Authorship.   I. Kesselman-Turkel, Judi.
II. Title.
PN147.P467   808'.02   81-21014
ISBN 0-13-543751-2   AACR2
ISBN 0-13-543744-X (pbk.)

This Spectrum Book is available to businesses and organizations
at a special discount when ordered in large quantities. For
information, contact Prentice-Hall, Inc., General Publishing
Division, Special Sales, Englewood Cliffs, N.J. 07632

A SPECTRUM BOOK

10 9 8 7 6 5 4 3 2 1

ISBN 0-13-543751-2

ISBN 0-13-543744-X (PBK.)

Interior design by Linda Huber

Prentice-Hall International, Inc., *London*
Prentice-Hall of Australia Pty. Limited, *Sydney*
Prentice-Hall Canada Inc., *Toronto*
Prentice-Hall of India Private Limited, *New Delhi*
Prentice-Hall of Japan, Inc., *Tokyo*
Prentice-Hall of Southeast Asia Pte. Ltd., *Singapore*
Whitehall Books Limited, *Wellington, New Zealand*
Editora Prentice-Hall do Brasil Ltda., *Rio de Janeiro*

Books by Franklynn Peterson and Judi Kesselman-Turkel

Research Shortcuts (Contemporary Books, 1982)
The Author's Handbook (Prentice-Hall, 1982)
The Magazine Writer's Handbook (Prentice-Hall, 1982)
Study Skills (Contemporary Books, 1981)
Test-taking Strategies (Contemporary Books, 1981)
Homeowner's Book of Lists (Contemporary Books, 1981)
How to Improve Damn Near Everything Around Your Home (Prentice-Hall, 1981)
I Can Use Tools (Elsevier/Nelson, 1981) *illustrated by Tomas Gonzales*
Good Writing (Franklin Watts, 1980)
Vans (Dandelion Press, 1979) illustrated by Paul Frame
Eat Anything Exercise Diet (William Morrow, 1979) *with Dr. Frank Konishi*
Handbook of Snowmobile Maintenance and Repair (Hawthorn, 1979)
The Do-It-Yourself Custom Van Book (Contemporary Books, 1977)

Books by Franklynn Peterson:

Children's Toys You Can Build Yourself (Prentice-Hall, 1978)
How to Fix Damn Near Anything (Prentice-Hall, 1977)
The Build-It-Yourself Furniture Catalog (Prentice-Hall, 1976)
Handbook of Lawn Mower Repair (Emerson, 1973; 2nd edition, Hawthorn, 1978)

Books by Judi R. Kesselman:

Stopping Out (M. Evans, 1976)

CONTENTS

Chapter One

Three Keys to Successful Magazine Writing

L ET'S START BY OFFERING YOU THE SAME DEAL WE make with students in our magazine writing courses:

1. experience life to the fullest and with a child's questioning mind,
2. keep setting your discoveries down on paper, and
3. do it with the professionalism we're going to teach you, and we'll turn you into magazine writers able to sell your articles to national magazines.

We're not promising you'll make your living writing for magazines. By latest estimates, there are only a few hundred successful full-time free-lance magazine writers and a few thousand others who regularly sell articles part time. But if your goal is to see your name in print, make some money, or share your point of view or wisdom with thousands of readers, your drive and our direction will get you close to that elusive brass ring.

1·1 A Love Affair with Life

The first ingredient you'll need to succeed is zest. Of the several hundred successful magazine writers we know, not one goes through a day without noticing something new or looking at something in a new way. Every one of them is constantly asking "Why?" and "How?" and "What next?"

We're just like the rest. Even though we've already jotted down enough story ideas to keep us busy the rest of our lives, we leap from our typewriters at the first sniff of something new or untried. We've traveled through nearly all of the fifty states and into foreign countries just to see what's there. We've been down in coal mines, up in hot-air balloons and open-cockpit biplanes, in jail, and on TV. We've questioned Nobel laureates and con artists, movie stars and Bowery bums, then raced home to fix our experiences on to paper.

But zest involves more than just physical activity. Most writers are *intellectual* activists. They keep coming up with ideas for doing

1

things differently or enjoying a better life. We've experienced the thrill of believing in something, writing about it, and watching it improve —just a little—the quality of other people's lives. Our articles have helped integrate hospitals in Sunflower County, Mississippi. They've helped save a progressive screening program for North Carolina preschoolers. They've helped find decent housing for the mother of a Vietnam War casualty. They've alerted women and social agencies to a new way of prosecuting rape cases.

Approach life not as an observer, but as a wide-eyed participant, and you'll have grabbed hold of the first key to successful magazine writing.

1·2 Time at the Typewriter

A young cousin of ours backpacked through all the countries of Europe, keeping track of her adventures in her diary, and her family called her a hippie. A friend backpacked through all of Europe, selling articles about his adventures, and *his* family introduced him as a magazine writer. He had found the second key to success—the discipline to sit for hours pounding words out of an unyielding typewriter. It's the same key we'd found early in our own careers.

The two of us combine over three decades of making our living as professional magazine writers. Over the years, we've sold several hundred articles to magazines of all sizes and just about all interests: *Family Circle, Woman's Day, McCall's, House Beautiful, Playgirl, Popular Science, Popular Mechanics, Seventeen, Writer's Digest, Science Digest, Elks, Sepia, Yankee, Family Health, Family Handyman, New York, Chicago, Pageant, Money, Physician's Management, Hospitals,* and many, many more. In addition, we've written fifteen books for adults and two for children. Three times in our careers we've been given coveted national awards for our hard work: the Brotherhood in Media Award from the National Conference of Christians and Jews, the Journalism Award from the American Optometric Association, and the Jesse H. Neal Editorial Achievement Award from the American Business Press Association. We didn't start out skilled with words, but after all these years at our typewriters, there are few writing problems we can't solve.

Since the early 1970s, we've been taking time off from our typewriters to make students just like you work hard in writing classes in New York and Wisconsin. In weekly lectures, we've told them everything we know about magazine writing, just as we'll be telling you here. But we've also impressed on them, as we will on you, that they would succeed at writing only if they went home and wrote and wrote and wrote. . . .

One of our magazine-writing classes at the University of Wisconsin started out with forty-two adult students, all eager to see their work in magazines. After they heard that we demanded an article and a query letter from them every week, half dropped out. Barely twenty students made it to every class, and only twelve did most of the assigned writing tasks. But *every one* of those twelve sold an article to a national publication, and two now work full time at magazine writing. They're not solid pros yet, but they're on their way.

Holding a daily one-way conversation with a typewriter might be fun for people who don't like other people. But writers are generally among the most gregarious folks on earth. We're no exceptions. For the reinforcement, as well as intellectual and professional stimulation, we get best from other writers, we stay active in as many writers' organizations as time and energy allow, especially the American Society of Journalists and Authors, a national group of pros that is more than thirty years old. The ASJA members and meetings are drawn on abundantly throughout this book.

Every year we participate in as many different writers' conferences as possible, for a chance to meet fledgling writers from other parts of the country. We figure it's part of the dues we owe the people who worked hard teaching us when *we* were beginners. We're not the only ones who recognize a debt. Fellow ASJA member Alex Haley said at one of our meetings that he might not have persevered in writing *Roots* had it not been for advice and encouragement from ASJA writers who'd already made it.

Then Alex told us that he hadn't met a single young, aspiring writer who "really was prepared to work five, eight, ten years to achieve this; most of them seem to have the impression that it's something quick—maybe six months or two years. Now the hard, realistic fact is that it is at least as difficult to become a writer as it is to become a surgeon. Hardly anyone who is successful at writing has come to be so without at least a decade of hard, hard work . . . the rejection slips, the psychic put-downs, and all the rest of it."

If your goal lies short of becoming another Alex Haley, you may not need a decade of preparation. But to succeed at magazine writing, you will need to log *hundreds* of hours at your typewriter. There's just no other way.

1·3 A Professional Outlook

Many people who haven't yet made it into the inner circle of professional writers are embarrassed to think of demanding dollars in exchange for words. For those people, we'd like to engrave—on placards to be nailed forever above their desks—the following words from a pro:

No man but a blockhead ever wrote
except for money.
—SAMUEL JOHNSON

Writing is the endeavor we like best. Not having Rockefellers for fathers or brain surgeons for spouses, we're obliged to earn a living from what we write. Fortunately, we live in a time when that's not only possible, but an entirely respected pursuit.

In sports, if you're not paid for what you do, you're dubbed an amateur—no matter how long you've been playing or how good you are. The same holds true for writing. Professional writers are not paid *enough* for what they contribute to the commercial successes of the publishers they write for, a fact we'll say more about later. But they are *paid,* and should be. Begin to demand payment for your words, and you'll have unlocked a very important door on your way to developing professionalism.

A mature gentleman who took one of our writing courses had been publishing for years. His scrapbook was bulging with his letters to the editor, but he'd never collected a penny for any of his writing. We taught him how to package his prose like a pro, and by the fourth session he proudly showed the class his first fifty-dollar check. He was finally on his way to learning what all pros learn early in their careers: it takes nearly as much time and energy to research and write for free or for low-paying magazines as for higher-paying ones. And it's more rewarding, too, to see your by-line in higher-paying, bigger-circulation magazines.

The way to reach the better-paying magazines is by studying them just as thoroughly as a farmer studies the food market before he decides which crops to plant. That's why the first thing we're going to teach you, even before we ask you to write a word, is a thorough understanding of your marketplace.

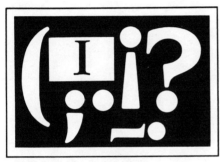

The Magazine
as Marketplace

Chapter Two

What a Magazine *Really* Is

N OW EDITOR-IN-CHIEF OF *POPULAR SCIENCE*, C.P.
(Ken) Gilmore recalls that as a free-lancing magazine writer, he
wanted to break into *Reader's Digest*. "So I spent two weeks studying
a year's worth of that magazine. By the time I was finished, I knew its
approach to ideas, subjects it liked and didn't like, how it handled
quotes and anecdotes. . . ." And Ken sold to *Reader's Digest* with his
first query letter—not only because he had a great idea (the tantalizing
variety of programs that innovative FM radio stations were starting to
introduce back in 1959), but because he knew that an idea is great only
if it's sent to the right *market*.

It's this acceptance of the magazine world as a marketplace that
separates the pros from the hopefuls who simply choose something they
know about, put their knowledge on paper, send it off to a magazine
they admire, and wait for the big check to arrive. A pro chooses from
two marketing methods:

1. He *studies* a magazine he'd like to write for, *searches* for ideas that are
   likely to appeal to the magazine's editors, *sells* the best idea via a
   query letter, *researches* the assigned article's contents, and only then
   sits down to *write* the article.
2. Or else he *develops* an idea that he feels confident will appeal to
   particular magazines, *pinpoints* exactly which magazines are likely
   buyers, *sells* the idea, *researches* the assigned article, and then *writes*.

Some would-be writers do know that magazines must be studied.
But they've never been told *what* to study, so they look for all the
wrong things. One of our students spent dozens of hours analyzing
magazine markets she wanted to crack. She read fastidiously through
Cosmopolitan, Redbook, McCall's, Ladies' Home Journal—all the big
women's magazines. When she was finished, she could tell us how long
the average article was, whether the magazine preferred long or short
sentences, how many articles it ran each month, and which numbers
were shown in figures rather than spelled out. She went so far as to
count how many cooking features ran in each issue, since she hoped to
sell her favorite recipes for a start.

Trouble is, she did all the wrong homework. (1) Details like
article length are generally covered in editors' assignment letters to

writers. (2) Questions of style for things such as numbers are the copyeditor's responsibility. Writers are not expected to know every magazine's style intimately. (3) The big women's magazines she studied almost never run recipes from nonstaff writers—and she could have discovered that easily if she'd known how.

The first major mistake we see would-be writers make is to turn every idea into an article and try to sell that, when they should sell an idea first and *then* write it up. Their next big mistake is to send a potentially great idea to the *wrong* magazine. To correct that, we're going to devote this entire section to teaching you how to study a magazine the way a professional writer does.

This chapter will explain how to tell one magazine from another and how to find out who its many editors are and what they do. Next you'll learn what to look for when you read a magazine. And Chapter 4 will assist you in picking markets for yourself.

Throughout this entire book we ask you to keep in mind that writing is an art: it requires a personal touch. We can share examples of techniques and conclusions that have worked for us as well as for our students and professional friends. But it's important for you to try them just as a jumping-off point. To etch your name in the roster of pros, you're going to have to develop your own techniques and your own style.

2·1 Consumer Publications

Of the four kinds of magazines, these are the best known. They're in business to sell advertising space to manufacturers who want to reach the *consumers* of their products. It is extremely important for the would-be pro to keep in mind that the hefty $2.50 cover price of a magazine like *Playboy* doesn't cover the cost of paper, ink, printing, staff salaries, and checks to free-lance magazine writers. The forty thousand dollars and more per page such magazines charge advertisers pays most of the bills.

We break down consumer magazines into several useful subcategories based on general editorial format:

GENERAL INTEREST
These magazines reach wide audiences with articles of fairly universal appeal. Their circulations generally number up in the millions. We lump into this category even most of the weekly tabloid-format newspapers such as *National Enquirer* and *Grit*.

Reader's Digest is still America's preeminent general interest magazine. Its U.S. edition alone has a circulation of 18 million. A typical issue's topics range from sex ("Straight Talk About the

Living-Together Arrangement") to the occult ("Rescue from a Fanatic Cult"), from politics ("China Behind the Guided Tour") to personalities ("Ray Bolger: Leprechaun of the Light Fantastic"), from the light ("André the Sociable Seal") to the weighty ("Needed—Tax Reform to Create Jobs"). On the surface, these articles seem to have nothing in common. But Ken Gilmore was able to make some generalizations about them. With careful study, along with the advice you read in this section, you can too.

Woman's Day is another general interest magazine, despite its mostly female readership. A typical issue includes not just recipe, decoration, and housekeeping articles but budget tips, pet news, even automobile advice. Magazines that attempt to attract *all* women or *all* men (such as *Playboy* and *Esquire*) must be classed, from a writer's viewpoint, as magazines of general interest. Personality magazines such as *People* and *TV Guide* belong here too.

SPECIAL INTEREST

What separates these magazines from the ones above is that, rather than appealing to many kinds of advertisers, they've zeroed in on a narrow range of special advertisers and, to attract those advertisers, have promised to appeal to consumers of their products. Therefore, they stay within rather narrow editorial guidelines.

Generally these magazines cater to their readers' *avocational* passions: *Field & Stream* to hunters and fishers, *Ski* to active or armchair skiers, *Sports Illustrated* to spectator sports fans, *Antique Monthly* to collectors (and their suppliers), *Audio Magazine* to hi-fi fanatics. In recent years, the number of general interest magazines has declined, while special interest magazines have proliferated dramatically.

Don't forget that practically every idea that appeals to readers (and editors) of general interest publications can be adapted to the narrower confines of special interest magazines. While general interest magazines aimed at women often feature cooking and recipes, why shouldn't *Field & Stream* be interested in how to fillet and fry trout afield, or *Ski* readers be warmed by how to use an insulated backpack to serve up a hot lunch during an all-day ski trip?

REGIONALS

Regional magazines are general interest publications for readers who live in a particular area of the country. Most major cities have their own regionals: *New York, Chicago, Boston, Indianapolis, Philadelphia, St. Louisan, Orlando-Land* . . . Broader regionals are: *Colorado, Arizona Highways, Adirondack Life, Wisconsin Trails, New West*. The number of regionals has grown geometrically in the past decade and shows no signs of tapering off.

To write successfully for a regional, you can choose practically any broad topic you'd see in a general interest magazine, but the article must apply specifically to the region for which it is written. For example, an article for *Wisconsin Regional* might have a regional *slant* (how the Wisconsin-based Oscar Mayer plant makes salami) or use regional *authorities* (the president of Oscar Mayer tells how to buy good salami) or use regional *statistics, anecdotes,* and *examples.*

Many large newspapers publish their own Sunday magazines, while others distribute *Parade* or *Family Weekly,* which are nationally published general interest newspaper supplements. These local newspaper magazines fit neatly into our regional magazine category. They include *New England* in the *Boston Globe, Empire* in the *Denver Post,* and *Star* in the *Indianapolis Star.* Since they're published weekly instead of monthly, they are attractive markets for free-lance writers with timely stories to tell.

COMMENTARY

Harper's and *The Atlantic* are two of the better-known magazines devoted almost exclusively to articles of opinion. At times the opinion is bolstered by solid mountains of fact, albeit carefully sifted. At other times the emphasis is on the rhetoric, and authoritativeness is stressed less than clever construction or reconstruction of analyses of facts. In either case, the viewpoint of the magazine determines whose opinions on what subjects it purchases.

Every magazine in this category does have a definable viewpoint. The magazines cited above sit politically just above the center, and seesaw a bit to the midright and sort-of-left. *The Progressive, The Nation,* and *The New Republic* report on the near-left, while *Mother Jones* oversees issues further left. *American Opinion* and *National Review* are on the solid right. Not all magazines of commentary are politically motivated. *Present Tense,* for example, is subtitled "The Magazine of World Jewish Affairs." *New Scientist* and *Fusion* are magazines of commentary on science, and pay just as poorly as most of the other opinion magazines.

2·2 Trade, Technical, and Professional Magazines

Many courses in magazine writing still overlook or down-rate this broad, very large, and important group of publications because most of them used to pay writers so poorly. Many still do, but times have changed within this second large category of magazines.

Some magazines for people in businesses or professions are big-time operations. *Men's Wear* has a circulation of close to 30,000 retail store managers. *Drug Topics* is read by more than 70,000 drugstore executives. *Medical Economics* mails to almost 175,000, as does *Juris Doctor: Magazine for the New Lawyer.* Advertisers pay, often handsomely, to appear in these magazines. And to guarantee steady readership for their ads, publishers must rely on professional writers who demand professional rates.

Writers researching markets must keep in mind two major distinctions between trade and consumer magazines:

1. Consumer publications generally concentrate on *pastime* interests of readers, while trades concentrate on their occupations.
2. Although you'll find a great many consumer magazines on local newsstands, you're not likely to find trade publications there.

The trades are sold almost exclusively by subscription. Fortunately, many public libraries subscribe to a generous selection of trades, so you may be able to research this lucrative market category at the library near you. College and junior college libraries are also good places to look for them. If you can't find a particular trade publication locally, write to its editor and ask for a sample copy or two.

2·3 House Organs

Exxon, Ford, DuPont, and many other major corporations put up the money for publishing this third category of magazines, aimed at employees, stockholders, customers, or the general public. Many are handsome—well written, beautifully illustrated, and creatively designed. Some are influential in charting the political, social, or economic course of the country.

A house organ doesn't accept advertising from other companies. The entire magazine is a form of low-key advertising to impress, as well as to inform, its readers. Its editors may have a sizable budget with which to recruit top free-lance writers. To give you some idea of the scope of interest of the classier, higher-paying house organs, we've reproduced the editorial requirements recently sent to an aspiring writer by *Exxon USA.*

You won't find house organs at newsstands. Libraries generally have only spotty collections of them. But knowing this, house organ editors usually cooperate with writers who request free sample copies.

2·4 Little and Literary Magazines

Often self-appointed guardians of our literary heritage, the editors of these journal-like publications devoted to short stories, satire, essays, poetry, humor, and belles lettres make up in enthusiasm what they lack in budget. Mostly they are sponsored by foundations or institutions of learning. They are "little," generally, in two respects: their

Ill. 2.1

WRITING FOR EXXON USA

Exxon USA is an advocacy journal published four times a year by
the Public Affairs Department of Exxon Company, U.S.A., a division of Exxon Corporation. Exxon supplies fuels and petroleum-
related products to wholesale and retail markets. Exxon USA is
a medium through which the company communicates to the American
public on matters of mutual concern. Prior to the company's name
change in 1972, the magazine was published as The Humble Way.
Exxon USA is distributed to employees and annuitants, but its
primary audience is one of thought leaders throughout the United
States. It is not distributed abroad. The magazine is sent on
request without charge.

Subject matter for Exxon USA is derived from three principal
areas. All are related to Exxon's public affairs interests and
concerns. Some articles explore contemporary issues affecting
the company. Examples: environmental conservation, national
energy policy, or business economics. Others originate in the
company's support of, or work in, cultural, social, or educational affairs. Examples: Opportunities for minorities, public
television programs, or higher education. A third source stems
from the company's need to establish friendly relations with
specific audiences with which the company may be directly involved. Examples: residents of states where Exxon's activities
are concentrated, ethnic or racial groups whose interests are
affected by the company's policies or actions, or organizations
working in areas of mutual interest.

Stories must have fairly strong company tie-in, or fall within an
area of specific public affairs concern. Queries are advised.

Exxon USA does not sell products. Editorial coverage is restrict-
ed to the United States. It does not publish articles of general interest, or travel articles where specific company involvement and concern cannot be demonstrated. It does not publish
poetry, cartoons, fillers, short items, current events, announce-
ments or straight news.

As the magazine is circulated to people who know little about
Exxon and the oil industry, and have no special interest in
either, the magazine strives for literary quality and readability.
An article should be a pleasure to read, as well as informative
and pertinent.

Preferred length is 2,000 to 2,500 words. Payment on acceptance
of a first article is $750; for subsequent acceptances, $1,000.
Exxon USA will pay expenses incurred on assignment. Exxon USA
buys all rights to an article, including the right to use it in
other corporate publications, and the right to grant reprint permission to other corporate or commercial periodicals outside the
company.

Downs Matthews, Editor   Otto W. Glade, Coordinator
Exxon Company, U.S.A.   Exxon Company, U.S.A.
P. O. Box 2180   P. O. Box 2180
Houston, Texas 77001   Houston, Texas 77001
A/C 713/656-5828   A/C 713/656-2749

Editorial requirements for *Exxon USA*.

short-page formats and the smallness of their circulations. Payment to writers is little, too, often meted out in copies of the issues in which the authors' cherished works appear.

The majority of literary magazines concentrate on fiction and poetry and are, therefore, beyond the scope of this book. Many, however, welcome essays, literary criticism, personal experience of an intellectual nature (such as having discovered a new way of interpreting Joyce's *Ulysses*), as well as sharp reporting about trends or events of current or historical interest.

Some, such as *Antioch Review* and *The American Scholar,* have been around for many years and pay modest honorariums to writers. Others in this category suffer distressingly short lifespans.

Closely akin to literary magazines are the scholarly journals such as *American Sociological Review, American Psychological Review, Sewanee Review,* and *New England Journal of Medicine.* Not markets for free-lance writers, they take contributions only from recognized scholars in their fields. The scholars, in fact, often have to *pay* production costs to get their articles into print. Frequently the only way to find out for sure what a publication's policy is, is to study its printed statement on editorial requirements.

One of our students spent several dollars on postage to learn one very important lesson about the little magazines. He'd sent some of his articles to high-paying mass circulation magazines, and they'd been promptly rejected because his ideas and his writing both needed lots of work. He'd sent off the same material to lesser-paying markets, and they too had shipped it back. Figuring, "Well, I won't get paid, but I will get my name in print," he sent his pieces to what he thought was the bottom of the barrel—the literary magazines. Not only was his work returned, but one editor scrawled a note saying, "Try again when you've learned how to write."

The lesson Jerry finally learned: never gauge editorial *quality* by editorial *budget.* Study the magazines!

2·5   Magazines Are Periodical

When you study magazines as markets, their periodical nature is an important aspect to keep in mind. Monthly magazines are the norm: *Popular Mechanics, Field & Stream, National Geographic,* and *Popular Photography* are familiar examples. We'll devote a major portion of this book to teaching you how to write for and sell to the monthlies.

Some magazines such as *National Enquirer,* and all the Sunday newspaper supplements, come out weekly. Their article requirements, in terms of writing technique and format, are little different from those of the monthlies. But editors of those publications have to have on hand four times as many articles as comparably sized monthlies. This means that, all else being equal, your chances of selling to a weekly periodical may be four times greater than your chances at a monthly. Also, a weekly editor can rush a timely idea into print four times faster than a colleague editing a monthly, which is important to bear in mind when you're marketing ideas that may become outdated quickly.

A few magazines are fortnightly now: *National Review* and *Fortune,* for example. Some former monthlies have added so many extra issues they too may eventually publish every two weeks. *Family Circle* and *Woman's Day* were on a standard monthly schedule in the early 1970s. But by the mid-1970s their advertising space was so much in demand they each added a thirteenth "monthly" issue. By the late 1970s, they were up to eighteen issues a year and still climbing. On the other hand, many house organs and literary magazines appear only quarterly.

A few magazines, catering to devotees of seasonal activities, publish on a seasonal schedule. Most publications in the field of snowmobiling, for example, come out only during winter months. *Snowmobile Week* publishes seventeen issues between September and March, and *SnoTrack* six issues between September and April.

There are even a few annuals that qualify as magazine writers' markets. The 13-30 Corporation, for example, publishes a number of titles distributed once a year to high school and college students. Titles include *Sourcebook, On Your Own,* and *Nutshell.*

Aside from the two aspects of periodicity that we've already covered here—the handling of fast-breaking stories and the overall number of stories editors are in the market for each year—*timing your submissions* depends on knowing in advance what various editors' publication calendars look like. You can make an intelligent guess based on publication frequency. As a rough rule of thumb, assume that editors are lining up stories that will appear six issues away. The editor of a weekly magazine is most likely receiving stories for issues six weeks from now, whereas the editor of a monthly is probably finalizing story ideas for issues half a year away.

If you submit a New Year's resolution story to a monthly magazine during January, you're probably either half a year late or half a year early. Most editors are much too busy to seriously consider stories or story ideas they won't be able to use for six or nine months. Besides, few editors' budgets permit them to buy stories so far in advance.

We try to suggest seasonal material to monthly editors about eight months in advance, and almost never send ideas for seasons closer than five or six months away. We hit editors of most weeklies eight to ten weeks in advance of a forthcoming event. And if a magazine doesn't publish in May, we don't suggest stories that depend on May Day,

Mother's Day, Armed Forces Day, Memorial Day, or Victoria Day in Canada. If a magazine is a quarterly or an annual, we know it probably isn't interested in seasonal material at all. That's how *we* work; you'll have to figure out what works best for *you*.

2·6 How Magazine Staffs Are Organized

One of the saddest faces we've ever seen was on Susan R., a young student who learned the hard way what magazine organization is all about. She'd had a truly great idea for an article for one of the larger general interest magazines. Not knowing who to send it to, she'd checked the magazine's *masthead*—the organizational listing found somewhere in every issue of most magazines. Seeing a name listed as contributing editor, Susan assumed that her idea for a contribution to the magazine ought to go to that person. Months passed, and she got no reply. Then one day she saw her idea written up in the magazine, by-lined by the contributing editor. "She stole my idea," Susan told us the first day of class.

Some questioning led us to a different conclusion. Susan hadn't made it clear in her letter that *she herself* expected to write the article based on her idea. And the contributing editor, being little more than a steady free-lance writer for the magazine, assumed that Susan was offering the idea to her as a gift. When we explained what contributing editors do—and don't do—Susan nearly cried at her innocent mistake. Her example is just one reason why you have to not only study the masthead, but know *how* to study it.

There are generally two sides to magazine organization. Purely business aspects are the responsibility of a publisher and her staff. This includes buying paper, choosing a printer, hiring typesetters, soliciting advertisements, selling subscriptions, distributing to newsstands, determining how much can be spent—all those details that keep a magazine from going broke.

All the nonadvertising content of the magazine is in the hands of editors. They decide on the free-lance articles they want to run, when to run them, and where to lay them out in the magazine. They order photos and artwork to illustrate articles, create titles for them, write catchy subtitles or "blurbs," design the cover (often in collaboration with an art director), and handle similar jobs that keep most editors at their desks for fifty or sixty hours a week. In addition, some magazine editors also write one or more articles for each issue. We've both been magazine editors and can attest that most are harried, hassled, and constantly battling deadlines.

At small magazines, there's just one editor and maybe a secretary or assistant. The large-circulation magazines have entire family trees of editors. Titles and duties vary according to tradition and whimsy. As Susan discovered on her own, the names and titles of major staff members are listed on a masthead, almost always on a page near the front of every issue. In order to publish nearly 200 pages every four weeks or so, *Family Circle,* for example, employs dozens of editors organized into very specific departments. If you can decipher that magazine's editorial maze, you'll be prepared for any you might encounter elsewhere.

At the very top of *Family Circle*'s masthead is Arthur Hettich, editor. On some other magazine he might be called editor in chief. Hettich is ultimately responsible for the magazine's entire editorial content. And along with that responsibility, he has the final power over what articles are assigned, which ones run, and what the writers are paid—although he has to follow the publisher's guidelines as to total expenses for the year or for each issue. He also comes up with ideas for articles—though Hettich delegates a great many of his responsibilities. Hettich has delegated executive editors Lawrence L. Kane and Myrna Blyth to watch over the execution of the service features and general articles. Most magazines don't have executive editors. The editor (or editor in chief) has to cope with administrative matters single-handedly.

A great many magazines do have managing editors, a spot filled at *Family Circle* by Aaron Schindler. Briefly, the managing editor does whatever the editor assigns to him, which at *Family Circle* is to oversee the deadlines and other day-to-day technical functions of the entire editorial department. Typical functions of other magazines' managing editors include organizing the story ideas that will be discussed at editorial meetings, taking charge of all manuscripts ready to be published, acting as liaison with typesetters and printers, directing letters and queries to the proper editor.

At *Family Circle,* the next lower organizational echelon assumes responsibility for smooth issue-by-issue functioning of each department. Food and equipment features, for example, are devised, often written, and edited by Jean Hewitt and her staff, health features by Maxine Lewis, beauty features by Barbara Winkler. All of the general nonfiction is assigned, with Hettich's okay, by articles editor Kathy Fury as well as by the two senior editors whose names appear alongside hers. At other magazines, senior editors lend a hand with editing and write "in-house," or staff-prepared, articles. (Other staff members may write too. Ms. Fury occasionally has a by-lined article in *Family Circle.*) At many magazines, staff written articles don't carry a by-line.

Another shadowy but vital staff position is that of editorial assistant. *Family Circle* employs a dozen of them, listed on the masthead as editorial associates. In the publishing industry, this entry-level position encompasses chores such as typing, proofreading, and acting as gofer. Many editorial assistants, in between handling other responsibilities, act as secretary to someone higher up on the editorial ladder, and it's in that capacity that most free-lancers encounter them.

Other titles on the mastheads at *Family Circle* and elsewhere are self-explanatory, except for editor-at-large and contributing editor. They're so similar we can lump the two. Technically, neither is on the magazine's staff. People with these titles have negotiated formal or informal contracts that call, as a rule, for them to write a certain number of articles per year. The magazine may write certain restrictions into such contracts. Judith Ramsey, one of *Family Circle's* editors-at-large, told us that her contract permits her to write for anyone else but the competition, *Woman's Day*. Like most people who land such a deal, Judith became editor-at-large after chalking up a long string of successful free-lanced articles for *Family Circle*. Unlike most contributing editors, however, Judith also buys ideas or manuscripts from other writers.

What about the many, many magazines whose mastheads display only an editor, an assistant editor, and perhaps an editorial assistant? The editor then has to divide up *all* the work among the three of them. When you see such a short masthead in a hefty magazine, you can be sure that the editors have little time for in-house writing and rewriting. If you write well and have good ideas, you'll be very much in demand there—but be forewarned that the publisher's editorial budget for free-lancers is probably as chintzy as his budget for in-house staff.

It's paradoxes like this which help make free-lancing the challenge that it is.

Chapter Three

How to Study Magazines as Markets

BACK IN OUR EARLY DAYS AS MAGAZINE WRITERS, some of our editors used to tell us, "You've gotta write for that Milwaukee beer truck driver," or "You've gotta write for that Milwaukee beer truck driver's wife." In those good old days, many editors decided who their readers were by the reader mail that rolled in. These days, editors refer with the same degree of passion to the *demographics* they get from computerized readership surveys.

3·1 Demographics: Who "The Reader" Is

When Jim Morgan was editor of TWA *Ambassador,* we asked him who read the magazine. He replied, "We are aimed at the traveling executive and professional person, who represents about 80 percent of our audience: 64 percent are men, 71 percent are between the ages of 18 and 49, 46 percent are college grads, and 43.5 percent have household incomes of $25,000 a year or better." What was the importance of all of those numbers? "You can tell what kind of people those are. You can extrapolate what kind of stories might interest them."

Sitting right next to Jim Morgan at the time was the executive editor of *Kiwanis Magazine,* David Williams. He echoed how important it is for writers to study a magazine's demographics. "The best reader response we've gotten in a long time was with an article called 'Simple Secrets of a Better Lawn.' " Williams explained that 82 percent of his readers own homes—and the grass that goes with them—so "just a simple thing like how high do you set the lawnmower blades can fascinate our readers." You can be sure Dave Williams wants to hear more from the writer who so cleverly dreamed up the article idea that fit into so many of his readers' front yards.

All editors want to buy articles that will appeal to their readers. And they will remember your name too once you've learned the three steps in using demographics:

1. identify the type of reader a magazine aims at;

2. select types of ideas that appeal to that reader;
3. suggest selected ideas to the editor.

Only then, with few exceptions, should you start to write your magazine article.

There are reference books that tell a little about magazines and their demographics. (The last part of this chapter will introduce you to many of them.) But after using reference books, you'll still have to decide what kinds of articles each magazine editor believes his particular readers want to read. To tell what the *editor himself* has concluded from his demographics, study issues of the magazine. As people become top-notch magazine writers, they become top-notch magazine readers and analyzers. You'll go further faster if you learn how to read a magazine right now.

3·2 Creative Content Analysis: Cover Lines

Before you even flip open the magazine, carefully read the cover. Cover lines are an editor's best friend. They *sell* the magazine to newsstand browsers; they make subscribers pick up the magazine before snapping on the TV. That's why the editor features the best articles on the cover and pays more for stories that suggest terse, eye-catching cover lines. Editors tell us repeatedly that they're looking *most of all* for ideas that can be cover-lined.

Cover lines tell a clever writer exactly what ideas an editor thinks appeal most to his readers—what ideas he's most in the market for. If you looked at the cover of *Redbook* for July 1979, could you quickly pick out ten things its editors believed about the magazine and its buyers when they planned the cover? These were the features and tag-lines that caught our eye:

1. "The magazine for young women" told us that *Redbook* aims at young females, or at least at readers who *consider* themselves young or want to read what the young women are reading these days. (It doesn't tell us *Redbook's* exact definition of "young.")
2. "The Happiness Report" clued us that upbeat ideas may have been in demand at the time. Magazines tend to vacillate between a preference for happy titles like this one and gloomy titles ("Beware this . . ." and "The horrors of that . . ."). Sharp writers stay up to date on which mood is preferred.
3. "Gail Sheehy tells how 52,000 women feel about life, work and love." This *tag line* to "The happiness report" showed us that *Redbook* editors must have believed: 1) their readers were among the millions of women who read *Passages* and wanted to read something

else by Gail Sheehy; and 2) their readers wanted to know how other women thought—the more women the better. "Life, work and love," we conclude, was the editors' picturesque way of saying "everything."

4. "30 Fantastic Make-Overs" showed that one of *Redbook*'s mainstays is beauty material, also that editors here considered thirty a goodly number of tips. (On the other hand, using techniques you learned at the end of Chapter 2 you would find that most of it is staff-written.)

5. ". . . tips *you* can use." The rest of the make-over tips line alerted a pro that the editors thought it important to aim advice at a very practical level, at things their average reader felt capable of doing.

6. "How to deal with a whining child" told us that *Redbook* editors knew that many of the young women in their readership had young children. The "how to . . ." lead-in confirmed our comments in number five above.

7. More "How to deal with a whining child." The really careful writer would get a second message from studying this cover line. If he checked inside, he'd have found that it was one installment of Dr. Benjamin Spock's long-running monthly column. We concluded that the editors believed their readers were so interested in *practical* child-raising advice they didn't care who was giving it. It could have been your neighborhood pediatrician as long as his advice was authoritative and practical.

8. "Mary Gordon: the friendship of women." Although Mary Gordon's first novel was superb, it didn't float her into superstardom. Editors here must have been more intrigued by the *subject* of Gordon's essay.

9. "Ella Leffland's new novel." Although the editors left off Dr. Spock's name, they featured both Mary Gordon's and Ella Leffland's, no doubt because they're women. If you turned to the story that goes with our next annotated cover line, you'd find that it was written by psychologist Carol Tavris.

10. "A psychologist talks to Sylvester Stallone" alerted us that *Redbook* was still pitching psychology. These fads come and go. One year every topic seems to need a psychological approach; another year it's health—fitness, health foods, healthy minds, even healthy relationships.

3·3 Creative Content Analysis: Stories Already in Print

Writers seldom have direct access to an editor who can tell them what the magazine's looking for. Instead, we've learned to read the published articles to find out that information. We remember Bob

Bahr, a top writer from Philadelphia, saying, "Skim the best-seller list and you'll find that the top ten are all based on ideas that came along at just the right time." That applies to magazine articles too. But with magazines, your sale also depends on how you approach the idea.

During 1979, country singer Dolly Parton was an idea whose time had really come. In June of that year, three magazines arrived in our mailbox that had Dolly Parton cover lines: *Ms., The Country Gentleman,* and *Writer's Digest.* The writers of those three pieces (we, like all pros, use *article, piece, story,* interchangeably) must have carefully read past issues of the magazine they'd each queried with the idea of writing about Dolly, because their approaches were as different as the magazines' readerships. There was very little overlapping information in the three Parton pieces.

Margo Jefferson's standard-length article in *Ms.* was titled (most likely by the editors) "Dolly Parton: Bewigged, Bespangled . . . and Proud" and subtitled "I think of Dolly as a genial, playful female impersonator. . . ." Its focus was the exploitation of Dolly's female-ness, a *Ms.* kind of topic, and was written in the first person—a common *Ms.* style.

The title and subtitle for Alanna Nash's standard-length article in *The Country Gentleman* played up the sexual jokes about Parton's parts that Margo Jefferson castigated in *Ms.*: "By Golly, It's Miss Dolly! Great Balls of Fire—Here She Comes Again, Looking Better Than a Body Has a Right To." Ms. Nash stuck to the third person and kept herself out of the article.

For the Writer's Digest article, Alanna Nash was again the author. The editor's title, "Goodbye, Dolly!" was followed by a long subtitle that let the reader know the author had written an unautho-rized biography of Dolly. This very long article was in the first person when Ms. Nash talked about researching and writing her book, and in the second person when she offered advice to other authors of unauthorized bios.

These three Parton articles exemplify just a few of the insights you can gain by careful article analysis:

LENGTH

Most editors use two kinds of articles. The first, called *standard length* or *feature length,* can vary from about 1,000 to 6,000 words, depending on the publication. The shorter kind is called a *one-pager, two-pager, short, quickie,* or sometimes even a *filler.* Length is often an indication of how much *depth* the editor expects readers to want on the subject, although in the *Writer's Digest* Parton piece, it signified how much detail Alanna Nash was able to include. As a writer in search of assignments, you needn't worry much about length since the editor will generally indicate expected length in your letter of assignment.

FIRST PERSON, SECOND PERSON, OR THIRD PERSON?

In *Writer's Digest,* Alanna Nash started in the first person. That's what editors there like. But when she got into giving advice, the article switched into the second person: ". . . read everything that's ever been written about your subject . . ." and "Don't be afraid to ask other reporters to do a bit of interviewing for you. . . ." The same writer's piece in *The Country Gentleman* was entirely third person, which is the way they like it unless the article is by-lined by a celebrity or the "expert" giving advice in the story. We know that Ms. Jefferson's use of the first person tells us that her personal assessment of the Parton phenomenon was endorsed by *Ms.* editors. That tells us a lot about the editors' likes and dislikes at *Ms.*

By watching for the voice in magazine articles—first, second, third person—you too can gain valuable insight into what approaches the editors like, and into their readers' biases—which become their own biases as editors.

FOCUS AND SLANT

We will explain all the differences between these two terms in Chapter 7. For now, let's just say that *focus* is the objective aspect of a topic that interests an editor and his readers, and *slant* is the subjective approach they take to that topic. An example is the question of Parton's sex appeal (focus) handled unabashedly (slant) by *The Country Gentleman* and a bit disapprovingly (slant) by *Ms.* Focus and slant reveal as much as cover lines do about what the editors perceive their readers to be like. For example, in the same issues of the three magazines we've been studying so far, *Writer's Digest* did one piece on the joys (slant) of turning lawyer's jargon into English (topic). *Ms.* took a scathing look (slant) at the right-wing (slant) girls (slant) meddling (slant) in the women's movement (topic). *The Country Gentleman* ran a politically conservative (slant) piece entitled "Are Your Property Taxes [topic] Too High? [slant]"

3·4 Creative Content Analysis: Ads

In the same three magazine issues studied above, creative reader analysis takes us beyond the covers and articles, to the ads. In many cases the ads give a faster, more graphic picture of a magazine's readers than article content does. *The Country Gentleman,* for instance, has a back-cover ad for high-powered rifles and a large ad inside for machine guns. Other ads offer for sale pitchforks, horse pictures, Norman Rockwell reproductions, weather vanes, red suspenders, wheelbarrows, garden supplies, antique supplies, and investment opportunities. After a glance at these ads, we reached the quick conclusion that *The Country Gentleman* advertisers, the folks who keep the magazine financially alive, believe that in these pages they can reach an audience that is mostly the male, outdoorsy, fairly well off landowner who likes the conservative, old-fashioned way of life. You can be sure its editors are eager to provide reading matter that will keep this particular reader group buying their magazine.

Ms., on the other hand, features more ads for liquor, cigarettes, and cars than we're used to seeing in a women's magazine. From that we conclude that the readers are independent, with some disposable income and strong tastes for high living.

Writer's Digest ads, at first glance, seem to appeal to professional writers. But look more closely. In the issue we've been studying here, we see two full-page ads for writers' schools, two for literary agents who charge reading fees (agents belonging to the professional Society of Authors' Representatives are not permitted to advertise), and five for "vanity" book publishers (companies *you* pay to print your books)—all in all, not the kind of ads that established professionals are likely to look at twice. From the ads, the sharp marketing pro would have to conclude that *Writer's Digest* is aimed largely at dilettantes and beginners.

3·5 Reference Books About Magazines

Professional magazine writers learn to use every research tool available to help them study their markets thoroughly. How you go about researching magazines depends not only on what tools your nearby libraries have available, but on how hard you're willing to work to make it in a field that has little room for the lazy. J. Wandres, who used to edit *Retirement Living*, now free-lances out of his Brooklyn, New York, home for *American Legion, Family Circle, Parade, Saga, TV Guide,* and other top magazines. J. told us, "When editors say, 'Study the magazine to see what our needs are,' first I go to *Magazines for Libraries.* Second, I go through two issues of *Standard Rate and Data* about six months apart to see what growth there has been in a magazine's advertising and circulation, since a magazine that's showing steady growth is one that I'd care to write for. Third, I go to the library and take out a year's issues of the magazine."

J. Wandres is lucky. He lives a few blocks away from the well-stocked Brooklyn Public Library. Our students Phyllis E. and Eileen B. live in rural Beaver Dam, Wisconsin, where the library's hours are as limited as its collection. But like so many states, Wisconsin has an active interlibrary loan program, giving Phyllis and Eileen access to practically any book ever published. It just takes them a little longer to get their books. And like libraries large and small, the Beaver Dam library does have a copy of *Writer's Market,* a professional writer's most-used tool except for the actual magazines. It's published by the same company that brings you *Writer's Digest.*

WRITER'S MARKET

This is a Sears, Roebuck catalog of thousands of the magazines published today: consumer, trade, house organ, Sunday supplement . . . It lists the name, address, and phone number of each magazine, plus names of key personnel such as editor, articles editor, photo editor. Then each entry offers a few lines of terse information about the magazine's major subject areas, likes, dislikes, seasonal deadlines, etc. Finally, payment policies may be presented.

The inch or two of space devoted to any one magazine is just enough to whet the serious magazine writer's appetite. Without also studying copies of the magazine, it's seldom enough to initiate a major query letter. But by browsing through *Writer's Market,* you'll know which magazines seem to be in the right subject and payment range for you. You'll discover the names of magazines you never knew existed. And people we know find that their idea juices often start flowing after a few minutes of reading about editors' needs.

Ill. 3.1

ELEMENTARY ELECTRONICS, 380 Lexington Ave., New York NY 10017. (212)949–9190. Editor-in-Chief: Julian S. Martin. For electronics hobbyists, amateur radio operators, shortwave listeners, CB radio operators and computer hobbyists. Bimonthly magazine: 96 pages. Estab. 1950. Circ. 250,000. Buys all rights. Buys 350 mss a year. Payment on acceptance. Free sample copy. Will not consider photocopied or simultaneous submissions. Reports on material accepted for publication in 2 to 4 weeks. Returns rejected material as soon as rejected. Query first. SASE.
Nonfiction and Photos: Construction articles are most needed; also, theory and feature articles related to hobby electronics. How-to and technical articles. "The writer should read our book and decide whether he can be of service to us; and then send us a precis of the story he wishes to submit." Length: as required to tell the story. Pays $150 to $250. No additional payment for photos used with mss.
How To Break In: "I would make three suggestions. First, how-to pieces are always winners. The same goes for construction projects. But they must be to fulfill some need, not just for the sake of selling. Finally, installation stories are very good —something that you buy and where the installation takes some degree of know-how that can be illustrated with step-by-step photos. The author will have to take the photos as he does the job. Theory pieces are tougher—you have to really know us and sense our needs and the sorts of things our readers want to learn about. Feeling and timing are key. We are about 98% freelance and most of our material originates in queries. Please read the magazine first!"

When you can't find copies of a particular magazine at your local library or newsstand, its circulation department often will send you one. Sometimes it's free (especially if it's a trade magazine, house organ, or other smaller magazine whose editors know its copies are hard to find); often it's at cover price (particularly if it's a consumer magazine). *Writer's Market* tells you the policy on sample copies for many of its listed magazines.

WORKING PRESS OF THE NATION

This expensive multivolume annual reference tool is designed for public relations executives who want to reach the right editors with their press releases. The volume devoted to magazines is of value to magazine writers as well. Like *Writer's Market*, *Working Press of the Nation* offers thumbnail sketches of each magazine editor's preferences, key editorial personnel, addresses, phone numbers, etc. It doesn't generally cover what editors pay for articles. Larger libraries are likely to have it on the shelves.

Ill. 3.2 ───

All Outdoors
(Southwest Holiday), Southwestern
Assn. Inc., Box 700, Denison, TX
75020
Ed. Ralph Dice
1947 M $5 Circ 150,000 Adv
Allegheny Flightime
East/West Network, Inc., 5900
Wilshire Blvd., Suite 300, Los
Angeles, CA 90036 (213) 837–5810
Publ. Jeffrey S. Butler
Aimed at the business executive.
Contains articles on business, travel,
sports, human behavior &
leisure-time activities.
1968 M $12 $1 per copy Adv $1,590
8 1/8 x 10 7/8 Web Offset Color

Aloft
Wickstrom Publishers, Inc., 2701 S.
Bayshore Drive, Miami, FL 33133
(305) 858–3546
Ed. Karl Wickstrom Adv. Dir.
Robert Mitchell
Edited for National Airlines
passengers.
BM $3 .75 per copy Circ 330,000
Adv $3,140 8 3/8 x 10 7/8 Web
Offset Color
Alpine Information
P.O. Box 4875, Washington, DC
20016 (202) 966–6379
Ed.-Publ. Joe H. Wagner
1976 M $24

Working Press of the Nation entry. Copyright © 1980, Working Press of the Nation, published by National Research Bureau, Inc., 424 South 3rd, Burlington, Iowa 52601.

STANDARD RATE AND DATA SERVICE

This biweekly directory keeps advertisers abreast of advertising rates, circulation, and similar information. Generally only very large libraries subscribe to it due to its substantial cost and limited appeal. Radio and TV, newspapers, and magazines are covered in separate volumes. For larger publications, the editor's name is not listed, since the publisher or ad manager is of more interest to advertising space buyers. It does offer a professional writer more timely information than any other reference tool about circulation, address, phone, etc., since it's published ten times more often than any volume like it. *SR&D* also provides a circumstantial peek at the magazines' financial states of health: look at the ad rates and the circulation figures.

ULRICH'S, AYER, ETC.

Most libraries of any size will have *Ulrich's International Periodicals Directory* and/or *Ayer Directory of Publications* since librarians, like us, use them as guides to periodicals. *Ulrich's* and its quarterly supplements divide magazines topically. The *Ayer* volume is principally organized by state and city of publication.

You may find one or more of these other general directories too: *The Standard Periodical Directory* bills itself as "the largest authoritative guide to United States and Canadian periodicals," a claim we won't quibble with. *International Directory of Little Magazines and Small Presses* and *Directory of Small Magazine/Press Editors and Publishers* each provide names and addresses of sometimes hard-to-find publications.

Ill. 3.3

MISSOURI

	Rate	Cols	Width	Depth	Sub	Circ

JEFFERSON CITY† (H5 1/2), pop. 32,407.
*Cole Co. (C). The State Capital. On Missouri River, 30 m SE of Columbia. Bridge to Cedar City. Lincoln University. Poultry, fruit, grain farms. Wheat, corn. Manufactures underground transformers, electrical appliances, structural steel, steel fabrication, wood products, dairy, drugs, bricks.

*Capital News (offset) . . . Estab. 1910 . . . Morn. ex. Mon. . . . Independent

	Rate	Cols	Width	Depth	Sub	Circ
		9	21	301	41.40	**5,023

Combination rate with Evening Edition. Color advertising accepted.
Donald S. Norfleet, Editor; Wm H. Weldon, Publisher

*News and Tribune (offset) . . . Estab. 1932 . . . Sunday . . . Independent

	Rate	Cols	Width	Depth	Sub	Circ
	.21	9	21	301	15.60	**21.418

Color advertising accepted.
Donald S. Norfleet, Editor; Wm H. Weldon, Publisher

*Post - Tribune (offset) . . . Estab. 1865 . . . Evg. ex. Sat. & Sun. . . . Independent

	Rate	Cols	Width	Depth	Sub	Circ
	.21	9	21	301	41.40	**16,160

Color and comic strip advertising accepted.
Donald S. Norfleet, Editor; Wm. H. Weldon, Publisher, 210 Monroe St. (65101) 314 636–3131

Construction Advisor, The (offset) . . . Estab. 1928 . . . Monthly . . . Construction

	Rate	Cols	Width	Depth	Sub	Circ
BW	350.00					
4C	750.00	2	33	126	10.00	‡2,910

Color advertising accepted.
Chris Wrigley, Editor; Duane A. Kraft, Publisher, P.O. Box 94 (65101) 314 636–3188

*Journal of the Missouri Bar . . . Estab. 1945 . . . 8 ti. a yr. . . . Legal

	Rate	Cols	Width	Depth	Sub	Circ
BW	180.00	2	28	107	8.00	‡12,000

Color advertising accepted.
E. A. Richter, Editor; The Ovid Bell Press, Publisher, 326 Monroe St. P.O. Box 119 (65101) 314 635–4128

Ill. 3.4

**IOWA-ILLINOIS GAS &
ELECTRIC CO**
206 E 2nd St Davenport Ia 52801
Gas and electric service

Newscaster: Sam E. Wilson, editor.
Monthly, 12-page, offset magazine, 8½
x 11, circulation 2,200, circulated to
employees, stockholders, others.
Industry news; general items with or
without company tie-in. Pictures.
Printer: Wagners Printing Co., 1515 E.
Kimberly Rd., Davenport, IA 52807.

Monthly Employees Magazine: Sam E.
Wilson, editor. Monthly, 12-page,
offset magazine, 8½ x 11, circulation
1,500, circulated to employees, dealers,
stockholders. Industry news; general
items with company tie-in. Pictures.
Interests: cheesecake; home appliances;
new products; public service material;
science. Printer: Wagners Printers, 1515
E. Kimberly Rd., Davenport, IA
52807.

Standard Periodical Directory entries. Copyright © 1979, Oxbridge Communications, Inc.

Ill. 3.5

Hub Publications Ltd. (see also ORBIS; IPSE), Robin Gregory, Cal Clothier,
Youlgrave, Bakewell, Derbyshire, England, United Kingdom. 1969. Poetry, articles,
reviews. avg. press run 1,000. lp/of. Reporting time: varies. Payment: varies.
Copyrights for author.

THE HUDSON REVIEW, Paula Deitz, Co-editor; Frederick Morgan, Co-editor, 65
East 55th St., New York City, NY 10022, 212–755–9040. 1948. Poetry, fiction,
articles, criticism, reviews, parts-of-novels, long-poems. "Although we have developed
a recognizable group of contributors who are identified with the magazine, we are
always open to new writers and publish them in every issue. We have no university
affiliation and are not committed to any narrow academic aim; nor to any particular
political perspective." circ. 3,500. 4/yr. Pub'd 4 issues 1977; expects 4 issues 1978, 4
issues 1979. sub. price: $10.00; per copy: $3.00; sample: $3.00. Back issues: varies.
Discounts: bulk rates and discount schedules on request. 160pp; 4½ × 7½; of.
Reporting time: 8–10 weeks maximum. Payment: 2½ cents per word for prose; 50
cents per line for poetry. Copyrighted, reverts only upon the author's request. Pub's
reviews: 80 in 1977. §Literature, fine and performing arts, sociology and cultural
anthropology. Ads: $175.00/$100.00/no class. CCLM, COSMEP.

International Directory of Little Magazines and Small Presses entries. Copyright © 1979, International-
al Directory of Little Magazines and Small Presses (Dustbooks), 14th edition.

MAGAZINE INDUSTRY MARKET PLACE
This reference book is so new—and so expensive—it's hard to say yet
how many libraries stock it. Many top professional magazine writers we
know have bought copies.

Ill 3.6

**Chrysalis: A Magazine of
Women's Culture**
635 W Lake Ave, Los Angeles, CA
90057
Tel: 213–413–4330
Subn Address: Box 28761, San
Diego, CA 91218
Ed: Kirsten Grinstad
Man Ed: Debra Marrow
Art Dir: Sheila Levrant de Brettevired
Adv Magr: Georgianne Cowens,
Geraldine Hanon

Circ Mgr: Fern Leaf
Circ: 13,000 paid
Frequency: Quarterly
128 pp; $4.50 per issue, $15 per yr,
$18 insts
Advertising: b&w & color, b&w page
$600, trim 7 3/4 x 11
Member: WPA
Coverage of poetry, theater, visual
arts, film, literature & analyses of
social & political developments from a
feminist perspective.

Magazine Industry Marketplace 1980 entry, with permission of R.R. Bowker Company. Copyright
© 1979 by Xerox Corporation.

MIMP has fewer listings than *Writer's Market,* but more details within each listing. One advantage we find is that *MIMP* is under the wing of R. R. Bowker, a company with a reputation for publishing serious reference guides. Magazines may be more likely to share candid information with Bowker than with the company that publishes *Writer's Digest*; one mention of a magazine in the *Digest* is guaranteed to drown an editor in mail, not all of it up to professional standards. We've known several editors to return their *Writer's Market* questionnaires with "We are not a free-lance market," when in fact they are. How can we be sure? We've sold to them.

Chapter Four

How to Pick
The *Right* Magazines
to Be *Your* Markets

S ALLY WENDKOS OLDS IS TODAY AN EXPERIENCED
professional writer who can just about choose the magazine she
wants to write for and land an assignment there. But it wasn't always
that way. Sally recalled for us recently, "I got started when I was
working for a civil rights organization in Chicago. Civil rights was very
new then, so I wrote up what we were doing, sent it to a church
publication, and they ran it. They didn't pay me a cent, but they gave
me a hundred free copies of the issue."

That "sale" was all Sally needed for her start. "After that, my
cycle was to write and learn, write and learn." Part of her learning was
in a Chicago writers' workshop. The major part came from writing for
the smaller markets until she got good at it, then for middle markets
such as *Parents* and regional editions of *McCall's* and *Good Housekeeping,*
until she knew how to turn out material suitable for them. And then,
finally, regularly, for top-paying markets.

4·1 Markets Beginners Should Avoid

The late great Mort Weisinger used to urge us, when we ourselves were
climbing from small to middle markets, "Start at the top. It's as easy
to write for a thousand bucks as for a hundred." That was true when
Mort got started in the 1940s. It's still true today: the writing's the
same. It's the chance of getting your idea *noticed* that's changed since
then.

"We get 1,200 unsolicited manuscripts and queries *every month,*"
Family Circle's articles editor Bobbie Ashby explained to a recent
writers' conference. "On top of that, we get several hundred story ideas
from writers we have already worked with. So the competition here is
very tough."

There's more to keep in mind if you think a top-paying market
like *Family Circle* ought to be your first goal. They typically offer a 25

percent guarantee on assigned articles. That means that, even if the completed article can't be used, an author is paid over $400—called a *kill fee* by pros—just for trying. Nice? Yes, but there's a catch: it means they have to be very selective, and generally can't afford to take a chance on anybody but an established professional.

At the same writers' conference, Roy Herbert, *Reader's Digest*'s managing editor, listed for a large audience the three ingredients he and other *Digest* editors look for: quality of the writing, quality of the research, and quality of the basic idea—"and *that's* the toughest of the three. You must *really* know your market and tailor each suggestion to the magazine."

4·2 Ideal Markets for Aspiring Writers

Some kids collect stamps, coins, or beer cans. By the time coauthor Frank Peterson had graduated from high school, he had collected a thick stack of printed rejection slips from *Reader's Digest, Saturday Evening Post, The New Yorker, Esquire,* and similar biggies. When Frank decided to start earning his living at writing, however, he approached it the way any young person would approach any career—working his way up. The place he decided to start, out of an interest in social activism, was a social-activist weekly magazine called *Ave Maria.*

Frank's first query to *Ave Maria* suggested a critical look at high-rise apartment buildings done in allegorical format—through the eyes of a twenty-first-century archaelogist discovering the ruins of twentieth-century high-rise buildings. It was a trifle lofty for the down-to-earth magazine, and editor and publisher Monsignor John Reedy wrote a two-page letter explaining to Frank what the problem was.

Next Frank queried *Ave Maria*'s managing editor Dan Griffin about a civil rights organization in Louisiana that used guns to protect civil rights demonstrators. He'd earlier received turndowns from *Look, Life,* and *Ebony,* no doubt because the editors were afraid—and rightly so—that Frank couldn't have turned in *their* kind of story. But *Ave Maria* assigned it. Frank wrote it. They paid seventy-five dollars. Then Dan edited the manuscript into a far better story than the original. Reading it taught Frank a lot about writing for magazines. By the end of his first year, Frank was selling at least one story a month to *Ave Maria*—and Dan no longer needed to edit or rewrite the manuscripts.

Dan Griffin needed Frank's stories to fill up his magazine with lively ideas as much as Frank needed Dan's editing, guidance, and checks. Both were shooting for bigger markets than *Ave Maria.* But they both knew that they had to master their trades at that level if they were going to jump up to the next plateau. Dan Griffin moved to the international desk at the *Washington Post,* and Frank moved to magazines that paid more than $100.

Frank had learned how to pick an appropriate focus for a story idea before he queried *Science & Mechanics* about hot-air ballooning—an undiscovered sport back then. He got the assignment, and because he'd also learned well enough how to write a basic magazine story, his efforts resulted in a $250 check. *Science & Mechanic's* editor put Frank through another apprenticeship, this time in picking story ideas slanted to the magazine's market. Before long, Frank was cashing one or two of their $250 checks every month.

From *Science & Mechanics,* the editor who bought Frank's ballooning story moved up to the best-seller lists; he's Lawrence Sanders, author of top novels beginning with *The Anderson Tapes.* And Frank, a bit older, and much wiser, landed solidly in a couple of $400–500 markets. This is how most of the pros we know worked up from the low-paying into the lucrative markets—and they're still moving up. We endorse it as the best way for you too.

4·3 Pros Sell *Ideas*

So far, we've mentioned only one article that was sold after it was written—and that was Sally's first. All our other anecdotes about writers tell about selling *ideas.* That's the professional way.

Professional writers think in terms of selling ideas. Editors think in terms of buying them.

Of course, if an editor assigns a story based on an acceptable idea, she assumes that the turned-in story will also be acceptable. Otherwise the writer will lose all or most of his payment—and part of his reputation as well.

We're going to devote all of Part III to selling article ideas. For now let's concentrate on how pros match up good ideas with appropriate magazines.

First, let's briefly define what an article idea is to a writer:

1. It's a subject worth writing about for 1,000 or more words. (Even most shorties are worth 1,000 words. They're just *very* tightly written.)
2. It is narrow enough so almost everything important and interesting about it can be said in a few thousand words.
3. It appeals to the narrow interests of an individual magazine's readers.
4. It has something new to say.

Remember, there are two ways that pros go at marketing ideas. Sometimes they come up with exciting ideas and then search for one or several magazines to assign articles based on those ideas. Or they have a magazine already in mind—either a steady market or a market they'd like to add to their list—and brainstorm for appropriate ideas.

4·4 How to Pinpoint Magazines for Your Story Ideas

Eve Merriam, prolific author of adult nonfiction books and articles, children's books, plays, and poems, told us she is sometimes assigned an article based on an editor's idea. But most of the time, "I am on a soapbox for something that's captured my attention and try to persuade an editor that his magazine should offer a forum for the idea. It may be something as frivolous as forecasting the next turn in fashion or as serious as an analysis of changing patterns in family life by an examination of what several hundred American middle-class children think of working mothers." But how does a writer decide *which* editor to try to convince?

Here's how it's done by Bill Nelson, free-lance writer and articles editor of the *Milwaukee Journal*'s *Insight* magazine. Bill spends one day every month researching at the library to pinpoint five new markets for his story ideas. Keeping in mind his mental file of ideas he'd like to write about (or already wrote about once), Bill studies magazines pretty much the way we advised you to in the last chapter. "In fifteen minutes to a half hour, I have a pretty good idea of the pulse and personality of the publication." He jots down assessments in his marketing notebook along with names and addresses. One February day, his market research netted Bill $795.60 in story sales.

His first sale on that otherwise dreary afternoon came about because Bill glanced once more through *Reader's Digest,* a magazine he'd read a thousand times, and noticed for the first time that *Reader's Digest* runs one-page features. Bill had recently done a short feature for a Wisconsin newspaper about the famed Burlington Liars Club. Two months after "library day," Bill was cashing his $400 *Digest* check for "The Truth About the Liars Club."

Bill also researched markets that day for a photo essay he was working on which lamented the passage of windmills from rural America. At the library he scouted *Magazine of the Midlands* (Sunday supplement to the *Omaha World-Herald*) and *Prairie Farmer,* both strong markets for rural pieces. Bill also saw that the "People" page in *The Christian Science Monitor* runs occasional glances at contemporary Americana. He sold the windmill yarn to all three noncompeting markets for a total of $150.

Bill had always wanted to write the hair-raising saga of life with his feisty foster son Kevin, so that afternoon he identified *The Lutheran* and *Catholic Digest* as likely markets for such a story. Two weeks later

The Lutheran bought the domestic adventure piece. And a year later, *Catholic Digest* reprinted it from *The Lutheran,* the two sales adding another eighty-five dollars to Bill's "library day" proceeds.

Many writers, pros and beginners, like to jot their ideas down on index cards or onto lists. Other writers find it limiting to formulate story ideas on paper at an early stage. Like Bill Nelson, they outline each idea loosely in their heads and then spontaneously reshape it, alter its emphasis, or selectively choose specific aspects of it in order to match the idea to the special demands of the chosen market.

On the other hand, no matter how good an idea is, it's almost impossible to sell it to a magazine that pays staff writers to develop articles in that subject area. The arts and crafts, recipes, and needlework sections of many large magazines are created and executed almost exclusively in-house. You can quickly spot situations like that by comparing by-lines to names on the masthead. If cooking articles, for example, are almost always by-lined by the cooking editor or another member of her staff, you'll have small chance of selling your recipes to that magazine. If major articles have no by-line at all, they *probably* are staff-written, but this rule isn't as hard and fast as the previous one.

When matching ideas to markets, always compare the masthead entries to names of authors of articles in similar subject areas. Submit your ideas first, as a rule, to magazines that use the greatest number of free-lance contributions in your preferred department. You *can* occasionally break into magazines that rely on staff writers for their departments, but it's a tough route to take.

For every rule in this business, there's an exception. Deanne Raffel is the exception to the one above. An avid do-it-yourselfer, she decided to turn what she'd learned about remodeling her own home into a monthly column. She suggested it to *House & Garden,* which of course had plenty of staff writers in that subject area. But Deanne stressed that she could provide a woman's touch to home repair; that was something new back then. Deanne's "House Craft" column became a steady feature in *House & Garden.*

4·5 How to Develop Ideas for Your Chosen Markets

Beginners are often at a loss for what to write about. In our classes we hear, "I don't know anything but mothering, and I can't even qualify as an expert on that," or, "I press buttons all day, but I'll be darned if I want to write about that." What can beginners write about? Here's what we assign to our students:

1. Go through the magazines you like to read and find five (or more) articles you enjoyed and could have written yourself. Ask yourself

how you would have written them differently. Develop ideas based
on those differences.

2. Read your newspapers for ideas. Clip every article that sparks your
interest. Ask yourself how you could turn each subject into
magazine format and length.

3. Notice, as you go through your day, the things that make you react
emotionally. Does the mail carrier never get there on time? Are the
flowers in your neighbor's yard extra bright this year? Does the third
cup of coffee taste worse than the first? Ask yourself why. The answer
is probably an article idea.

4. List all the things you'd really like to know more about. You're not
the only one. Each is an article idea.

Once you develop these four tips into habits, finding ideas will
come easy for you.

Unlike so many beginners, professional writers are rarely at a loss
for ideas to write about. How often a bunch of us have sat around over a
glass of something cool and mused that we ought to form a corporation
to sell our unused ideas to fledgling writers. At a dollar an idea, our
Ideas Unlimited would generate millions.

Frankly, we *need* to start with thousands of ideas a year just to
come up with enough assignments to pay the bills, because the ideas
we'd like to write about aren't necessarily what the magazines are
looking for. Some magazines we want to write for because we can count
on them for steady income; others we attempt to crack because of their
pay scale, their prestige, or simply the challenge of that particular
market.

Editor Pamela Fiori once told us, "The most frequently heard
word around the editorial staff of *Travel and Leisure* is a simple one:
'No.' Conservatively speaking, we say no fifty times a day: On the
phone, in person, and by letter." Bonnie Remsberg recalls that when
she and Chuck were launching their careers, they mailed out between
twelve and fifteen query letters for every assignment they got. Without
a fertile supply of ideas, magazine writers are doomed to destitution.

A few years ago, Frank wrote twenty to twenty-five stories a year
for a syndicate of Sunday newspaper magazines. They depended on him
for story material as much as he depended on them for income. During
their peak advertising seasons, he was expected to write a story every
week. He had to come up with—or at least help develop—most of the
story ideas. That meant weekly brainstorming sessions with the editor,
the late Don Feitel. Here's the give-and-take of a typical session.

Frank knew the newspaper group liked dramatic personal sagas
set in traditional blue-collar American situations. So, "What about a
family of steel mill workers?" he began.

"What about 'em?"

"They're in Pittsburgh. It's hot work. It's well paid. It's dangerous. . . ."

"So?"

"Well then, how about a family of dairy farmers?"

"What about 'em?"

"Well, for the first time in the family's history, they're able to make a good living from dairy farming."

"Okay, that's a handle. Go find one."

"Is it an assignment?"

"Yes."

That would be easy. Frank's uncle is a prospering dairy farmer in northern Wisconsin. But he tried to get some more assignments while he was at it. "How about coal mining?"

"What about it?"

"Why not a story about a modern coal miner?"

"What about him?"

"He's caught between the company and the union."

"Yah, but that's not enough for a story. We need a handle."

"Like what?"

"Like the third generation in a coal mining family."

"If we find one, do we get the story?"

"Yup, we'll call it 'Three Generations in the Mine.' "

It took him a year to locate a third-generation mining family, and then only by one of those lucky breaks that make all writers fanatic believers in luck. But it turned into one of the most touching stories Frank was ever privileged to write.

Like so many publications, this newspaper-magazine group wanted more consumer information articles than it could get. Most writers' suggestions fell short of the mark because the ideas had to take unusual approaches or lend themselves to eye-catching titles. In hunting out story ideas, Frank didn't look for importance or even freshness of information as much as for drama.

While everybody else was writing about how consumers can do their own doctoring, he wrote "The Dangers of Self-Medication." Every spring, consumer magazines run something about buying lawn mowers. He wrote "Beware the Lawn Mower." While all of his friends were encouraging people to find creative hobbies, he wrote "The Hazards of Hobbies."

At Christmas, everybody wrote about toys. But he asked what happens to all the battery powered toys *after* Christmas, and wrote an exposé about how batteries are marketed: "The Caustic Truth About Batteries."

Most magazines feel obliged to run some seasonal material. After a few years on the job, editors run out of fresh-sounding ideas for Christmas. Frank's newspaper group editor was no exception. One year

Frank wrote up the coldest spot in the nation, the next the snowiest. What next?

Well, there was this northern Wisconsin town that was red-light district from one end to the other all during summer's tourist season. What went on there in the depths of winter? He called the article "There's No Hot Time in This Old Town Till Spring."

Then too, editors—and readers—love predictions. So in "Where Are the Snows of Nexteryear?" he predicted, with help from the federal government's weather and climate experts, how much colder the United States was becoming, and how fast, and on which states the big snows would fall.

He did the prediction bit again the next year. Thanks to the nation's number one weather expert, an M.I.T. professor, he predicted that we were in for a record cold winter. Title: "It's Going to Be a Red Flannel Winter." He even sketched maps, based on the expert's prognostications, which showed how much colder various parts of the country would be and where the heaviest snows would fall. It was a marvelous story idea, incorporating practically every ingredient editors love. The only hitch occurred months after the story was written and paid for: the expert had been one year premature in slipping half the country's readers into red flannels. The story ran in Sunday magazines all over the U.S. during one of the warmest winter days in history.

It's stories like that one that make us glad we're writers. Since Frank only quoted the expert, he can sit at his typewriter and chuckle about the meteorological miscue. If he'd been the weather expert, he'd still be banished to Siberia.

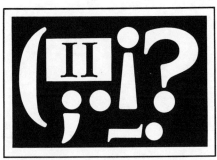

The Article
as Marketable
Property

Chapter Five

There's More
to Writing Than Typing

L IKE A MERRY-GO-ROUND, THE FIELD OF WRITING
rarely stands still. While Part I's *guidelines* for studying markets
will always be true, the conclusions you reach today about a particular
market may be outmoded by next year. Learning everything that's
important to become a successful magazine writer is like photograph-
ing all of a merry-go-round: there's no logical beginning to the subject.
You have to take it all in before any of the parts fit properly into place.

Some teachers jump on at the writing stage. First they help
students learn how to write articles. Then they show the various kinds
of markets, if any, that exist for the students' articles. Since we're
convinced that people take our courses primarily because they want to
appear in print, we start, as we did in Part I, by discussing the markets
for articles. Without a market, no matter how exciting the idea or how
beautiful the execution, your article won't get published.

In Part II, we still won't have you writing finished copy. First, we
feel, you have to learn to visualize your magazine articles from the same
perspective that works for successful magazine writers and editors.
You'll need this skill so you can judge whether your own ideas are
salable and can present them so they will sell.

The one activity most novices associate with writing—the actual
application of words to paper—takes up relatively little time in a
professional magazine writer's work week. Flora Davis, a New Yorker
who writes regularly for *Redbook* and *Woman's Day,* estimates that she
spends four to six weeks on an article, generally with at least two
articles in the works at one time. And even though Flora carefully
writes and rewrites, she logs in little more than a quarter of her time at
her typewriter. "I spend a heavy amount of time on research," Flora
told us. "That's where I get my psychic rewards." Although we've
never kept a log of our hours—that sounds too institutional for
free-lance writers—we know that barely half our working time, on
average, is spent in front of our Sears, Roebuck typewriters, and
perhaps half of that time is devoted to writing letters.

For the series of forty-odd monthly articles we wrote for
Physician's Management, for example, we had to interview fifty doctors

each month. The interviews took up three or four working days on the telephone. Organizing our research took several hours. The writing, both first and second drafts, was done in eight hours or less of actual writing time, with an hour or two in between for editing the first draft.

For some articles, the research may involve just an hour on the phone and half an hour at the library; the actual writing may be the major part of such a job. But for most articles, a week or more is spent chasing down information and only two or three days writing. You have to add onto all of these times the many hours—often many days—spent selling the article idea.

We've found that most people who want to break into this field want to spend as little time as possible selling. We've organized our courses and this book to accomplish that goal. Part I, which concentrated on magazines as markets, should have helped you locate salable article ideas. But those ideas are only the bare bones of what magazine editors want to know before they'll buy. Even though a pro rarely writes any article until after landing an assignment, he does know a great deal about every article he wants to sell and eventually to write. He decides in advance which of the various *formats* can best show off his idea (Chapter 6 takes care of this). He finds a simple *focus* and a suitable *slant* to the idea, and singles out a possible *lead* (all covered in Chapter 7). He does preliminary research (Chapter 12) to ensure that he can deliver what he intends to promise. Then, when *querying* an editor (explained in Chapter 10), he shows off his mastery of the *techniques* (detailed in Chapter 8) that make articles leap off the typed pages.

All of these devices work to the writer's advantage. Just as corporations have developed standard ways of organizing personnel, magazines have developed standard ways of organizing words and ideas. You'd be labeling yourself less than professional if you were to write to an editor, for example:

> *I want to tell you what's wrong with school buses. I want to investigate why they don't put seat belts inside, and I want to interview mechanics about how often the buses leave the garage with defective brakes and bald tires. I want to check into the driving records of men and women who drive them. My article will alert parents to the dangers their children face every morning on the way to school.*

A pro might write instead:

> *I'm planning an exposé on school buses that documents drivers' poor driving records, bald tires, questionable brakes, lack of seat belts. My digging may make parents nervous when they kiss Sis or Junior good-bye, but I've located organizations and officials who are working on solutions, and concerned parents can join them.*

The second paragraph uses twenty fewer words—important in a field where tight writing is revered. But the second paragraph includes one more—important—idea than the first. It incorporates *exposé*, a word that signals to editors that you plan to do a lot of hard-nosed investigation into what's dangerous about school buses and write it up in a highly dramatic manner. The editor knows all that without your having to say it because the professional writer and editor speak a special vocabulary.

The instinctive writer discovers this vocabulary—formats, pegs, elements, techniques—and the rituals of magazine writing by trial and error, reinventing the wheel as he learns his craft. But they're just as standard as chemical formulas and, as you'll see, can be learned quickly and easily once they're understood.

Chapter Six

Ten Standard Article Formats

BEFORE YOU SUGGEST YOUR FIRST IDEA TO AN editor, you have to know what kind of format it must have and which elements and techniques you'll be expected to employ with that format. The late Beatrice Schapper, in her *How to Make Money Writing Magazine Articles* (Arco, 1974), reflected how diversified the terminology had become. She listed nineteen article formats linked to subject matter and another fifteen formats linked to treatment, We've reclassified the material into ten standard article formats with at least one example of each for study. (The examples, excerpted from published articles, are all bylined except for those written by one or both of us, and will be referred to again later in the book). We have not necessarily reprinted the articles in their entirety. Learn these formats, and you can talk and think like a pro.

6·1 How-to

This is one of the easiest types of article to sell—and write too. There must be thousands of them published every month, because nearly every consumer magazine uses them.

"Build Your Own Luxurious Plastic Furniture," which we've reproduced in part, (Ill. 6.1), is in a classic how-to style. It opens with a *rousing promise:* you too can build elegant, expensive-looking plastic furniture. It describes the *materials and tools* needed, and finally it moves into *step-by-step directions* for building actual furniture.

During the exposition—which is one of the three writing techniques explained in Chapter 8—we balance the article's *point of view* by covering some of plastic's shortcomings—it scratches, and it's expensive. We also, at the end, tell readers *how to locate suppliers of materials* in their local phone directories and, in case that fails, the name and address of a company that will mail them information and supplies. Editors who publish how-to's like to see as many of these elements as possible worked into their articles. *Family Handyman's* Editor, Gene Schnaser, must have found everything he wanted. He published the article exactly as we submitted it, and invited us to submit more story ideas.

Ill. 6.1

Build Your Own Luxurious Plastic Furniture

If a home handyman finds a lovely-to-look-at but expensive piece of wooden furniture, he'll try to build one just like it and usually he achieves a neat creation. Wood has always been a favorite of do-it-yourselfers. Plastics, however, being relatively new, still frighten a great many people. But working with plastic is in many ways easier than working with wood, once you learn the basic differences.

By the time you've finished this short article, you'll know these differences. Better still, you'll know how to build the $575 luxurious shelves for about $150 (closer to $100 if you shop carefully; closer to $200 if you take the easy way out). You'll be able to build the $100 coffee table for $10 to $15.

The Materials.

Furniture shown here is built from a clear acrylic type of plastic sold under brand names such as Plexiglas, Lucite and Acrylite. Acrylic plastic is just as clear and sparkling as glass, yet it is incredibly hard to break. It comes in sheets of various thicknesses. The thicker your plastic, the more luxurious your finished furniture will look.

However, price is a big factor too. Acrylic plastics aren't cheap. So in designing the furniture here we've kept thickness to a minimum.

Acrylic plastics scratch more easily than glass. That's the major problem you'll find in building and enjoying furniture like this. However even glass will scratch if you slide gritty or sharp-edged metal or glass objects over it. With plastic you can do something about the scratches; with glass you can't. If you do happen to get a scratch on some highly visible part of your plastic furniture, you can buff it out.

Most acrylic plastic you find on the market is sandwiched between lightly glued protective papers. Leave the paper in place while you're working to avoid scratches.

Tools and Methods.

You can cut acrylic plastics with any saw that cuts soft metal—hacksaw, coping saw, sabresaw or circular saw. However, when you're building furniture such as the two items shown here, many local plastics suppliers will cut pieces to size if you don't ask for too many different-sized cuts.

Cut with the finest-toothed blade you have available, be sure it's sharp, and use the slowest speed possible. You have to be sure that your blade is cutting through the plastic and not melting its way along. Best approach of all is to buy an acrylic-cutting blade for your saw.

How-to's can be about *physical actions:* how to build plastic furniture, extra closet space, bird houses. . . . how to fix cars, bikes, refrigerators . . . how to make fancy pies, strawberry shortcake, lined drapes for the living room . . . . But they can also be about *intangible actions* that improve our mundane lives or provide guidelines for once-in-a-lifetime events: how to save money, find a job, pick a husband, choose a divorce lawyer, catch a trout, sue a doctor, fly a kite, drive safely. . . . Judi's article "12 Ways to Get More out of Studying" is also written in classic how-to format. In fact, since *Seventeen* magazine's editor laid out the story to feature Judi's numbered tips, you can graphically appreciate the simple, logical way in which a good how-to almost organizes itself.

Ill. 6.2

12 Ways to Get
More Out of Studying

Effective studying is the one element guaranteed to produce good grades in school. But it's ironic that the one thing almost never taught in school is how to study effectively.

For example, an important part of studying is note-taking, yet few students receive any instruction in this skill. At best you are told simply, "You had better take notes," but not given any advice on what to record or how to use the material as a learning tool.

Fortunately reliable data on how to study does exist. It has been demonstrated scientifically that one method of note-taking is better than others and that there are routes to more effective reviewing, memorizing and textbook reading as well. Following are twelve proven steps you can take to improve your study habits. We guarantee that if you

really use them, your grades will go up.

1 Use behavior modification on yourself.

It works. Remember Pavlov's dogs, salivating every time they heard a bell ring? Just as association worked with them, it also can work with you. If you attempt, as nearly as possible, to study the same subject at the same time in the same place each day, you will find after a very short while that when you get to that time and place you're automatically in the subject groove. Train your brain to think French on a time-place cue, and it will no longer take you ten minutes a day to get in the French mood. Not only will you save the time and emotional energy you once needed to psych yourself up to French or whatever else, but the experts say you'll also remember more of what you're studying!

2 Don't spend more than an hour at a time on one subject.

In fact, if you're doing straight memorization, don't spend more then twenty to thirty minutes. First, when you're under an imposed time restriction, you use the time more efficiently. (Have you noticed how much studying you manage to cram into the day before the big exam? That's why it's called *cramming.*)

Second, psychologists say that you learn best in short takes. (Also remember that two or three hours of study without noise or other distrac-tions is more effective than ten hours trying to work amid bedlam.) In fact, studies have shown that as much is learned in four one-hour sessions distributed over four days as in one marathon six-hour session. That's be-cause between study times, while you're sleeping or eating or reading a novel, you mind subconsciously works on absorbing what you've learned. So it counts as study time too.

Keep in mind that when you're memorizing, whether it's math for-mulas or a foreign language or names and dates, you're doing much more real learning more quickly than when you're reading a social studies text or an English essay.

Seventeen, September 1976. Copyright © 1976, Judi R. Kesselman.

When writing about *physical actions,* how-to's are almost always organized in *time* sequence: readers must follow directions in order, or they won't get the promised results. When writing about *intangible actions,* however, the logic of which comes first is often much more subtle. Sometimes the progression is from the general act to the specific, or from easy to hard. Sometimes the most interesting points are interspersed with less interesting ones, to keep the reader moving along. The *Seventeen* article combines several of these techniques. Whichever logical organization you choose, you must do it consciously and carefully to achieve a well-written how-to.

How-to's should be kept as simple as possible. Readers (and editors) are looking, first of all, for easy-to-follow instructions. Intricate organization and flowery language only get in the way. Readers want *reassurance* that what you're advising them to do is within reach, *proofs and promises* that lead them to anticipate with pleasure the finished pro-duct or action, and *referrals* for required supplies or additional infor-mation. It's better by far to leave the readers wishing you'd said more (especially if you tell them where to find out more) than to have them wishing you'd stopped 300 words ago.

How-to articles should be as short or as long as your subject requires—no longer, no shorter. The editor can be counted on to know how much information on the topic the magazine's readers want and she'll provide you with guidelines as part of the article assignment. For *House Beautiful* we did 500 words on how to buy lumber and, for *Popular Electronics,* 500 words on how to build a simple record stand. On the other hand, our *Popular Science* story about how do-it-yourselfers can add dormers to their houses required 4,000 words.

6·2 Profile and Interview

These are popular twin formats, found in a majority of consumer magazines and a large proportion of trades. You have to be careful with them, because they look deceptively simple. We've watched our students stumble repeatedly before understanding the elements that make them come alive for the reader.

First of all, it's important to comprehend the difference between the two terms. A *profile* is simply a prose sketch of one or more aspects of someone's personality or life. (Don't try to reveal the *whole* person or tell the *whole* life story. Nobody can be revealed totally in article length.) Pros often call a profile of a celebrity a *personality profile* or a *personality piece.* Editors rarely publish profiles of anyone who is not considered by the publication's readership to be celebrated or otherwise outstanding.

To research a profile, the writer usually interviews the subject and, often, other people—spouses, managers, coworkers, children, neighbors—anyone whose observations provide further insight into the aspects he has chosen to reveal. Good writers rarely limit themselves to interviews. They draw on newspaper clippings, previous magazine stories, books, and anything else that may provide anecdotes, suggest clues to the subject, or spark questions for follow-up during the interview. But the profile ordinarily relies heavily on the interview, and is most often written up using the interview's time and place as the frame of reference and the subject as the story's organizing backbone.

Many people use *profile* and *interview* interchangeably when referring to article format. The two are slightly different, however. Unlike the profile, which is written in conventional article style, the *interview* often mimics the actual give-and-take of a live interview by using a question-and-answer format, called *Q&A* by the pros. Q&A has become popular with editors. It looks embarrassingly simple to write, but is far more difficult to bring off than you might think.

The benchmark of Q&As is *Playboy*'s regular feature, "The Playboy Interview," in which a person of some national importance is explored in great depth through probing questions and *carefully edited* answers. A while back, Barry Golson, editor of the *Playboy* interviews, explained the work that goes into these seemingly off-the-cuff Q&As. When he has selected an interview subject, either himself or from a writer's query, he asks the writer to show him between 100 and 500 questions in advance. Then Golson discusses all aspects of the subject with the writer. Only then does the first face-to-face meeting with the interviewee take place. Usually between thirty and forty hours of taped interview sessions are expected of the writer, from which the spontaneous-looking Q&A is pieced together. "We make no bones that a *Playboy* interview is a serious discussion put together from various tapes to retain the flavor and integrity of the original conversations," he said, adding, "A conversation as you hear it can *never* be printed verbatim."

Ill. 6.3 ——————————————————————————————

{This part of the interview was conducted within five days of the nuclear accident at the Three Mile Island plant near Harrisburg, Pennsylvania.}

PLAYBOY: What do you make of this catastrophe?

TELLER: I would not call it a catastrophe; I would not call it a disaster; I would not call it an accident. I would call it a malfunction.

If I undertake something really dangerous, such as driving a car, and the car stops and I can't make it work, but no one is hurt, that is called a malfunction. If someone is hurt, that is called an accident. In the Three Mile Island malfunction, no one was hurt.

PLAYBOY: But there is great fear that people will be hurt in the future.

TELLER: I am very confident that no one will be hurt. Should I be invited to visit there, I would do so, and I wouldn't feel like a hero, as I have every confidence that I would be all right.

In the functioning of many reactors, health-damaging accidents have been avoided. There is no exception. It just so happens that the antinuclear movement, lacking a real

accident, has latched on to this one, promoting it into something that is isn't.

PLAYBOY: Nevertheless, it is the most serious malfunction—if that's what you want to call it—that has occurred so far.

TELLER: Indeed. I estimate that the financial damage will be even greater than it was in the Browns Ferry malfunction, which cost $120,000,000. My hunch is this will cost even more.

PLAYBOY: For which, of course, the utilities' customers will be paying.

TELLER: If we don't have nuclear reactors, the utilities' customers will be paying much more, because even counting in these costs for shutdowns, nuclear reactors are still cheaper than the next cheapest source of electricity, coal, and much cheaper than oil or gas.

A $500,000,000 loss, while it may hurt the customers in the long run, has an immediate and severe impact on the utility concerned; it will suffer loss, compared with other utilities. Therefore, the utility has the most direct financial interest in seeing that such a malfunction never occurs again. Right now, there are enormous numbers of responsible engineers who are carefully analyzing the questions: What has gone wrong and what other things may still go wrong? When the story is over, we will know how this kind of nuclear plant might malfunction, and therefore, we will know more about how to keep it safe. Utilities will be more careful in seeing that every component is safe, that instruments are employed in the reactor that will appropriately inform the operators, so that wrong judgments can be avoided. They will train operators to avoid mistakes that may have been made here. So, as a net result, we will have bought added safety for our money, without sacrificing human life or human health.

Playboy interview with Dr. Edward Teller, August 1979. Copyright © 1979, Playboy.

There are many degrees of variation between the strict interview format and the classic profile. Sometimes a writer incorporates his questions into the actual text of the article, instead of standing them starkly aloof as in the *Playboy* format. Answers may be quoted exactly, with comment or without, or interpreted through the writer's words.

Interviews may cover many aspects of a person, jumping from topic to topic without the need for transitions. Profiles, as a rule, focus on a single major aspect of the subject's experience. When Judi profiled Lynn Redgrave for *Weight Watchers Magazine* (reproduced in part, in Ill. 6.4), she built the story around one theme. The editor highlighted it in the article's subtitle: ". . . Growing Up Fat with the Fabulous Redgraves." Judi's article goes into Lynn's childhood, of course, but covers almost nothing beyond its food- and weight-connected aspects. Lynn's equally famous older sister Vanessa fits into the story too, but only in terms of *her* eating problems while they were growing up. Later in the article, Judi talks about Lynn's acting career—but again she sticks to its weight-related aspects.

Ill. 6.4

Ladies and Gentlemen . . .
Meet the Girl Who Made It
As a Fat Movie Star

I was a food junky," Lynn Redgrave announces.

She sits across from us, all sleek and attractive, her long bony arms obvious proof of the fact that her past lies far behind.

Behind—but not forgotten. "The pain, the hysteria, the self-hate

—they're things you never forget," she admits, emotion softening her clipped British accent.

Lynn Redgrave made it as a movie star on her fat. In *Georgy Girl,* as the overstuffed English bird who can't attract her own man but gets a friend's cast-off on his rebound, she won an Academy Award nomination in 1967. And now, padded all over for the title role in the Broadway play *My Fat Friend,* she's having to relive every night that fat-girl feeling again. "The only consolation," she says, "is that by the end of the play, I've shed 60 pounds and am my thin self again."

She clasps the tips of her long fingers, crosses her long legs at the knees and sighs. "If anybody had offered me this play six years ago, I would have said, 'Play a fat girl? I can't, can*not* do it. I cannot go through that again.' It's only because I haven't been a fat girl for years, and have some distance from my pain, that I could take it on at all now."

Anger, aggression, pain, hysteria, hate. It was all there, from the time Lynn was 13 or 14. She hadn't always been fat. In fact, born in 1943, in the midst of the bombings on England during the second World War, Lynn came into the arms of her actor-parents enormously anemic, with huge calcium and iron deficiencies.

"When my mother was pregnant with me, people were uninformed about iron and vitamins. Food rationing was on. We were allowed one egg a week, and, of course, my 3-year-old brother Corin and my 6-year-old sister Vanessa got to share it. Of meat, I think you were each permitted two ounces a week, and, of course, extra milk was unheard-of. Oh, I was born a good size and the right weight, but I was always so tired as a baby, I literally couldn't take a walk." Whenever Nanny took the children out to the park, Lynn had to be pushed in a stroller—right up until the age of 6. She was tall and straight, but she couldn't manage the few blocks under her own steam.

But then the war was over, and gradually food became more plentiful and nutritional knowledge began filtering down to the local doctors. "By the time I was 7 or 8, they were feeding me full of pills and of eggs from chickens Nanny kept in the garden, and by the time I was 8 or 9, I was packing in the starchy foods and getting quite chubby."

We've picked up a random stack of old magazines to demonstrate, just by their cover lines, the important point that a good personality piece captures a single major theme. In each case, we've underlined the key words that tell the theme:

Ladies' Home Journal: "John Travolta: A Career in Crisis" "Barbara Walters Takes You Behind the Scenes of her TV Triumphs" "Shirley MacLaine: Warren Beatty Is Looking for a Woman Like Me."

McCalls: "Dinah Shore: How to Look Your Best All Your Life" "Kristy McNichol: Her Real 'Family' Is Stranger than TV."

Good Housekeeping: Jackie Kennedy at 50" "Michael Landon: "How I Got Back the Daughter I Lost."

As we said before, most published profiles are about celebrities or outstanding persons in their particular vocations or avocations. But the rule isn't hard and fast. The same technique—singling out those aspects of a person that illuminate a central theme—can be used with utterly unknown people. *Reader's Digest* often runs articles of this type.

When Frank wanted to do the exposé of the continuing miseries of coal mining mentioned in Chapter 5, he chose the profile as his format. Locating a Pennsylvania coal miner whose father and grandfather had been miners too, a man whose name hadn't been in print since a local newspaper had reported his marriage many, many years earlier, Frank spent two days interviewing the miner, his father, and his son (who was about to become the fourth generation of miners), and others important to the story. Frank wrote the article the same way he would have had a notable been involved. The only difference was, the Sunday newspapers that ran his story headlined the subject's occupation instead of his name: "The Miners: Been Down so Long".

Ill. 6.5 _____

The Miners: Been Down so Long

As an occupation, coal mining has taken its lumps ever since the Industrial Revolution sent men to attacking underground seams of black coal to feed the machines that make things. From the once green valleys of Wales to the eroded hills of Appalachia, coal miners have endured deprivation and danger as a steady diet. In lore as in life, a miner's lot has been described as 16 tons of debt-ridden existence with disaster and black lung disease as companions. Bad enough, they say, for a man who can't scratch out a living otherwise, but a foolish choice for a job if he can drive a truck or sell shoes.

Yet, mine crews around Western Pennsylvania don't suffer from a labor shortage, and the interesting fact is that now, possibly for the first time, a miner can make a decent living. There is also a proud tradition that goes with coal mining. Call it coal dust in the blood or a dogged determination to follow a trade, the fact is that new coal miners tend to come from the families of old miners. The Guza family of Amity, Pa., reflects this tradition for four generations. They've got complaints against the system, of course. Volumes of them. But the mine is their life, and they don't ask for much more than steady employment at fair wages.

Back in the early 1900s, when a German immigrant named Daniel Guza went to work in the coal pit at

Marianna, Pa., miners were paid $2 for a 12-hour day. To old Daniel, whose specialty was erecting oak timbers to shore up tunnel roofs, it seemed foolish after a while to have a healthy, half-grown son just sitting around the house. So he got a job in the mine for his son. Soon, young Frank learned to handle the mules that pulled carts of coal out of the mine. "It was considered a good job," recalls the son, who's retired now, "because the mine bosses cared more then about mules than men. The mules, after all, cost $100 or so."

Perhaps it's the stories told on wintry evenings that set a youngster's course. Frank's son, Francis, who's 48 now, grew up on tales of muscle pitted against rock, of John Henry-type achievements with shovel or pick. He knows by heart the details of the great disaster at the Marianna in '07, when a short circuit in an electric cable ignited a gas pocket, blew up the mine, and killed more than 100 men. Long before Francis graduated from high school, he was determined to be a miner, like his father, maybe even a mite better one. It didn't seem to him, he recalls now, there was another choice worth considering.

Chicago Tribune Magazine, April 16, 1972. Copyright © 1972, Franklynn Peterson.

6·3 The Informative Article

All articles give information, of course, but this format is designed to emphasize information for its own sake. It uses expository writing, anecdotes, quotes, facts, figures—any of the journalistic and literary techniques that we will examine in Chapter 8—to inform the readers about a subject they want to know about. Some magazines, especially the big women's publications, have adopted the term "service article" to include both the how-to's and this format, which we probably could have labeled the *what-to, why-to, and when-to.*

Science magazines lean heavily on this format, using it to relay new developments. Health magazines use it to talk about diseases (whereas they use how-to's to talk about regimens for better health). Sports magazines use it to titillate readers about such things as great salmon streams in the Northwest. Business magazines rely on it to reveal trends. With a bit of scanning, you can spot it in almost any magazine you pick up.

The informative article, like the how-to, has to be organized *logically.* Sometimes chronological order is possible; most often, the movement is from major point to next logical major point. The best writers instinctively find a subject's internal logical progression. But it's a knack that can be developed through lots of writing and rewriting, testing alternate organizations and judging them critically.

Like the how-to and the profile, the informative article must concentrate on one unique aspect of the subject—in editorial jargon, the *handle*. (See Ill. 6.6)

Ill. 6.6

Tornado Factory

On April 3, 1974, one of the most ferocious tornado storms ever to hit the United States screamed across the Midwest. By the time the winds died down, more than 148 separate twisters had bulldozed a path through 13 states—killing at least 300, injuring thousands, and destroying several billion dollars' worth of property.

Despite its ferocity, that storm may mark the first step toward the taming of tornadoes. For as the winds subsided, meteorologists at Purdue University learned that Wally Hubbard, an Indianapolis TV cameraman, had taken some remarkable movies of the storm.

Driving home from an assignment, Hubbard spotted a twister several miles away. Steadying his camera against the car, he filmed the twister as it approached—and as it swept by him, barely a mile away. Hubbard took some of the clearest films ever made of tornadoes. More importantly, his lens captured one of the twisters breaking up into four separate cones, all of them barking and biting as they sped counterclockwise around the spot where the single funnel had vanished. For the first time, the Purdue meteorologists had documentary proof to back up what many had suspected—that a tornado, especially a highly destructive one, often has several cones rampaging in concert.

Some 9000 people have been killed by tornadoes in the United States in the past 50 years, according to Dr. Waltraud A. R. Brinkmann, geoscientist at the University of Wisconsin. And property damage averages between $200- and $300-million a year.

Despite such visible devastation, until very recently tornadoes have remained an enigma to weather scientists. Part of the reason is their utter unpredictability. Even fulltime tornado scientists, who strive mightily to be where the tornadoes are, consider themselves lucky if they observe two a year.

And with winds of 200 mph or more and a funnel that spans two miles across and often stretches 10 miles up into the sky, tornadoes don't lend themselves to easy study. So when Purdue meteorologists saw Hubbard's breakthrough films, plus the many still photos that had been taken during that April storm, they decided on an alternative to field study. Professors Ernest M. Agee, Christopher R. Church, and John T. Snow started to build themselves a tornado-making machine right in their laboratory.

Popular Science, July 1978. Copyright © 1978. P/K Associates, Inc.

The handle of the "Tornado Factory" article we wrote for *Popular Science* was the aspect of the general subject *tornadoes* that focused on the *why-to*: why tornadoes behave the way they do, as understood by Purdue University's tornado scientists who built a giant tornado simulator inside their lab. It employed *anecdotes* such as the one about the TV reporter who photographed the 1974 tornado, *quoted* experts such as Dr. Brinkmann (even though we didn't put quotation marks around her figures), and also used *exposition*. For *Family Health* (Ill. 6.7) we again wove *anecdotes* (such as the opening story about Wade Barnes) and *exposition* into an *informative* article about a new piece of medical hardware. The *handle* was: do our hospitals really need this expensive new piece of equipment? It was a *why-to*, though it also answered other questions.

Ill. 6.7

Miracle Machine

Wade Barnes is a big, likable, middle-aged man who used to make television commercials before he became a successful New York real estate dealer. Despite the pressure of his current job, he is usually in excellent health—except for periodic, but painful, gallstone attacks. The last time he had one, the standard gallbladder dye tests failed to produce positive findings and Barnes's doctor, concerned about ulcers or colitis, ordered a complete GI, or gastrointestinal, series. Barnes obediently swallowed some evil-tasting liquid barium and posed in a variety of uncomfortable positions as technicians took x-rays of the thick fluid passing through his intestinal tract.

When the radiologist examined the x-rays, he suddenly became less interested in Barnes's gallbladder than in a peculiar shadow he spotted on the pancreas. He told Barnes's doctor, "I don't like it. Looks like there might be something growing in there." The physician passed the bad news on to Wade Barnes. *Something growing? Cancer!* was Barnes's first, frightened thought.

But how were they to find out for sure? X-rays, like the ones Barnes had just had, can hint at a pancreatic growth, but cannot define it. The reason? Unlike bone and other hard body tissues, which reflect radiation onto an x-ray plate, soft body tissues, such as the internal organs, absorb almost uniform amounts of radiation. Thus, the differences between diseased and healthy tissues in an organ like the pancreas will be barely distinguishable even to a specialist's trained eye. Barnes would have to undergo risky, expensive and painful exploratory surgery so that a doctor would see with his own eyes if there was, indeed, a growth.

Fortunately, however, Barnes was acquainted with a team of radiologists who had recently bought themselves a fancy new machine that was capable of taking readable x-ray pictures of parts of the body never clearly photographed before. Barnes called the radiologists at their Queens, New York, office and asked if their machine could help him. He was told it could, so he made an appointment.

The doctors, however, couldn't see him for two weeks and, during that time, Barnes lived with fear of the disease and apprehension about the complicated new machine that would determine his fate. His nervousness didn't abate when he walked into the scanning room, changed into a paper examining gown, and was asked to lie on a table and insert the lower half of his body through a donut-like ring and into a huge, rectangular steel device. He was prepared for the worst—certainly for more discomfort than a GI series.

Instead, as the noisy machine started up and the rectangle began clicking and circling around his stomach like a robot from some science fiction novel, the only discomforts Barnes experienced were those of having to remain motionless for several minutes at a time and of holding his arms stiffly behind his head. After half an hour, the technician who'd helped him onto the table helped him off. It was all over and, by the time Barnes had dressed, the radiologists, Drs. Herbert Rabiner and Jeffrey Kaplan, were ready for him. "Wade," Dr. Rabiner said, "there isn't a thing wrong with your pancreas. It looks as healthy as mine."

The machine that saved Wade Barnes from exploratory surgery is called a CT or CAT whole body scanner. (There are also scanners designed to photograph only the head or the torso; the whole body scanner, however, does both.) The initials stand for Computed Tomography or Computerized Axial Tomography, different terms for the same process. The *computing* is done by minicomputers similar to the ones used in rocket ships. The word *axial* refers to the fact that, unlike conventional x-rays that produce a two-dimensional, lengthwise picture, CT scanners use the patient as an axis and rotate the machine around him. The result: a crosscut image. And *tomography* is a Greek word meaning "to write a slice," which is exactly what the CT scanner does—it writes a detailed description of what a thin slice of the patient would look like if a doctor could section him the way a cook slices tomatoes.

But when Barnes had his pancreas scanned, he wasn't even poked. Instead, the CT scanner made a series of 180 degree arcs around his stomach, pausing every so often to direct a tiny amount of radiation—no greater than that of conventional x-rays —through him. The x-rays were then fed through an electric eye into a computer terminal, where the information was translated into a front-to-back photo of the inside of Barnes's torso, as well as a numerical print-out and a magnetic tape to be filed for future reference. Within seconds, a slice of Wade Barnes could be viewed on a TV screen—either in black-and-white or, with the press of a button, in psychedelic colors. His pancreas, his stomach and his backbone and spinal cord were all clearly distinguishable. And with assurance of 95 percent accuracy, the radiologists could tell Barnes that his pancreas was not malformed, that it was not diseased and that there were no blood clots or other foreign bodies that shouldn't be there. Only surgery could give more precise information —but that, fortunately, was no longer necessary.

The CT scanner can bring to light organs other than the pancreas, too. It can examine the liver for hematomas (tumors containing effused blood). It can detect benign cysts in the kidneys, which can then be drained to cure the patient without surgery. And it can show the extent of cancerous tumors and ascertain whether or not they've spread. For example, after an ordinary chest x-ray, one patient was told that she had a lung tumor. An operation would have followed almost automatically, except that a CT scan revealed that the tumor had spread to the chest wall, making surgery useless. Although the woman wasn't cured, at least she was spared a needless operation.

Surgery isn't the only unpleasant diagnostic tool that CT can replace.

A patient suspected of colonic tumors, polyps or diverticula (sacs produced by abnormal protrusions through organ walls) may be scanned instead of having to take an uncomfortable barium enema. Scanning is also a possible alternative to tests involving the injection of dyes or radioactive materials via painful catheterization of the artery that supplies blood to the liver, pancreas, spleen or kidneys. (Sometimes dyes *are* used in conjunction with CT scanning but, on those occasions, comparatively small amounts are administered by simple needle injections.)

Valuable as it is, CT body scanning is only a babe-in-the-woods compared to its older sibling, CT head scanning, which has revolutionized the diagnosis and treatment of brain disorders.

Until seven years ago, a doctor had few alternatives—none of them pleasant—if he wanted to find out what was happening in the soft tissues hidden behind a patient's skull. He could order an encephalogram, a technique that involves forcing air into the patient's brain to outline the convoluted tissues on an x-ray plate. (The patient would. . . . .

continued in Ill. 8.1

In writing informative articles, you should be prepared to answer those classic canons of journalism: who, what, why, when, where, and how. Occasionally, these articles end with brief how-to sections or referral lists—if there's information that ambitious, inquisitive readers might want to investigate further to try out for themselves. We've added these brief how-tos to many of our stories for *Popular Science,* as well as to articles on such topics as rape (listing crisis centers), alcoholism (listing helping agencies), and test-wiseness (listing books that provide more information). Many editors love to receive extra tidbits that add to the *service* aspect of the articles and often treat them as *boxes* or *sidebars*.

When we tackled geodesic-dome homes for *Popular Science,* we stuck almost entirely to the *handle* of what was *new* and *exciting* about the subject, since the magazine had done dome stories almost biennially since Buckminster Fuller had invented the concept. As you can see in the article's ending (Ill. 6.8), we were able to carve the story almost entirely from *anecdotes* and *quotes,* using *exposition* merely to glue the other elements together. At the end, as we'd promised the editors, we offered a central source of additional practical information. We also prepared a list of more than two dozen dome home manufacturers, with their addresses, to whom readers could write for help in buying their own domes. Editors wisely sidebarred the list, setting it apart from the story because a long series of facts, presented simply as facts, makes for boring reading. And the first commandment for good writers and editors has always been: keep it exciting.

Ill. 6.8

There are two basic construction methods in use today among dome suppliers. The hub-and-strut method is closest to the early Buckminster Fuller models. Conceptually it's very much like building with Tinker Toys. A steel hub, typically a short length of a six-inch pipe, is bolted to a collection of 2×6 pine struts that fan out until they link up to other struts via other hubs. The network of resulting triangles curves gracefully into the famous dome shape.

Stresses from the weight of the hubs, struts, snow, wind, and other building loads are evenly distributed through the network, coming finally to rest on the ground. Alternately, the dome can be set upon a foundation of poured concrete, cement blocks, or specially treated wood [PS, Sept. '72]. Some domes are built on top of risers that increase the height of the outside walls.

The second basic dome construction method uses the panelized approach. This hybrid technique combines the early Fuller concept and traditional frame carpentry. Buckminster Fuller approves of the method.

Wisconsin dome manufacturer Ray Shultis explains how his version of the panelized dome developed: "My dad got interested in domes five years ago, and he took me along. But about all that anybody knew about domes back then was in *Dome Book I* and *Dome Book II,* produced by the counter-culture. So our first dome came right out of *Dome Book II.* It was nice, but it was also too hard for your ordinary building contractor to work with. So I spent 18 months educating myself about the math and design of domes. And we redesigned our dome so it fits into the experience of your ordinary frame carpenter."

Four times better

Says Bob Koger, a Florida architect who's collaborated on Shultis' design: "We've designed our domes to be four times better than the building codes require. We have them out for third-party testing now, and when the results are in, we won't have to go through so much red tape at local building departments."

An informal survey of building departments finds that inspectors *are* willing to okay domes, but many of them do want to see studs every 16 inches like the old frame construction. A Madison, Wis., building code supervisor chuckled as he said the major problem he'd have with domes was deciding where the roof (requiring 30-pound snow-load capacity) ended and the wall (requiring only a 20-pound wind load capacity) began! He added, "I don't see any problems that can't be tackled easily."

The U.S. Department of Housing and Urban Development is starting to okay the structural soundness of a few dome manufacturers' designs. HUD approval is generally required before an FHA-insured home mortgage is possible.

You can get more information by writing the National Assn. of Dome Manufacturers (Suite 470, 1701 Lake Ave., Glenview, Ill. 60025) or by contacting individual manufacturers below.[A list of names and addresses follows.]

Popular Science, April 1979. Copyright © 1979, P/K Associates, Inc.

6·4 The Exposé

One specific kind of informational article has evolved into a separate format with its own structure: the exposé (a word often written without the accent that reminds us to pronounce the final *e* as *ay*). Exposé writers use *investigative reporting,* which is simply any kind of research for facts that will in some substantial way shock the readers. Too many would-be exposé writers think their jobs are done at that, which is really only a first step. Next, the exposé writer must present the facts in a manner that *does* shock the reader, while staying carefully within the bounds of accuracy and discreetly hedging when necessary to avoid needless libel suits or nasty letters to the editor.

Not much exposé research is of the mind-boggling Woodward-and-Bernstein variety. Exposés of Watergate magnitude generate newspaper headlines and laudatory pickup stories by other writers. But startling statistics, authoritative quotes, and shocking anecdotes work well for stories with more modest pretensions, as long as they add to the exposé's end result: to shock readers. Since early efforts in your writing career will probably be confined to exposés that don't shake the world, we'll work with such examples here.

"The Skateboard Menace," an article Judi prepared for *Family Health* magazine, highlighted what was then a new fad, the broken bones, torn muscles, concussions, and fatalities. In among the exposition for parents who didn't yet know a skateboard from a Ouija board, Judi strung out statistic after statistic, anecdote after anecdote, each more shocking than the last.

Judi researched the story by asking selected police and medical officials about skateboarding problems. She asked skateboard officials about them, too. Using newspaper indexes and friends, as well as other resource people (quoted in the article), she found dozens of horror stories. She made sure she studied medical journals and authoritative accident statistic compilations. Her research did not reveal anything press-stopping (skateboards had not become the number one crippler of children), but Judi used classic exposé writing skills to shock parents nonetheless. Let's pinpoint these techniques.

In Judi's *lead* paragraph, she establishes skateboarding as a big and growing hobby, as well as a multimillion dollar business, thus providing *framework of magnitude*. After all, unless skateboards are used by a significant part of the population, the dangers—no matter how great—are of insignificant concern. Then she quickly (first full paragraph on the article's second page) introduces the *statistics,* which show the *reason for concern.* Notice that Dr. Coll, her *authority,* doesn't actually say that 20 percent of all accidents are caused by skateboarding. He says, in fact, that in a *typical weekend*—(typical, of course, being whatever the doctor and author choose to call it)—20 percent of *only certain accidents* are from skateboarding. But as it is worded, the *quote* shocks the quick reader. That's what readers like—and pros give readers what they want to read.

Later Judi offers another *statistic:* she mentions that, thanks to polyurethane wheels, skateboards can hit fifty miles per hour. *Do* they ever attain that neckbreaking speed on neighborhood sidewalks? Judi sidesteps the question, qualifying her figure by saying, "on a race track."

Statistics are a powerful device in the hands of the good exposé writer. Editors and readers alike want to look into the future. Judi found definite figures for the previous year's skateboard accidents —27,522—but what about the *current* year? No way to know for sure, of course, since the article was to run in the August issue (which means it was written before June). Instead, Judi informally surveyed several hospitals and got the report that in a three-month period they had patched up as many skateboarders as in the previous twelve months.

Quick readers would conclude that there could be four times as many accidents this year. They could be right. A pro never ever fudges on statistics—but she *does* learn to use them to best effect.

Ill. 6.9

The Skateboard Menace

Business is booming for orthopedists all over the country this year. Broken wrists, splintered elbows and smashed ankles are just three com- common hazards of the reborn skateboard craze.

Skateboarding became a short-lived fad about 10 years ago, when out-of-season surfers attached roller-skate wheels to their surfboards and took to the hilly roads. As other young people took up the sport, manufacturers began to offer mass-produced skateboards. But as quickly as the fad blossomed, its popularity faded.

Two years ago, a California enthusiast tried something new: He screwed a set of new polyurethane wheels to an old board, achieving a faster, smoother, quieter ride. Almost instantly, a whole new generation of skateboarders emerged, and this time close to 150 manufacturers undertook to meet their needs. Today, skateboarding is a multimillion dollar business. In June, 26 top skateboarders met in New York to vie for $7,000 in prizes at the first World Masters Invitational competition, and in September the first open World Invitational meet will take place in California—with a $50,000 purse! At least one magazine for skateboarders or "hot doggers" is being published, the first skateboard movies are making the rounds and a TV series is in preparation. *Newsweek* magazine estimates that between 6 and 10 million Americans are now on the boards.

But for most of these fans, generally boys in their teens and pre-teens, skateboarding is neither business nor semi-pro sport; it is a popular neighborhood pastime—and a very dangerous one. As Dr. Geoffrey Coll, orthopedic resident at Long Island Jewish-Hillside Medical Center in New York, says, "The year before last we saw no skateboard injuries in emergency orthopedics. Last year I remember only one or two. This year the numbers are significant: Out of twenty bad strains, sprains and broken bones in a typical weekend, I'd estimate that 20 percent are from skateboard accidents. And," he pointed out, "I only see the more serious injuries. Minor scrapes and bruises are treated by the interns in our general emergency room."

Little accidents happen mostly to beginners, according to a Great Neck, New York, pediatrician. "The novices are cautious at first. They choose their roads carefully and avoid dangerous tricks. They fall on their fannies or scrape their hands and knees, but, in general, they get no more banged up than beginning bicyclists. When they think they've mastered the boards, that's when they start taking chances and really hurt themselves."

A Long Island policeman reports that people are complaining about teenagers trespassing upon neighbors' drained swimming pools to "ride" them. In this gravity-defying trick, picked up from a California skateboard movie, necessary momentum is gained to make the skateboard wheels cling to the curved upper sides of the pool, while the rider spins dizzily atop—or, more accurately, aside—his board. So many children perform "nose wheelies" and "tail wheelies" (tipping back or front) that some skateboards are now being manufactured with snubbed noses and flipped-up tails.

Tricks like these were not possible a decade ago, when skateboards were made of wood and wheels were steel or clay. Today's good-quality boards are flexible fiber glass, aluminum or Lucite, and boast sophisticated "trucks," the mechanisms to which wheels are attached. The polyurethane wheels themselves provide the remarkable traction necessary for "riding" pools, and on a race track can carry their passengers as fast as 50 miles per hour.

Since mechanical advancements make it possible for almost any experienced skateboarder to do some fancy tricks, intense pressure insures that youngsters will try. In fact, a cult glamorizing both risk and pain is rapidly developing around the sport. According to the code, if you haven't been badly hurt at least once, you haven't attempted a really difficult trick. "Wiping out is considered neat," explains Bill Colvard, a salesman in the Durham, North Carolina K-Mart sports department, where skateboards are the season's biggest-selling merchandise. "A kid who's experienced the pain of skateboarding is really big stuff. His image is definitely enhanced."

Enhancing or not, a wipe out can be a serious matter. In New Haven, Connecticut, a young teen's braces cut right through his lip; a Chicago youth, swerving to avoid a dog, collided with a parked car and broke both knee caps. In Haverstraw, New York, a high school junior struck a rut and wound up hospitalized for two days with a concussion. Severe scrapes and bruises are common enough to be referred to as "road rash," and so many youngsters have suffered arm injuries that, according to *The Physician and Sportsmedicine* magazine, doctors now call a shattering of the olecranon, "skateboard elbow." At least two fatalities have been recorded in California, and on a national level, skateboards caused a spectacular 27,522 injuries requiring hospital treatment in 1975—a record that promoted them from eighth to third place in accident frequency for all children's toys (except for bicycles, which are in an accident class by themselves). A recent three-month survey showed more skateboard casualties in some hospitals than in an earlier twelve-month period.

Another modest exposé, reprinted in part, points out that almost no topic is outside the purview of this journalistic technique. In "Household Hotlines" (Ill. 6.10), an attempt to scare people into being careful with the ubiquitous extension cord, Frank's lead sentence starts right in by stating that every year there are *hundreds* of serious fires resulting in *millions of dollars* of damage (*framework of magnitude* and *reason for concern* all rolled into one). But those are very indefinite figures. Even more indefinite is the clause within that sentence that tells that deaths occur, too—but not in every one of the hundreds of fires. Had Frank explained, or used very precise statistics, the reader's eye would have to slow down, slowing down the story and generating less shock.

In the last line of the first paragraph, Frank creatively uses National Fire Protection Association figures: he doesn't say, "Extension cords cause X many fires, TVs Y many fires, and microwave ovens Z many fires." Nor does he say, "Extension cords cause one-fourth as many fires as all appliances put together." Both of the preceding are true—but not exciting. With the indulgence of the National Fire Protection Association, Frank chooses his words accurately but carefully, and concludes that the lowly extension cord "is the most dangerous electrical item in common use." You too will be able to select and present facts with maximum impact after you've cut your piranha teeth on a few modest exposés of your own.

Ill. 6.10 ⎯⎯⎯⎯⎯⎯⎯⎯⎯⎯⎯⎯⎯⎯⎯⎯⎯⎯⎯⎯⎯⎯⎯⎯⎯

Household Hotlines

Every year hundreds of serious fires resulting in deaths and millions of dollars of damage can be traced to faulty extension cords or their improper use. Innumerable incidents involving these connectors go unreported. They include minor fires, major scares and damage to household furnishings and appliances. Damage and tragedies caused by the innocent-looking extension cord have increased to such an extent that now it is the most dangerous electrical item in common use, according to figures compiled by the National Fire Protection Association.

Basically extension cords become dangerous under three conditions: when they are old; when they are used permanently; when they are overloaded.

In Washington, D.C., a mother wanted a reading light for her side of the bed. She found an old extension cord and ran it under the bed to a wall outlet. Months later, the forgotten old cord overheated or shorted, ignited the bedding and mattress, and in the fire which resulted the family's five children perished.

The National Fire Protection Association (NFPA), a major spokesman in the electrical safety field, warns that extension cords must never be used near combustible materials such as a mattress or clothing. They advise that before using any extension cord, "look for frayed, broken or brittle insulation," all of which can lead to shorts which generate such intense heat that fabrics can be ignited in seconds.

A Seal Pleasant, Md., family's TV was connected to a cord which often sent out a shower of sparks when somebody stepped on it. Early one morning, a six-year-old son went down to the living room and tried to get the TV and extension cord to work. Sparks ignited the living room draperies. Before the morning was over, $16,000 in fire damage had been done to the house. The mother and two children died.

The Maryland family, among its other misjudgments, had also violated the National Electric Code (NEC) by using an extension cord as a permanent installation. Most insurance companies follow the NEC in making electrical safety inspections. The Code recommends that extension cords be avoided whenever possible and forbids their use for anything other than strictly temporary jobs.

Used Permanently

An extension cord was wedged into an out-of-the-way crack under the stove in a Maywood, Ill., kitchen. A combination of wear and heat gradually destroyed the extension cord's insulation. When it short-circuited one night, three children died in their upstairs bedroom be-

cause of the ensuing fire. The mother and two other children escaped with injuries.

Heat and most chemicals are murder on extension cord insulation. Electrical cords should never be used near radiators, heat pipes, stoves or even near the back or bottom of TV sets which also generate considerable heat. And if a cord is going to be used near moisture (such as in a damp basement or outdoors) or near oil (such as in the kitchen or a garage), the NFPA recommends that you "use only cords marked water-resistant or 'oil-resistant'."

Overloaded

During a chilly November night in Stillwater, Okla., a college fraternity hooked up a 1650 watt electric heater to an ordinary light extension cord. To keep members from tripping over the cord, it was laid under a rug in the bedroom. During the night, the small cord which was forced to handle too large an electrical load overheated and set fire to the rug. Fortunately, an automatic alarm system alerted fraternity brothers in time to escape, but $600 in damages resulted.

"Portable electric heaters need special extension cords designed to carry heavier loads," says the NFPA. Most common cords are made of number 18 size wire and should not carry more than 700 watts of power, according to the NFPA. Heaters, toasters, broilers, vaporizers and similar home gadgets require more than 700 watts of power. It is safest not to use any extension cord with heaters and such appliances. But if you feel that you must, buy a heavy-duty extension cord made of wire large enough to handle the load. Every extension cord on sale should be clearly marked with a label designating the maximum electrical load it can safely handle.

6·5 Personal Experience, Reminiscence, and As-Told-To

When one of our students set out to write an article about a weight-reduction program fairly new to Milwaukee, he decided that the liveliest way to relate the story was by telling his own personal experience in shedding forty-seven pounds. The *Milwaukee Sentinel* feature editor agreed that he'd have a lively story if he could present *his own* experience along with sufficient *general information* for readers who might want to consider doing likewise. We've reproduced the first part of John's "Food Greaser Loses 47 Pounds" (Ill. 6.11) so you can see for yourself how well he succeeded.

Ill. 6.11

Food Greaser Loses 47 Pounds

by John L. Hirsh

I used to be a greaser. A food greaser.

On a typical day I ate several quarter pounders with cheese, extra crispy fried chicken, deep dish pizza and a couple of ham sandwiches. In between, I kept myself going with refined sugar products. I munched chocolate bars with almonds, sweet rolls and cream filled cupcakes.

My stomach started to jam up against the steering wheel of my car. Then my stomach began to rebel. To neutralize the acid and gas, I gobbled Rolaids, Alka 2, Tums and Pepto-Bismol—whatever was handiest.

When I walked a block or two, I'd huff and puff and say, "I have this asthma condition, you know."

At 5 foot 10½ inches, I weighed close to 250. On some days I denied every pound of it to myself. On others I decided it was really macho to be that heavy.

Being a food greaser also led me to the dentist's chair. My teeth were rotting. I had to have root canal work and new fillings. The incredible pain I suffered convinced me that I had to get some grease relief. I had to abandon "gut bombs" and sugar. I had to start eating the right food. I had to go on a . . . on a . . . on a diet.

BUT WHICH ONE? There are so many. And each is different.

The "more of" diets suggested an increase in wine, liquor, vegetables, lollipops, ice cream, candy or liquid protein. The "less of" programs recommend no breakfasts, no meat, virtual starvation or just plain wiring the mouth shut.

About a year ago, when I was in a pharmacy buying a chocolate bar with almonds, I made the decision to "degrease." Spotting "Consumer Guide to Rating the Diets" by Theodore Berland helped me make that decision. I checked to see which diets rated high. Based on Berland's criteria of high protein, a maximum of 30% fat (mostly unsaturated), low carbohydrates and sugar, he gave a four star rating to 21 programs. Of the top three programs, two had branches here—Weight Watches and Diet Workshop.

I had tried to lose weight in groups before. I'd been moderately successful, once almost going below 200, but the "confession" aspect of the meetings turned me off. I always *knew* I was doing things wrong. What I wanted now was a program to change my behavior.

I REVIEWED Berland's book again, discovering that Diet Workshop could tell me what to eat, how to use behavior modification principles, and I liked its emphasis on exercise. Eleven months ago I joined Diet Workshop. I lost and I won.

I had been a member of Weight Watchers in 1974 and then again in 1976. As to which is better—Weight Watchers or Diet Workshop—I can only say that it really depends upon you and the group leader. What follows is my experience with Diet Workshop.

A good diet, I discovered, does NOT reduce the amount of food. It teaches you HOW to eat and WHAT to eat. It changes your lifestyle. I was amazed at the quantity of food I could eat. I learned about low fat meats which I had never heard of or was too poor to buy: antelope, buffalo, caribou, venison, elk, goat, moose, pheasant, quail, squab, squid, tripe, finnan haddie, chicken haddie, butterfish.

I learned that I could eat high fat proteins—beef or frankfurters—only three times a week. At first I splurged once a month and ate sirloin steak. Then I learned that I could lose weight faster by eliminating beef from my diet altogether.

FOR BREAKFAST I got an egg and toast on one day, cheese and cereal on others. Never having thought of cheese as breakfast food, I soon discovered delicious varieties like gouda, edam and ricotta.

I also could eat five fruits a day including bananas, cantaloupe, peaches, pears, plums, raspberries and strawberries.

I got to eat as much as I wanted of asparagus, bean sprouts, broccoli, cabbage, celery, chard, cucumber, endive, lettuce, mushrooms, onions, radishes, spinach or zucchini. But I was limited daily to 4 ounces or one-half cup of artichokes, brussels sprouts, carrots, eggplant, kohlrabi, peas, pumpkin, squash or tomato.

Occasionally, as a bonus, I could

substitute frozen yogurt or ice milk (from stores like Dairy Queen or Boy Blue) as a 4 ounce substitute for an 8 ounce milk requirement. Best of all, I learned I could drink up to 1 ounce of liquor or 3 ounces of wine two or three times a week!

Milwaukee Sentinel, January 11, 1979. Copyright© 1979, The Sentinel Corporation.

The personal-experience story combines some elements of both the profile and the informative article, especially in that it is usually organized chronologically and highlights an aspect of a person. In fact, it's possible, although not common, to do exposés and how-to's based on personal experience. Do a personal how-to, for example, if you've learned how to build a Saran Wrap flying machine and are willing to share your unique techniques with other readers. Do a personal exposé cum personality profile if a KKK Grand Dragon locked you in a bathroom with Richard Pryor for eighteen hours, during which he told you one bad joke after another. If you could expose southern public restrooms and Richard Pryor's humor all in the first person, you'd have a selling article for sure.

A majority of students begin by trying to crank out personal experience stories. Some, we're sure, do it because they think it's the easiest kind of format. But we get the haunting feeling at times that many enroll in writing courses simply to write letters to the world and expect us to get them published. The number one requirement for selling a personal experience story is not that you want to *write* it, but that enough people want to *read* it. In short, you have to have had a personal experience that in some substantial way sets you aside from the day-to-day lives of quiet desperation that Thoreau felt most people live. Reminiscences don't sell either, except sometimes locally for a few dollars.

How many of us can survive enough falls off twenty-eight-story buildings, or recover from enough near-fatal illnesses, to make a living writing personal-experience articles? The pros who do make a living at it write about *somebody else's* tragedies and triumphs. Sometimes the person who's lived the experience gets the entire by-line. Other times the actual author is listed second: "as told to. . . ." Rarely can the author count on a traditional by-line—usually only for articles involving celebrities.

The dean of personal experience storytellers must be Terry Morris, ex-president of the American Society of Journalists and Authors. About 1950, Terry abandoned short-story writing in favor of human-interest magazine articles about people in crisis. Her genius for telling a touching story carried over from fiction to nonfiction, and she sold her first two articles to *Cosmopolitan* and *McCall's* early in 1951. Not a bad beginning!

Terry's all-time favorite is "Please Don't Lose Faith in Me," an as-told-to article from the viewpoint of the mother of a schizophrenic son. *McCall's* ran it in July 1953; we've reproduced the beginning (Ill. 6.12) so you can study how a master molds somebody else's personal experience.

Ill. 6.12 ───────────────────────────────────────

> On Sunday, rain or shine, my husband and I
> drive twenty-five miles through a pleasant country-
> side to visit our first-born, our son Jamie. Jamie
> is 30 years old. If he should ever again, by the
> grace of God, raise his head and stand erect he
> would measure six feet two inches. He has broad
> shoulders, a lean waist, and the strong, bold
> features of a man of decision. Looking at him
> we see what he might have been -- but what he is
> not and never will be.

McCall's, July, 1953. Copyright © 1953, Terry Morris.

6·6 The Essay or Personal Opinion

Back when Judi was tending her two sons' intellectual curiosity and the family's tight budget too, New York City museums initiated a not entirely voluntary "contribution" fee. Judi got angry. Rather than write a letter to the editor, she typed her thoughts in personal opinion article format. *The New York Times* not only published it but paid her for it, because she had put into strong words an opinion that many of its readers agreed with. (Ill. 6.13).

Ill. 6.13 ───────────────────────────────────────

It Costs Too Much To Go
to a Museum

So the museums are doing poorly, are they? Well, I'm secretly glad to hear it. I've been doing poorly myself ever since they slammed their doors on me and my children several years ago.

I used to think that the Metropolitan and the Natural History museums were *my* museums. When I was a youngster growing up in lower-middle-class Brooklyn, those museums were where our family went on glorious excursions to New York. The dinosaurs in the cavernous halls are linked forever with the double-decker Fifth Avenue busses among my earliest memories. When I began traveling the subways alone, I met friends from the Bronx in the Egyptian tomb at the Metropolitan and we wandered the other corridors until we knew them by heart.

A school trip introduced me to the Museum of Modern Art, and I loved its paintings. But its entry fee, then 50 cents, was for the most part beyond my means. When I did splurge for a ticket, I felt like a poor relation in its intimate rooms —tolerated, but not really welcome. (These days, a visit to MOMA with my two sons would set me back $3.50 in all, so we're still poor relations.)

Then I married and moved to Manhattan to bring up my children on the borders of Central Park. I counted pennies while my first child was in the stroller. In the Museum of Natural History, I discovered, they allowed me in with the stroller, and on weekdays when the halls were empty of all but school groups, I'd push my son around the museum.

When he was very young, there were the stuffed animals; he'd look and I'd explain what the placards said.

Later on we graduated to the snakes and turtles in the live-animal room, the Indian displays, the oil rig, the nature hall, and the fine new Hall of Man. By then he was out of the stroller and his little brother was in it. I had widened his horizons to the Metropolitan, starting with the "Knights in Shining Armor." Then the Metropolitan opened its Children's Wing, with a ground-level door through which the Wing welcomed my stroller.

The children grew, our mobility increased and we widened our horizons to include all the exhibits of both museums. A yearly trip to the Guggenheim consisted of taking the elevator to the top and then chasing after the kids as they alternated a happy run down the ramp with an occasional long visit with a piece of art whose color or form caught their happy eyes. That delighted romp down the ramp was itself worth the 50-cent admission price: it reinforced their observations that pleasure went with art.

For the most part, however, even as we grew more affluent we ignored the museums that charged admission.

Just as your personal-experience stories have to involve some experience that a great many people want to read about, your personal-opinion article must contain opinions on a subject of consequence to thousands of people. As a rule, national magazines publish relatively few personal-opinion articles, and then almost exclusively on vital national issues written by people of national stature. Local editors are more likely to publish opinions by local authors on subjects of local or national importance.

The essay, classically, is a carefully constructed opinion piece in which *all* the facts, arguments, and conclusions are filtered through the author's unconcealed (and at times quite opinionated) viewpoint. This genre does not represent a substantial market for pros, but if you want to pursue it, we suggest you reread Chapter 2's comments on magazines of commentary and study the publications mentioned there.

6·7 Humor and Satire

There's nothing funny about humor. It's tough work. Most editors we've met have said they'd like to see more humor coming across their desks—but that they haven't seen much good humor yet. What is—or is not—funny is very subjective and always changing.

Humor can be applied to any of the other standard magazine formats. A humorous personal experience is out-and-out humor. A humorous exposé, a humorous how-to, a humorous interview, and so forth, are all called *satire*.

You may have considered writing humor because even your mother laughs at your jokes. In that case, we suggest you try writing movies or TV sitcoms where there's bigger money and a greater market. But if you're set on writing magazine humor, who are we to stand in your way? Write it and send it out. Unlike most other formats, you can't sell humor based on ideas alone. You must mail the finished article to an editor, with the hope that she thinks it's funny too.

Because we believe that humor is such a specialized, hard-to-sell field, we don't include an example here.

6·8 Inspirational

In a sense, one could call the inspirational article a form of how-to. It tells readers how to *feel good* or how to *do good things*: how to feel good about themselves, how to do well at selling vacuum cleaners, how to lead more exemplary lives. In another sense, such articles are personal experiences. A typical inspirational weaves the experience of some person, celebrity or not, around a moral message that leads readers to conclude that it's possible and worthwhile to achieve better lives.

Many people automatically associate inspirational stories with religious magazines. Those publications do, in fact, run a plethora of inspirationals. But business, civic, and other magazines use inspirational articles, too. (Ill. 6.14)

Ill. 6.14

One Teacher's Triumph

by Paul Martin

The school day at Westside Preparatory School sometimes starts as early as 7:30 in the morning. The students' rigorous work schedule includes recitation of passages from Shakespeare, Kipling and Emerson, discussions of Socrates. Grammar-school youngsters write themes about Sophocles and Dostoevski's *The Brothers Karamazov* that reveal a grasp of abstract concepts. Spelling and grammar are accurate.

An expensive private institution in Shaker Heights or Scarsdale? Not at all. It's a one-room school at 3819 West Adams Street on Chicago's tough west side. Students range in age from 5 to 12, and their enthusiasm for knowledge is the inspiration of a remarkable woman—Marva Collins.

Westside Prep opened three and one-half years ago, the vision of Collins who was "fed up after 14 years of teaching in the Chicago public schools." Using the family savings,

her husband, Clarence, remodeled the second floor of their two-family home, and the school opened in September 1975. It began with 6 neighborhood youngsters and grew to 14 by the end of the year. Today 31 students attend Westside Prep.

With boundless energy, Marva Collins encourages, jokes, cajoles and inspires her young scholars, telling them to sit up straight, speak up, look people in the eye and pay attention. While one group masters a drill in a workbook, another group of children receives personal instruction from her.

Marva Collins fosters a strong sense of individual responsibility among her students. "Success doesn't come to you," she declares. "You go to it. You don't buy it with Green Stamps. There's no paycheck until the work is done. You don't get a report card unless all the homework is in. Every moment here is going to be used."

The techniques for writing inspirationals are little different from those used to write profiles or personal-experience articles. In each of those other formats, writers concentrate on some single topic; in the inspirational, the focus is always the inspirational point that you (or your editor) want to make.

Markets for inspirational articles are bountiful. Payment, as a rule, isn't.

6·9 The Historical Article

Many beginning writers see this as a separate article format. They come to us—those who feel their own lives aren't exciting enough to warrant personal-experience stories—and say that they want to tell about this or that legendary character who lived in their neck of the woods, or this or that legendary event that happened nearby. It's a noble venture, to be sure, but a futile one unless your daddy grew up with the likes of Jesse James or John Dillinger and has a steel-trap memory.

A historical article is not *only* about something that happened a long time ago. It must also meet all of the criteria we detailed earlier for profile, personal experience, and informative articles. (History can also be fodder for humor.) It must, therefore:

> tell about events or people of interest to thousands or even millions of readers;
> focus on a single aspect of the subject;
> be organized logically (usually chronologically);
> tell readers (and editors) something substantial they didn't already know, and tell it in an exciting fashion.

To have discovered some previously unheard-of person or event is *not* reason enough to write a historical article—not if you expect to see it published. If that previously unheard-of person or event involved something terribly funny, dangerous, or historically significant, then you might be able to sell the piece.

When Frank was researching cartoonists, he discovered Louis Raemaekers. Attracted to the man's art as well as his caustic perspective on World War I, he started collecting Raemaekers' lithographed cartoons. Suddenly it occurred to him that if he'd never known about Raemaekers before, maybe a lot of readers didn't either. That proved true—but it wasn't salable. What *was* salable was that many credited the little-known artist with having started Belgium's involvement in World War I. Because Raemaekers fit the requirements for a historical article, Frank was able to sell a story about the cartoonist to *Mankind* magazine.

The national history magazines such as *Mankind* and *American Heritage,* and the regional magazines of history, are natural buyers for historicals—but they're an overcrowded marketplace. Magazines of more general interest also buy history if its subject fits into a publication's framework. For example, tired of space-exploration sagas, Frank sought relief in historic novels. He picked up Jules Verne's *From the Earth to the Moon* and noticed so many parallels between the story and real rocket launches that he sold an article to *Science & Mechanics:* "Who Planned Apollo II, Von Braun or Verne?" (Ill. 6.15)

Ill. 6.15

Who Planned Apollo II, Von Braun or Verne?

The space vehicle was just a nautical mile or two in the distance. All hearts on deck of the recovery ship paused for the duration of this momentous voyage. Breathing stopped as the small boats put out for the craft just returned from its trip around the moon. The Pacific Ocean itself seemed subdued and awestruck.

And as one recovery boat drew near, all ears cocked to catch a sound of life. What momentous scientific lore would the three intrepid space travelers be discussing at a moment such as this?

"Queen! How is that for high?" a nasal voice broke the calm with its twang.

It was followed by an even shriller response, cloaked in a bit of an accent. "King! My brave Mac! How is that for high?"

"Ace!" came still a third response. "Dear friends, how is that for high?"

High-Low-Jack! The three astro-nauts were so preoccupied with their game of high-low-jack they hadn't noticed the recovery vessels steaming toward them. A rousing game of cards was quite a fitting ending for a space voyage conjectured back in 1865 by none other than Jules Verne.

On their way to the moon, Verne managed to stow some very exquisite chow on board the space capsule *Columbiad,* including bottles of vintage wine like Chateau Yques and Clos de Vougeot. When Aldrin, Collins and Armstrong set out a century later for the same celestial body, the menu was hardly less exquisite than Jules Verne concocted for his three imaginary astronauts.

Colonel Collins, for instance, radioed back: "My compliments to the chef. That salmon salad is outstanding." Scalloped potatoes, shrimp cocktail and butterscotch pudding accompanied the three 20th century hardies on their way, but no wine. And no deck of cards.

Science & Mechanics, March 1971. Copyright ©1971, Franklynn Peterson.

In researching another story, Frank discovered an obscure but well-documented old book telling about African explorers who'd make it to America before Columbus. From that start, he discovered twenty-three other explorers who had probably touched North America before old Chris. That year, editors at the Metropolitan Sunday Newspaper Group presented a unique Columbus Day offering, "Goodby, Columbus, To No. 1." (Ill. 6.16).

Ill. 6.16

Goodby, Columbus, To No. 1

Everybody knows Columbus discovered America, and the year was 1492. But was he the first "foreigner" to land in the New World, or was he, as some historians reckon, about the 25th to discover America? And there are always new claims popping up, like Chinese claims of landings somewhere in Mexico around the year 1 a.d., and reports of various Polynesian drifters who might have gone eastward beyond Hawaii.

Since Columbus Day is near, it might be interesting to put together some of the accounts of prior discovery, which are more or less documented by more or less responsible sources.

The Vikings landed in the New World five centuries before Columbus. Eric the Red, former bodyguard to the Norwegian King, had a fight with his boss and fled to Iceland. From there, he sailed westward in 982, landing on then virgin Greenland. Like Columbus, Eric thought himself the first man to set foot in North America.

In 986, a Viking named Bjarni Herjulfsson made a wrong turn on his way to join Eric in Greenland and sailed all the way to Cape Cod before turning back. Seventeen years later, Leif Ericson, Eric's son, borrowed Bjarni's boat and led an expedition which landed on Nantucket. Leif wanted to settle there eventually but died before he could return from his Viking homeland.

Eric the Red's other son, Thorwald Ericsson, also borrowed Bjarni's boat and spent several happy years living among friends he took with him to Nantucket. The Ericsson family really didn't have to borrow boats, being well-to-do, but the Norsemen were a superstitious lot. Since Bjarni's boat had made the trip once, the sailors decided fate would guide it there again. And it did. In 1007, Thorwald's luck finally ran out when he was slain by unfriendly Indians.

Right where Wall Street is today, Thorfinn Karlsefni, another Norwegian, formed in 1010 what he hoped would be a permanent colony. A son, Snorri, was born there a year later. However, in 1014 Wall Street went through such a rough winter that the Viking settlers decided to seek better environs.

Other Vikings, including a Norwegian bishop no less, visited various parts of New York, Rhode Island, Massachusetts and Nova Scotia right up to the time of Columbus. In 1362, a group of 30 Norwegian and Swedish hunters actually made it as far as Kensington, Minnesota, a part of the country still inhabited by latter-day Norwegians and Swedes. In 1898, a Minnesotan discovered "the Kensington Stone," a rocky tablet on which was inscribed accounts of the hardships the 14th Century settlers faced.

Irish fishermen reached the

North American fishing banks in 1150, whereas their English counterparts didn't make it for another 330 years. Thomas Lloyd of Bristol, after finding good fishing in the New World, decided to make annual trips there between 1482 and 1491.

Columbus Dispatch Sunday Magazine, October 7, 1973. Copyright © 1973, Franklynn Peterson.

6·10 The Roundup

The roundup is a *collection,* really, of bits and pieces of information or anecdotes or quotations or opinions or recipes or anything else *from many sources* all tied together *with one theme.* We've reproduced pages from two of our own roundups (Ills. 6.17 and 6.18).

Editors love the roundup for three reasons:

1. It often can play up the *magic of numbers* in its title and on a cover line. The cover of *Family Circle*'s May 15, 1979, issue offers a potpourri of round-up ideas:

   "50 Big & Little Home Improvement Projects"
   "The 30 Best Plants for Hanging!"
   "20 Proven Ways to Save Money"
   "Magic with Muslin—12 Decorative Projects"

2. It often can play up the *magic of big names.* Our roundup for *Swank* magazine, using quotes as captions for photos of the "High Schools of the Stars," dropped nine celebrities' names. (A writer trying to produce a profile can consume days trying to coax a few hours from a celebrity who's hot at the moment. But when doing a roundup, it's easy to get a star's public relations firm to come up with the few appropriate lines you need.)

3. It often can play up the *magic of graphics and interesting layouts.* Although a flashy layout means absolutely nothing to the doctor-readers of *Practical Psychology for Physicians,* to the editor of *Swank* the graphics were as important as the words. In fact, our assignment included getting pictures of the stars' high school buildings.

   Writers, too, love a roundup—for the modest amount of writing time it takes to collect the same fee as any other article. But, as with every pot of gold, there a hidden crack: good ideas for roundups are tough to keep dreaming up because they have to stand the tests we laid down earlier for profiles, how-tos, and informative articles; the numbers aspect can be used only to enhance an already salable idea.

10 Questions Patients Are Afraid to Ask About Cancer

When Duke University of North Carolina plugged in its statewide Cancer Hotline last May—the first widespread information service of its kind in the nation—it was immediately deluged with phone calls. Within the first few months there emerged a pattern of most-frequently asked questions: by and large, these were all ones the callers felt they couldn't ask their physicians.

Duke's Cancer Hotline is an offshoot of its Comprehensive Cancer Center, one of 17 federally funded ones established by the 1974 Amendment to the National Cancer Act. Through outreach programs to the surrounding communities, these Centers attempt to help the public understand and deal more effectively with cancer.

A number of the Centers have Hotlines, but Duke's is the first to serve an entire state. It is also the first to insist that a Center physician approve every answer.

The Hotline personnel at Duke discovered that ten kinds of questions head the most-frequently-asked list, and that in many cases it is the anonymity of the phone call that permits people to express the fears and overcome the shyness that prevents them from going right to their doctors with these problems.

These ten questions may be the very ones your patients don't want to ask you.

1. "Is cancer contagious?"

Many patients don't really understand what cancer is. But they feel they ought to, so they're too shy to admit their ignorance to their doctors. The misapprehension that cancer is contagious is due to the oft-quoted statistics about a person's being more likely to get cancer if a family member had the disease. An all-too-frequent question to the Hotline is, "A family member has cancer. What can the rest of us do to avoid it?"

2. "How rapid is 'rapid growth'?"

People speak of cancer as if it were one disease with one cure, while it is, of course, many kinds of diseases, each with its own pattern and each requiring unique treatment. For example, very few people realize that there are 42 different kinds of cells in the lungs alone, and that each kind can go haywire in its growth to make 42 different kinds of lung cancers; or that cancers of the blood and lymph systems are very different from bone-cell cancers.

People are also confused about the role of cell growth in cancer. People hear talk of "growing cells" and "abnormal cell growth" in cancerous tissue, and many assume that all cell growth—certainly all abnormal cell growth—means cancer. The doctor must take the time to educate his patients so they understand that all our cells are constantly growing and that there are always a few abnormal cells in the body which are ordinarily destroyed by the body itself without outside intervention. The patient should understand what we mean when we say "uncontrolled growth" when referring to cancer.

Practical Psychology for Physicians, September 1976. Copyright © 1976, Judi R. Kesselman and Franklynn Peterson.

Ill. 6.18

High Schools of the Stars

Goldie Hawn

"All through high school I spent every afternoon in dance classes. I was a late bloomer, and not so pretty as my sister. I never clowned for my friends, and almost never had a date. I was—well, sort of small, underdeveloped. Boys didn't ask me out. Not that I really wanted to go, I wasn't really ready for it, but, uh, I sure wanted them to ask me."

Sally Struthers

"I overdid it in high school. I was an honor student, president of the girls' league, and head cheerleader. I would devise all the yells for our school events, even the wrestling matches. The thing I'm most proud of was forming the first girls' track team —we were so good, some of our girls even went to the Junior Olympics. I also worked as a waitress after school, and clerked in the drugstore on Saturdays. Why did I cram so much in? Well, I guess the busier you are, the less time you have to spend alone."

Muhammad Ali

"In high school the kids sometimes would make fun of me because I said I wanted to be a champion fighter. I guess I always liked attention and publicity, even then. I used to race the school bus 28 blocks, and beat it, that kind of thing. I guess I became the most popular kid in Central High School . . . but I was not the best student, because I saw fast there was no future for me in a high school education. As a matter of fact, I graduated with the lowest marks possible, not because I didn't study —which I didn't—but because I had other things to do. Boxing, for example, which even then made me feel like somebody different. I knew a lot of guys who had diplomas who were just laying around in the streets."

Peter Nero

"In four years at Music and Art, I once figured out, I rode 61,000 subway stops from Brooklyn to Harlem —and it was worth every stop. I'd leave home before seven in the morning, run three blocks to the elevated subway, and when I'd get to the end of the second block, if I saw that the train coming from the other direction hadn't reached the station yet, I knew I was going to make my train. If I missed that train, I knew I'd be late to school. School and subways, it was all tied together, an hour to get there and an hour to get home every day. They used to expect us to do three hours' homework and two hours' practicing our instrument each evening, and in addition I was earning money accompanying dance classes three times a week, three hours a night at 13 or 14, so high school was one long memory of being tired."

Swank, October 1976. Copyright © 1976. Franklynn Peterson and Judi R. Kesselman.

6·11 The Photo Story

This is a bonus to our Ten Standard Formats. So many writers these days pack cameras alongside their typewriters that we think you ought to keep the photo story in mind as part of your marketing armada. Technically, it isn't a genre all by itself; it can be a personality piece, a bit of an exposé, a graphic approach to history, humor . . .

In this format, the writing is often less important than the photos—although no editor will object to good writing. But the photos themselves have to satisfy all the requirements for a good article. You must create a *lead* photo that hooks the reader and sets a tone for the rest of the photos. Your pictures have to be *organized logically*. The story has to have a concluding photo too.

When we suggested to *Popular Science* an article showing how homeowners could avoid painting their palaces more than once every ten years, the editors liked the idea. But, they suggested, instead of supplying the information first in words and again in pictures, why not do it only *once* through pictures with comprehensive captions? The result, our first pictorial how-to story, satisfied all the criteria of a how-to from the lead photo showing lab research underway, down to the happy-ending photo of the almost completely painted house. Technical requirements preclude our reproducing the article here, but you can find it in the May, 1979, issue of *Popular Science*.

We don't have space here to cover photography thoroughly, so we'll limit ourselves to a few of the major problems we've seen in the way beginners handle photo stories. First, with black-and-white photos, the 8 × 10-inch single-weight glossy or double-weight semigloss print is *the* standard. While it's true that some magazines accept smaller prints, to submit them is a giveaway that you're an amateur. With color, transparencies (35 mm and 2¼-inch sizes) are standard; color prints are almost always the mark of an amateur.

Have the transparencies mounted in cardboard, and slip the cardboard mounts into plastic protectors. With 35 mm slides, the twenty-to-a-page plastic protector is standard. Be sure your name and a caption are on each slide. Some writers just number the slides and submit separate caption sheets keyed to the numbers. Ideally, you should do *both*.

Having been editors, we know the mayhem that prevails in editors' offices and always submit captions in duplicate (for black-and-white as well as color). When we type captions, we make two carbon copies. We submit the original captions typed in manuscript format on 8½ × 11-inch paper. For black-and-white cut up one carbon copy and fasten each caption to the back of the appropriate picture with rubber cement or double-sided scotch tape. (Regular Scotch tape is taboo. After a few years in the files, it sticks to the face of adjoining prints.) For color we submit two uncut caption sheets. The third copy of the captions goes into our file in case the editor loses the other two sets. After all, one way of advancing in this crazy career is to recognize that editors have problems too, and to encourage them to rely on you to solve some of them.

Chapter Seven

The Four Elements of a Good Article

I T MAY SEEM CONTRADICTORY THAT IN THIS BOOK for free spirits and idealists, we seem to keep telling you, "Do this, don't do that." But the fact is, a set of classic article formats, elements, and techniques has evolved over the years. Using them works to the advantage of everybody—writer, editor, reader. It makes writing—as well as reading—fun, fast, unfailing, and helps writer and reader walk together on familiar ground.

In your reading, you may never have consciously identified the four elements found in almost every good magazine article: lead, topic sentence, body, ending. But they're there. Most pros find it almost obligatory to use all four elements in all of their articles, although any literary rule can be broken successfully by a pro who's really studied her craft.

As an introduction to your study of the four elements, let's look at the reproduced part of the "Female Alcoholics" article Judi wrote for *New Dawn* magazine. (Ill. 7.1) As you read it, see if you can intuitively answer these questions:

1. How does Judi get the readers' attention and make them want to read her article?
2. What is the article about?
3. How specifically stated is the subject of the article?
4. Is there a subjective ingredient in how Judi handles the topic?

Ill. 7.1 ——————————————————————————————————

Female Alcoholics

Marie Neenan was a trusted legal secretary. She handled confidential files, important memos, and even, at times, large amounts of money. Her bosses never knew that sometimes she worked in a total blackout, unable to remember afterward what she'd done in her alcoholic stupor.

Pat Frye seemed like any other young mother, wheeling her baby carriage to the corner deli to have lunch with a friend. But that lunch was often four hours long and almost totally beer, and then she'd *weave* her carriage home, not wheel it.

These women are alcoholics. Although they haven't touched a drop in more than a decade, they know that they are uncontrollably addicted to alcohol—that one sip of anything harder than a Coke might send them right back to the hell out of which they dragged themselves.

Women alcoholics have always been around. It may be worse nowadays; one study suggests that the number of *known* female alcoholics has doubled in the last thirty years. Or it may be simply that women aren't hiding at home so much

anymore—that, as alcoholism counselor Ruth Maxwell (formerly with the Smithers Alcoholism Rehabilitation Center of Roosevelt Hospital in New York, and now a consultant to business and industry in setting up alcoholism pretreatment programs) suggests, now that women are working more, they are more easily recognized. At any rate, it's now an accepted fact that *just as many women are prone to alcoholism as are men.* Since one out of ten is an alcoholic, it may have already enmeshed *four million women* including you or your best friend. And the only way to defend against its ravages is to understand what it is and how it affects us.

New Dawn, October 1976. Copyright ©1976, Judi R. Kesselman.

7·1 The Lead

If you were to launch an expensive research project to locate the single trait that predicts the success of a magazine writer's career, we bet you'd find that trait to be the caliber of the writer's *leads.* The lead is built into the very first one or more paragraphs of an article. It's the article's jumping-off point, the bait that hooks both reader *and editor* into reading on into your story. A good lead is the best selling tool there is. It usually makes its sales pitch in one or more of three ways:

> It may bring a subject to life for the reader.
> It may intrigue, excite, or startle the reader.
> It may appeal to the reader's emotions.

We can still tell you how we stumbled onto each of our best leads. We still wince remembering the story or two we turned in without a great lead, after every trick in the book failed to produce a beginning that grabbed and shook. Every professional magazine writer we know can pick up an article and know instinctively, "That's a great lead!" or "Boy, what a washout of a lead!" But ask precisely *why* it's great or a washout, and you're likely to hear a minute of unbroken stammering.

Don't ask most fine writers *how* to create a great lead, either. Most likely, they do it instinctively.

We've grabbed a random stack of current magazines and, leafing through them, found ten articles by writer friends—all members of the American Society of Journalists and Authors—whose fine leads illustrate the various approaches that can be taken.

BRING THE SUBJECT TO LIFE

The easiest way to get the reader involved in your subject is to bring it to life for him. The writer's tool for doing that is most often the *anecdote,* a little story that illustrates one of the article's points.

So many top writers lead off with an anecdote that we like to think of it as the magician's rabbit of our profession. In Ill. 7.1, Judi's article on female alcoholics, her first three paragraphs seem to be about two women whom almost none of the readers has ever heard of. Yet readers know instinctively that the article is not about either woman per se; that their stories are a lively, personal, exciting way to get Judi's article rolling. Being experienced, Judi knows she'll hook her readers with that lead, that they'll read further to learn more about Marie and Pat.

Flora Davis's *Woman's Day* piece on how to cope with stress (Ill. 7.2), Lee Edson's true-life drama about an infant burn victim (Ill. 7.3), and Jack Galub's very practical information about how to prevent drowning (Ill. 7.4), all make effective use of anecdotes for leads.

A lead can include one anecdote or several. Often, the writer chooses the most dramatic examples uncovered by research. That's the case in Jack's lead, but not in Flora's. She opted not for drama but for greatest likelihood of grabbing the average reader's attention. And Lee was bound by the need to use almost strictly chronological organization. Still, he pulled off a beginning that grabs. In all three examples, the selected leads do the job of bringing the subjects—stress, burns, drowning—vividly to life. They say, "It's happened to somebody." They imply, "It could happen to you."

Ill. 7.2

How to Live with STRESS and Thrive

by Flora Davis

Sarah has a job on Wall Street that's one long crisis from nine to five. By the end of the week she's worn out. Her husband is worried about her and wants Sarah to look for less demanding work. "He says I'm under too much pressure," she said, "and that stress can make you sick. But I love my job. I don't want to give it up."

Like so many people, Sarah wants it all: a life crammed to the brim with work, family, fun. And like others, she's concerned about stress. In recent years researchers have concluded that stress can contribute to various medical problems—heart disease, high blood pressure, ulcers, asthma, headaches and more. Even the common cold is sometimes included in the list. The theory is that stress breaks down your natural defenses so you fall prey to every virus that comes along.

Ill. 7.3

Doctors Call Her the Miracle Girl

By Lee Edson

It was a snowy January morning in 1978. Having been up most of the night, Linda Short could barely keep her eyes open, but she would not give in to sleep as she watched over her eight-year-old daughter, Rena. The child was swathed in blankets in the emergency ward at Dorchester General Hospital in Maryland. The young resident doctor and local pediatrician who examined Rena agreed that the little girl needed to be moved immediately to a larger facility—to Baltimore City Hospital.

The doctors tried not to upset Linda (she had already been through an overwhelming ordeal), but they felt they had to be truthful. "Rena is badly burned," they told her. "If she lives two weeks, she may make it, but she'll be lucky to live two weeks."

Linda looked down at the tiny discolored doll that was her daughter. In her overfatigued state, different images came and went. Some were dreamlike; others, she knew, were all too real.

Ill. 7.4

Summer Water Safety—
Amazing New Facts
That Can Save Your Life

By Jack Galub

The child was found unconscious in a backyard pool. She had been underwater for possibly 15 minutes. Resuscitation efforts failed. But minutes after being given up for dead, the drowned two-year-old began to breathe. Sixteen hours later, she recognized her mother and spoke to her. A two-year follow-up showed the child growing normally, with no sign of brain damage.

An 18-year-old drove off a country road and crashed to the bottom of a 10-foot-deep, iced-over pond. Lifted out of the water 38 minutes later, he gasped spontaneously despite no detectable life signs. Intensive resuscitation efforts by a team of doctors started his heart beating. After two weeks, he returned to college, continuing as an A student.

These lives were saved by the "mammalian diving reflex"—an involuntary reaction developed by whales, seals, porpoises, sea lions and other animals that remain under water for extended periods of time. The reflex is present in all mammals, and recent discoveries confirm that it can operate in some human beings, especially those under age 20 when they are plunged facedown into cold water.

While the reflex is operating, water does not enter the lungs; blood circulates slowly between the brain, lungs and heart. A person undergoing the reflex may give every physical appearance of being dead—no discernible pulse, no breathing, blue skin, pupils dilated—and yet may *not* be dead. And such a person may be revived with *no lasting impairment of mind or body* after a much longer period than has been expected.

Such new knowledge has stimulated an intensive study of water-related accidents and has led to important new first-aid rules for drowning victims.

Family Circle, June 26, 1979. Copyright©1979, Jack Galub.

INTRIGUE, EXCITE, OR STARTLE THE READER

Nothing hooks readers faster than a question that asks something they've always wondered about. Next best is to ask something they've never wondered about, in such a way that they suddenly wonder *why* they never wondered about it. In general, people are accustomed to looking for answers in their magazine reading. They seem to pay special attention when confronted by a question in an article's lead.

Chicago's widely read Bonnie Remsberg begins her *Ladies' Home Journal* article (Ill. 7.5)—whose title promises answers about love and sex for the reader—with a question asking why couples rarely talk about sex. Her lead ends with two more questions. Is it effective? We sure think so.

Ill. 7.5 _____

Love and Sex: The 10 Most Often Asked Questions

By Bonnie Remsberg

Why is it so often true that the most intimate side of the relationship between a woman and a man is the one they talk about least? A tricky question, almost certainly with as many answers as there are marriages. But the fact remains that most couples, even when the marriage seems fine, can talk about everything—except their love life. Things can go along quite well this way for as long as both partners feel satisfied. But what if one or both of them want things to be different? How can they solve a problem they can't talk about?

To meet the needs of men and women who want their lovemaking to be the best it can be, a new breed of specialist has emerged—the sex therapist. Sex therapists, some of whom are psychologists, some psychiatrists, some gynecologists, are treating couples of all ages who have all kinds of sex problems. And they're doing so with great success.

What, the Journal wondered, are these experts learning, not only about troubled marriages, but about flourishing ones as well? What, specifically, leads people to seek their help? And in what ways can the knowledge and expertise of reputable sex therapists benefit even the most contented couple? To find out, we initiated a cross-country search to talk to, and learn from, the leading practitioners of this new, important and growing field.

Ladies Home Journal, July 1979. Copyright © 1979, Bonnie Remsberg.

_____

Claire Safran, too, incorporates three questions into her lead for *Redbook* (Ill. 7.6), a magazine where she was once an editor and whose audience she therefore knows well. She can be sure these are questions her readers have asked their own children. Why? Because she's seen lots of parents play this game.

How Children Feel About Their Bodies

By Claire Safran

"Where are your eyes? Your nose? Your toes?" In the little games we parents play with our young children we teach them about their bodies. In the ways we dress them, clean them, comfort them and hold them, we show them how highly we value and how deeply we care for those bodies.

And that is sex education—or the simplest and most important part of sex education. A mother may not think of it that way, but her hugs and kisses are the ABC's of the physiology of sex, a child's early lessons in physical pleasure and in feeling good about her body. The free flow of affection between parent and child is also a course in the sociology of sex, in what loving, caring and relating are all about.

There are other parts of the curriculum, though, and few people are at ease with all of them. The burgeoning sexuality of young children is rarely talked about. When it is discussed, there is confusion about what it means and how to deal with it. So a mother may feel uncomfortable, oddly disturbed in spite of all she's read, when she sees her young son exploring his body. Or a father may half enjoy, half worry about the ways his little daughter flirts with him. Even for parents who feel free and uninhibited in their own sexuality, the notion of their child as a sexual being can be discomfiting.

Today it is especially difficult for parents to be sex educators. Social change is everywhere. New ideas clamor to be sorted out. Old rules are challenged. For parents who want to raise their children to be at ease with their sexuality, there are few models to follow.

Across the country, doctors have as many questions as parents do, and they are finding many of the answers in a growing body of neonatal research. In recent years pediatricians, psychiatrists and researchers have been interviewing parents in depth and observing young children at their most intimate, unguarded moments. They are trying to fill in one of the last great gaps in our knowledge of human sexuality—the sexual behavior and feelings of young children. And many of the answers to parents' and doctors' questions can be found in the new insights researchers now have about what is *natural*.

It is helpful to know how the drama of sexuality unfolds for most children.

The scenario of sexuality begins at birth, if not before. Feeding, cuddling, touching and being touched —these activities may not seem strictly "sexual" but they are the ways a child learns to feel comfortable—or uncomfortable—about her body and her identity. According to Dr. Veronica B. Tisza, lecturer in psychiatry at Harvard Medical School, "If par-ents don't hug, hold and admire the child with their hands, their eyes, their mouths, then the child may be deprived in a number of ways, including sexually."

Readers, editors, and even writers like to puzzle over paradoxes of all kinds. These, too, make *intriguing* leads. Alan Haas's *Science Digest* paradox is posed in question form. His lead also *startles* the reader with facts and figures—in this case, large sums of money. After doing all his research, the New York pro organized his article on antique cars so that his flashiest data could be shown off up front. Then he used both question and startling statement to hook his readers into wanting to know more.

Ill. 7.7

For Fun and Profit (Lots)
Buy That Bonanza V8 Convertible
or a '55 Goldmine Coupe
by Alan D. Haas

If you had purchased it in 1972 for $50,000 you could have sold it currently for $235,000. What is it?

A Picasso or other modern painting? A Russian sable fur, a rare diamond or postage stamp, a mansion in Beverly Hills, several gold bricks?

No; none of these. The answer: an eight-cylinder, 1932 Duesenberg Phaeton SJ-261 vintage automobile, sold at auction in the Midwest for this astonishing price—highest dollars ever paid for a classic American car.

According to Frank (Skip) Marketti, director of the Auburn-Cord-Duesenberg Museum in Auburn, Indiana, where the auction took place, "Duesenbergs have increased at least 20 percent in value each year for the past ten years." This particular Duesenberg appreciated even more because its owner, Ed Lucas, an engineer in Detroit, spent thousands of hours lovingly restoring it to its original beauty.

What was formerly a hobby, the collecting of Locomobiles, Cords, Bugattis, Isotta Fraschinis, for the pleasure of owning, tinkering with, or simply admiring these splendid machines of the past, has, in the past decade, become a bonanza for knowledgeable car freaks.

For instance: A 1928 Mercedes-Benz SSK roadster worth $25,000 in 1968 would, in today's market, bring around $200,000. A 1925 Isotta Fraschini Type 8A Tourer, with a value of $8,500 a decade ago, would fetch $80,000 now.

Marvin Grosswirth's use of paradox, in his *Science Digest* article, is straightforward intrigue. Marvin knows that most people don't know much about osteopaths—which is why he suggested the story to ex-editor Daniel Button in the first place. To hook his readers, he startled them with three simple paradoxes. His three-paragraph lead looks so obvious it seems anyone could have written it; yet it took a top pro to recognize instinctively that within all the data he had collected about osteopaths there lay three paradoxes that would make any reader want to know more.

Ill. 7.8 ————————————————————————————

What Is a . . . Doctor of Osteopathy?

by Marvin Grosswirth

An osteopath is a fully recognized, fully licensed physician—but he is not an M.D.

He has been trained in the art of manipulative therapy—but he is not a chiropractor.

The number of osteopaths increases every year—but they are nevertheless in danger of becoming invisible.

Approximately ten percent of all people who visit physicians' offices go to osteopaths, but many of them are unaware of any difference between a Doctor of Medicine (M.D.) and a Doctor of Osteopathy (D.O.) But there is one, and the osteopathic profession is determined to preserve it.

Basically, that difference may be described as the allopathic approach to medicine as compared to the holistic approach. *Allopathic* medicine —practiced by most M.D.'s—treats a particular disease or condition. *Holistic* medicine treats the entire organism.

A really powerful quote can also make an exciting, intriguing article lead. David Zimmerman chooses a mother's candid remarks about her test-tube baby to lead off his *Woman's Day* article. David couldn't have dreamed up an opening more dramatic than this mother's quote. But it took a sensitive writer to give the quote its context—and its excitement—by artfully adding the phrase "first baby ever conceived outside a woman's body."

Ill. 7.9 ─────────────────────────────────

Are Test-Tube Babies the Answer for the Childless?

by David Zimmerman

"Dear God, she's so lovely!" exulted Lesley Brown, as she held her daughter, Louise, the first baby ever conceived outside a woman's body. "She's so beautiful, and she's mine!"

For Lesley, Louise's birth last July is a personal miracle. Without *in vitro fertilization,* the so-called test-tube baby procedure through which Louise was conceived in a laboratory dish, Lesley was hopelessly infertile. She lacks fallopian tubes, the organs in which conception normally occurs.

The birth of baby Louise has wider meaning, however. The in vitro method is one of three dramatic experimental procedures that represent a scientific revolution in the treatment of infertility. They offer real hope, for the first time, that millions of childless women one day will carry and deliver babies of their own.

─────────────────────────────────────

APPEAL DIRECTLY TO THE READER'S EMOTIONS

Though both foregoing types of leads appeal to the reader's emotions, neither is a *direct* appeal. But look at Michael Frome's *Woman's Day* travel story (Ill. 7.10). Mike chooses to begin his article ostensibly by appealing to the reader's *interest* in being like "women on the go." But read more closely; his appeal is to her *concern* about traveling alone. Appeal to the emotions, Mike knows, is much more of a hook than appeal to intellectual interest.

His second paragraph reinforces the concern he has generated by flashing specific visual images of conceivable situations—a sick friend far away, a business trip, a prize vacation, a dream getaway from women's cares and concerns. Notice the hidden emotional appeal of all these instances. It's all part of his lead.

Ill. 7.10

Traveling Alone

by Michael Frome

Like practically every woman on the go these days, at some time or other you may find yourself traveling alone.

You may be called to stay with a sick friend or a relative in a distant state. Or you may be sent out of town by your company on a ten-day business trip. Or your husband may be tied up with work just when you win a free ticket to Tijuana. Or you may just plain want to throw caution —cooking, cleaning, dirty dishes and diapers—to the wind and find out once and for all what it's really like to wing it on your own.

What's standing in your way? Nothing, according to travel experts, who maintain that with the new liberated attitudes and lifestyles —not to mention the growing number of singles across the country (close to forty-four million, according to latest totals, or about one fifth of all households)—more and more women are not merely traveling on their own, but wondering why it took them so long to give it a try.

The advantages, of course, are obvious. You can move at your own pace, shopping and sightseeing at will, waking up at the crack of dawn or sleeping late till noon, without having to worry about keeping someone else waiting or, worse yet, having to wait yourself. If you've always wanted to see New York and your husband has his eye on Los Angeles, you can both get your wish: Split for a week, then when you get back, put your heads together over a cup of coffee and compare notes.

If you've never had to learn about financial matters, you can get a first-hand crack at making reservations, booking flights, renting cars, using credit cards and tipping that will stand you in good stead not just when you're out on the road but once you get home. And best of all, you can acquire a new sense of independence, a stronger self-confidence and a broader range of experience and friendships that should endure for the rest of your life.

7·2 The Topic Sentence

It is important to let readers know early just what you plan to talk about in your article so they don't expect something more or something different from what you're prepared to deliver. Disappointed readers

—especially disappointed editor-readers—leads to loss of sales. The place to announce your topic is in your topic sentence, which always comes right after the lead.

We mentioned in Chapter 3 that there are two aspects to every topic. The *focus,* or objective parameter, is always part of the topic sentence. The *slant,* or subjective approach—your point of view toward the topic—may be stated in the topic sentence, or implied there, or not even mentioned at all but revealed later between the lines.

A topic sentence may be a phrase, or it may be several sentences long. It can be as simple and obvious as "now I will talk about" topic sentences in your school essays, or it can be disguised in a quote, question, or statistic. It may be smoothly sewn onto the end of the lead, stand by itself, or begin the next paragraph. In some magazines it's echoed in the title; in other magazines the title may have nothing to do with it.

Novice writers whose titles contain their topics often forget to also put in the topic sentence. Pros, who know that editors often change titles, leave nothing to chance.

In Judi's article on female alcoholism (Ill. 7.1), her topic sentence is found in the first part of her fourth paragraph. It narrows the *focus* from alcoholism (too broad a topic for 3,000 words) to female alcoholism (still a broad topic) and, further, to "what it is and how it affects us." It also promises to help the readers "to defend against its ravages"—the *slant.* By telling the readers, right after they're hooked, precisely what they're getting into, she avoids having to explain the purpose for each of her many statements and examples as they are introduced in the body of her article. And readers, spared from having to wade through dull, repetitive exposition, can still follow her points readily. Unless Judi tells them otherwise, they will know that every one of her sentences refers to what female alcoholism is and how it affects them so they can guard against it.

In every one of the articles shown in our discussion of leads, the author uses some kind of topic sentence. A study of them illustrates several different techniques for weaving them smoothly into the text.

Claire Safran has a long lead in which she says parents do give their children some basic sex education. But then, she uses a paradox ("The burgeoning sexuality of young children is rarely talked about") for transition into her topic sentence on the article's following page: "It is helpful [the slant] to know how the drama of sexuality unfolds for most children [the focus]."

In "Doctors Call Her the Miracle Girl," Lee Edson manages to disguise his topic sentence as a dramatic quote: "Rena is badly burned. . . . If she lives two weeks, she may make it, but she'll be lucky to live two weeks." This gives the focus, but not the slant. The slant is already implied in the tone of the lead.

Often the topic sentence is contained in a separate paragraph. In his traveling-alone article, Mike Frome does the unorthodox: he postpones that paragraph for several more hundred words. If you look up his article (*Woman's Day,* August 7, 1979) it's the paragraph beginning, "Planning a trip alone, in short, calls for some groundwork. . . ." For Frome, this long postponement works. For novices, it's a risky procedure.

Alan Haas uses a full sentence for his topic sentence beginning "What was formerly a hobby, the collecting of Locomobiles . . ." and ending with exactly what it is about those old gas buggies (his focus) he's chosen to highlight: ". . . a bonanza for knowledgeable car freaks [his slant]."

Marvin Grosswirth's and David Zimmerman's topic sentences are simple, obvious, and straightforward. They focus the fields about to be discussed down to manageable yet lively topics. David's topic sentence says he'll show "three dramatic experimental procedures that represent a scientific revolution in the treatment of infertility." He sets the slant of the article, too: "They offer real hope. . . ." Marvin's, after stating that people don't know if there's a difference between an M.D. and a O.D., adds, "but there is one . . ." and the rest of his article explains that big difference.

In her love-and-sex-question article, Bonnie Remsberg needs a very long topic paragraph to establish her framework. Instead of cutting corners (and possibly leaving her readers uncertain of the article's parameters), she prevents the long paragraph from getting dull by casting her topics into questions, a sure-fire device for exciting readers: "What, the *Journal* wondered, are these experts learning, not only about troubled marriages, but about flourishing ones as well?" After posing two more topic questions, Bonnie promises readers they'll get the answers if they read on. But she does it with the subtlety of a real pro: "To find out, we initiated a cross-country search to talk to, and learn from, the leading practitioners of this new, important and growing field" [sex therapy].

In her lead, Flora Davis uses an anecdote: the story of Sarah. Her topic sentence has to change the focus of readers' attention from Sarah to the entire, loosely defined population included in her story about stress. See how smoothly she makes the transition while establishing the parameters of her story. We've underlined the transition: "Like so many people, Sarah wants it all: a life crammed to the brim. . . . And like others, she's concerned about stress." *Topic* is the part not underlined: living a full life while managing stress.

Jack Galub's one-page water-safety article opens with two anecdotes that lead into a long explanation of the "new knowledge" he wants readers to understand, because their acceptance of "new knowledge" paves the way for his topic sentence. It's the last part of the last sentence in his long introduction: ". . . important new first-aid rules for drowning victims." Why not just offer his water-safety tips with no lead and no topic sentence? Because without the focus given by the topic sentence, and the illustrations offered in the lead, the reader may well take a fast peek, think, "There's nothing here I didn't already know," and flip the page. (If the editor thinks the reader will do that with *your* article, he won't run it in the first place.)

7·3 The Body

To comprehend fully how you get meat onto the body of an article—that long section between beginning and end—you must understand the techniques that every professional writer learns to use. A thorough explanation takes up all of Chapter 8. Here we'll explain in depth just that elusive quality so many beginners have trouble tying down—the article's *slant.*

We defined slant along with focus when discussing the topic sentence because, as we said, it's sometimes summed up there. However, when it comes to writing the body, there's no choice for the writer: the slant must pervade its every paragraph.

Because the novice confuses slant and focus, we'll redefine them once again:

> *Focus* is *what* you're writing about.
>
> *Slant* is *how* you write about it. It's the author's viewpoint, and it's essential to every article.

But if an author slants an article, what happens to objectivity, that foremost essential of good writing?

To answer that, we must define *objectivity* more precisely than it's been defined in school. Objectivity in magazine writing is not the bland, unbiased presentation of both sides of every issue. Objectivity is, instead, *fairness,* the sharing with readers of viewpoints opposing the writer's own *where they are significant.* (Obviously, they are more significant when dealing with whether children should be taught about sex than when writing about five ways to prevent drowning.) It permits readers to disagree with the author's viewpoint—but lets readers know clearly what that viewpoint is.

Many people become writers because they want to make their viewpoints more widely known. Most of us choose article topics that coincide with our viewpoints. However, even when we suggest an article about which we have no strong viewpoint, we make value judgments throughout: what's to be included and what left out, what's to be highlighted as more important and what given little space, what's to be dramatized and what merely announced. The *basis* for our value judgments—our slant—must, in all fairness, be shared with our readers. In marketing our idea, we must recognize that its slant is as important to the editor as the topic itself. He may not want an article whose slant—too radical or too conservative—will anger his readers.

When we wrote about new developments in geodesic-dome housing for *Popular Science,* we had no strong feelings for or against dome homes. Should we allow dome homes or not? was not a social issue. Still, after doing our preliminary research, we formed several subjective criteria that carried over into our query, and into our article. We gave greater emphasis to contractor-built domes than to do-it-yourself dome kits. We pointed out that building departments were finally okaying domes rather than relating incidents where domes were running into code problems. We chose to include, albeit with an editorial grain of salt, the anecdotes, unsubstantiated by scientific research, suggesting that domes are cheaper to heat than traditional houses. We signaled our slant in the last line of our lead-cum-topic paragraph. After warning of our provisos—"Thus far, however, the geodesic dome has proved too kinky to appeal to the masses of home buyers, too unproven to merit mortgages from conservative bankers, too unorthodox to satisfy zoning and building codes"—we announced our hopeful, optimistic, yet vaguely hesitant slant: "But now all that may be changing."

When we sold *Popular Science* on the dome-home story idea, we let them know our slant. We opened the query with, "Until we went to two home shows in the area recently, we never realized how readily available—and practical—the Bucky Fuller dome home has become." Further on we focused our stance more: "Frankly, they're not for just anybody. . . . They seem ideal for a second home, or a first home for the artsy or environment-oriented small family; for a home that you need erected in a hurry, or a place you can enjoy with a minimum of overhead." When *Popular Science* assigned the article, they knew not only what facts and figures we intended to present, but also the sort of coloration our presentation would have.

Pro or con? Moderate or extreme? Reasoned or impassioned? Writers don't often tell editors baldly, "My slant will be . . . ," but they make that slant clear when marketing. We're sure that clarifying our slant impressed *Popular Science* a great deal more than just writing, "We'd like to tell your readers about dome homes."

One time in particular, our slant was crucial to a sale. A lawyer we knew was advocating that rape victims hire lawyers. Any editor hearing that focus without the slant would have figured the lawyer was being self-serving, and would have refused the article. In our query to *Viva's* Ernie Baxter, we spelled out that our slant was twofold: to help put more rapists behind bars, and to help ease some of the agony of rape victims. It was exactly the slant Ernie needed to be able to run an article on rape. Imagine how the readers would have received that article if it had "objectively" given the rapists' side of the story equal space!

7·4 The Ending

When you've said everything there is to say, it's not enough simply to stop writing. When the time comes to end your article, it's important to create a proper *ending*—the fourth essential element in a magazine article.

The ending leaves readers feeling that the article has come to a successful, satisfying conclusion. This is not to say that you must save your *conclusions* about your subject for the ending. The general pros and cons of your topic are most often assessed within the focus and slant messages of your topic paragraph. The ending is a reiteration, a summation, or even in some cases a statement that there is more to be learned or to be said than the reader has been told.

But we can save a full treatment of endings until we get into Part IV, Chapter 14, and a full-blown discussion of the mechanics of writing an article. In selling your idea, you'll rarely need to discuss how it's going to end.

Chapter Eight

The Three Standard Writing Techniques

N OW THAT YOU KNOW THERE ARE ONLY FOUR elements to every article—lead, topic sentence, body, and ending—you are beginning to see the skeleton of every article you read (and write). To put some flesh on that skeleton, the magazine writer has use of only three basic techniques, the same three available to nonfiction book authors, short-story writers, and novelists: anecdote, quotation, and exposition.

When an author *sees* something happen, and narrates it for readers, that's an *anecdote,* the magazine writer's name for narration. When an author *hears* something worth repeating, and repeats it in writing, that's a *quotation,* the magazine writer's equivalent of dialogue. When an author *thinks* something, and reports it to the readers, backing it up with facts to prove it, that's *exposition.*

8·1 Anecdotes

Everybody loves a good story. Who can pass up a chance to hear a juicy tale about the next-door neighbors? And what's more exciting than a small bit of innocent eavesdropping? In lively magazine writing, too, little narratives—anecdotes—provide the juice. They are used with abundance in nearly every standard magazine format.

Many of our students start out confused not only about how to use anecdotes but about how to recognize them. So let's lead off with a good working definition.

> An anecdote is a complete story in miniature.
> It has a beginning and an ending.
> It takes place in a particular setting, and that scene usually has to be described in brief.
> It depicts a real person or real people.
> Something happens to the people—or they make something happen—during the anecdote.
> Time passes or the people move about.
> The setting, action, dialogue, and/or narrative contained in the anecdote make a point that belongs in the article.

The anecdote is the second most useful tool of a successful magazine writer. (The first is the lead. Writers are fond of anecdotal leads because they know that the combination is a powerhouse.) Effectively used, it *takes the place* of exposition, which is the laying out of your facts. It not only whets reader interest by spinning a yarn about interesting people in interesting settings doing interesting things, but it conveys some of the information the reader needs to understand the point of your article. Instead of writing that Mount Kilimanjaro is 19,000 feet high, tell the reader about a sixteen-year-old cheerleader from Secaucus, New Jersey, who climbed the 19,000 feet of that mountain to deliver homemade brownies to a guru. The reader is much more likely to remember the height of that mountain. If you tell how a machine saved a person's life, that's a story that will glue readers to the page. If you merely describe the dials and wires inside the machine, that's no story at all.

Two chapters ago, we reproduced the first two pages of our *Family Health* story on CAT scanners (Figure 6.7) as an example of the informative article format. Our article had to inform the reader about price, size, theory of operation, duration of a scan, and medical benefits. Most important, though, the article had to grab readers and hold them. So in the first page, absolutely every piece of information was given within an anecdote that told the experience of one man. Just look at the information we got across: that CAT scanners are new, that CAT scanning is painless, that traditional X-rays have trouble distinguishing between healthy and diseased soft tissue—and why. We also told what the machine looks like and gave a patient's-eye view of how it works.

We've reproduced another page from the same CAT scanner article (Ill. 8.1) and marked each of the anecdotes with a circled A. The first anecdote relates how the machine was developed. The second is a true, dramatic story about a four-year-old boy whose brain has been saved by a scan. (Notice the interweaving of hard facts about radiation danger in using CATs.)

The next anecdote describes the plight of thirty children born too soon to benefit from CAT scanners, but promises the possible prevention of similar misery in children born today. That ministory also tells the reader that there are several forms of infant brain damage.

Anecdote number four isn't just a story about a boy in a life-and-death drama: it informs about the CAT's TV screen as well as its computer printout capabilities. Then it tells just how precisely a CAT can measure the position of tumors. Our final anecdote on the reproduced page explains that the CAT works in conjunction with surgeons for on-the-spot emergency operations. But that fact is narrated via the drama of a stroke victim's brush with death.

Check how many of an anecdote's attributes, described at the beginning of this section, each one of our anecdotes has. Then reread the anecdotes, but this time keep in mind what an anecdote is *not*. Our students often have trouble figuring *that* out, too.

Ill. 8.1

(continued from Ill. 6.7)

suffer excruciating headaches for days afterward.) He could perform an angiogram by injecting dye into the arteries that supply blood to the brain—a procedure that sometimes triggered convulsions, stroke or even death. Or, if he was associated with a major research center or teaching hospital, he could request what was then called a brain scan. With this method, radioactive liquid, injected into the brain, is charted as it makes its way through the soft tissues. Not only are these techniques painful and/or dangerous, but they cannot be counted on to detect anything more subtle than a major stroke or a large tumor.

For years, medical researchers had played with the idea of a device that could collect a series of soft tissue x-ray pictures, and with the aid of computers capable of differentiating minute shadings, combine them into a well-visualized "slice." Little had come of it beyond one experimental machine that worked too slowly and projected too much radiation to be practical. But in 1970 an English scientist, Godfrey Hounsfield, who had been working on a CT scanner for three years, turned on his brand-new machine in a London hospital—and 20 minutes later gave the startled doctors mankind's first clear, detailed look at a tumor deep within the

interior of an uncut human brain.

Three years later, improved, faster-operating versions of Hounsfield's invention—capable of illuminating for the first time the soft tissues of the eyes, nasal passages and larynx—were introduced to American hospitals and laboratories and hailed as wonder tools.

According to Dr. Marvin E. Haskin, chairman of diagnostic radiology at Hahnemann Medical College and Hospital of Philadelphia: "The head scanner brings medicine out of the dark ages. Now we not only can look directly at the brain but we can do it so easily and safely that even a newborn infant can be scanned. With CT, we have picked up correctable abnormalities in children as young as four days old."

Dr. Haskin and his team of radiologists at Hahnemann have done much of the pioneer work in brain scanning and have written definitive medical texts on the subject. Since July 1974, when their hospital purchased a head scanner, they have examined over 6,000 patients, many of them youngsters.

Haskin's associate, Dr. Patricia D. Laffey, chief of Hahnemann's section on noninvasive imaging, department of diagnostic radiology, sees many of the pediatric patients. Recently, she examined a four-year-old boy who was behaving erratically following a fall and a sudden blackout. Positioning the child in her scanner, she discovered not only the blocked brain ventricle (cavity) that had caused the boy's blackout but a benign tumor the size of a tomato that nobody had known about. Had the child not been scanned, the tumor could have gone undetected until it caused irreparable brain damage. The boy might have grown up deformed or retarded—or he might not have grown up at all.

"As a result of our scan," Dr. Laffey says, "the doctors knew just where to operate to remove the tumor." And, after the operation, a follow-up scan made sure the entire growth had been removed. The small amount of x-ray exposure each CT series entailed—about as much as a dentist's x-ray—seemed a reasonable risk to take in return for what Laffey calls "every chance of complete recovery."

Scanning also led Drs. Laffey and Haskin to discover a surprising number of cases in which children, diagnosed as retarded, turned out to have unsuspected brain tumors or hydrocephalus (water on the brain). They promptly arranged to scan 30 children from St. Elizabeth's Home, a school for the educable and trainable retarded in West Philadelphia. Fully 20 percent of the youngsters—a much higher figure than anticipated—were found to have tumors, cysts, water on the brain, congenital malformations or structural abnormalities that could have caused the mental problems. Unfortunately, the diagnoses were made too late to help most

of the St. Elizabeth children. But Haskin feels that, as head scanners become more accessible, many similarly afflicted youngster will be discovered in time to be treated. "My experience has convinced me that every hospital with a patient load of over 100 should have a head scanner," Haskins says.

Dr. Stephen Rothman, director of computerized tomography at Yale-New Haven Hospital in Connecticut, agrees. He recalls the case of Chuck, a little boy whose only symptom was that he "behaved strangely." When Dr. Rothman settled Chuck into the head scanner, the TV screen promptly revealed a benign tumor as large as a grapefruit. "I not only could tell the surgeon there was an operable tumor but from the computer printout—which provides exact positions to within a millimeter—I could tell him just where the tumor was placed," Rothman says. "Today Chuck is alive and normal, but he would have had a dim prognosis before CT scanners came along."

Even more dramatic was the case of the adult patient rushed to Yale-New Haven's emergency room with a stroke. As the staff worked over the 50-year-old man, his vital signs deteriorated rapidly. Then, on impulse, the doctors rushed him to radiology, and shifted him to the CT scan table. While residents stood by, Dr. Rothman set his instruments in motion, and in less than a minute a "slice" of the dying patient's head appeared on the TV screen. Clearly visible were the eyes, both sides of the brain and the ventricles containing the cerebrospinal fluid that transports nutrients to the brain and toxic materials away from it.

Dr. Rothman's trained eye isolated the problem at once: A blood vessel in the brain had burst and was bleeding into a ventricle. The surgeon watched closely as Rothman pinpointed the endangered area. Right there in the CT scan room, the surgeon drilled a hole through the man's skull, inserted a needle and drained the cavity. "If that ventricle had filled with blood," Rothman says, "the patient would have died within minutes. Instead, he left the hospital some days later, completely well."

"After I did a thousand head scans I was excited by the tool," Dr. Haskin says. "Now that I've done six thousand, I'm six times more excited —and that's rare in medicine. This machine is revealing pathology we could only guess at before. And although no indirect diagnostic tool is 100 percent accurate, the CT scanner's record of 95 percent accuracy makes it 25 percent better than any other radiologic instrument!"

So enthusiastic is Haskin that he recommends a head scan if any of the following symptoms occur: sudden-onset recurrent headaches, seizures, sudden and continued behavior changes, concussion, sudden . . . .

Family Health, January 1977, Copyright © 1977, Judi R. Kesselman and Franklynn Peterson.

An anecdote is not:

a quotation in which an expert (or nonexpert) gives information or talks about something that happened;

a ministory that duplicates information already given through exposition;

a ministory spliced into the article simply to offer readers relief from straight, tiring exposition.

We know several writers who, while researching, put each anecdote they find on a single 3 ×5 card. To organize the article, they group their note cards into a logical layout. To complete the article, they just fill in the transitions and generalizations. That's how vital *you* should make anecdotes to your own writing if you plan to make it professionally.

Obviously, then, a large part of your article research should be the constant search for anecdotes. How should you go about this? One way is through interviews, to which we devote all of Chapter 13. When you ask people to provide you with anecdotes, they may not understand what you're talking about. But if you ask, instead, for *examples,* you'll get the same thing.

For our CAT scanner article, for example, we interviewed Dr.

Laffey for facts and opinions—but we were also looking for anecdotes. Like most scientists, she is accustomed to speaking in terms of the specific example. When she'd state a fact or figure, we'd ask, "Give us an example," and, "What's another example?" That's how she came up with the story of the four-year-old boy that gave the article so much pathos.

Another way to get true, exciting, believable, and informative anecdotes is to tell all your friends what you're writing about. You'd be surprised how many people have had experiences with your topic that they're dying to share. For a while, Judi was regularly doing features for *Playgirl* on contemporary subjects such as how to choose a divorce lawyer, how to handle a love affair, how to be assertive, how to avoid on-the-job molestation. As each new article idea was assigned to her, Judi would ask her friends about their experiences, and whether they knew anybody else who might share similar experiences. No matter how personal the subject of her article, she always came up with half a dozen solid anecdotes within her circle of acquaintances, plus leads to another half dozen.

Judi didn't name names in *Playgirl*, which is one reason her friends didn't hesitate to tell all. If your article is on a sensitive subject, your editor (and your readers) won't expect your personal confidants' full names. As long as your anecdotes have the ring of truth—achieved by getting all the details and making the reader see them too—nobody will doubt your word that "Janice P., who lives in a quiet suburb of Madison, Wisconsin, has been secretly plotting her husband's death for six years now. . . ." The only time you weaken an anecdote by not using complete, authentic names is when the names are easily recognized by your average reader. In an article on the hazards of living together, an anecdote about the damages Lee Marvin had to pay his ex-mate keeps readers more interested than an anecdote about anonymous Joe Blow's or Lee M.'s troubles. (Until you've built a reputation for yourself, editors may insist on being told your sources' full names and addresses for verification. But they'll promise not to reveal the identities.)

Well, if you don't need a full name, what's to keep you from making up an anecdote if it's harmless and illustrates the point? That's a question our students ask repeatedly. And we answer repeatedly, "Try it!" You'll find that *making up* a believable setting, history, experience, and voice of a fictitious character is much harder to pull off than getting on the phone and locating a *real* anecdote. Besides, the fictions you create are never as farfetched as the truth. In faking an anecdote about a man who studied books to trim his waistline, would you think to give intimate details about the improvement in his sex life? Or in faking an anecdote about a prominent southern mayor, would you try telling how he'd "gotten a girl in trouble" in his younger days? These and other stranger-than-fiction anecdotes rewarded our for-real research efforts.

Calling themselves *new journalists,* some writers openly (and sometimes not so openly) invent settings, people, and situations. As expected, the people described sound like stick figures and the articles fall flat. The true "new journalists" use real people involved in real happenings. Sometimes these writers set their subjects in their natural milieus even though the interview may have taken place somewhere else. That might be considered invention. But it works, because during the interview, as a rule, the successful journalist—old or new—has solicited enough facts to reconstruct the subject's natural habitat. In fact, the entire technique is not new at all.

Sometimes it's acceptable to amalgamate anecdotes. One magazine editor wanted a piece about a hooker's daily life. A noted writer who got the assignment researched prostitution without uncovering any one hooker with a memorable story to tell. *With* the editor's blessing, the author amalgamated parts of the lives of various prostitutes she had interviewed, until she'd fashioned one helluva hooker. She chose among her anecdotal data so artfully that very few people suspected her superhooker was about as real as James Bond. The magazine did not point out the amalgamation. (The editor, who told us this anecdote, asked that we uphold the fiction. That's why we haven't included any identifying data in this anecdote.)

Judith Ramsey was faced with a similar dilemma while working on a *Family Circle* article on incest. It was a new and rather touchy subject for that magazine. Judith and her editors realized they could show the ramifications of incest most effectively through a personal saga of one family. But no family had experienced everything they wanted to say in the article. So Judy amalgamated the experiences of several families and wrote her touching article as if it were about one family. Then, at the end of the article, *Family Circle* editors—unlike the editor in our earlier example—told readers how the piece had evolved.

Manipulating anecdotes is controversial. For some editors, it's taboo. Our philosophy on controversial techniques is simple: When in doubt, tell the editor in advance what you're doing, and tell the reader in print what you've done.

8·2 Quotes

We suspect that three quarters of all grammar school teachers do not know a quotation mark (") from an exclamation point (!). Since so many of our students come to us uniformly mistaking the one for the other, they must be mislearning in some standard place such as grammar school.

They insist on dropping exclamation points at the ends of sentences they began with hopes of initiating a great deal of excitement, but ended suspecting they failed. They slap " " around ideas which they suspect won't stir up much excitement, but to which they hope to draw some of the magic they've heard resides in quotes.

There's no magic inherent in either exclamation points or quotation marks. They do not cause excitement in themselves. They do not conceal boring, hackneyed writing. Exclamation points indicate strong emotion and are practically nonexistent in professional magazine writing. Quotation marks indicate *only* that the words between them have been borrowed.

The reason people think quotes are a magic device for lifting an article out of the mud is that in an anecdote we often quote the words of people involved in the action. A good anecdote, we saw before, is an exciting literary technique, one that you should strive to use. But it is not the quoted dialogue in anecdotes that makes them anecdotal. It is the action. The entire lengthy first anecdote in the CAT scanner article contains only two very short quotes.

If there is no action—if nothing is happening except for the transfer of information, experience, or opinion, and if the words involved in the transfer have been borrowed from someone else—the information is not an anecdote but a quote. We put quotations around the borrowed words to show that they are secondhand.

Just as you must learn to choose among possible anecdotes, you must learn to choose *only* the quotes that will make your article exciting. Improperly used quotations say as much about your writing as improper table manners say about your upbringing. They may say, for instance, that you lack confidence to draw conclusions on your own and lean on others to draw them for you. They may lead readers (and editors) to conclude that you lack originality to cast your own phrases. If you're quoting "in" intellectuals or obscure men and women of letters, they may smack suspiciously of name-dropping or of padding a poorly prepared outline.

Let's quote here the well-known authority on language, H. W. Fowler:

> *A writer expresses himself in words that have been used before because they give his meaning better than he can give it himself, or because they are beautiful or witty, or because he expects them to touch a chord or association in his reader, or because he wishes to show that he is learned or well read. Quotations due to the last motive are invariably ill advised. The discerning reader detects it and is*

contemptuous; the undiscerning is perhaps impressed, but even then is at the same time repelled, pretentious quotations being the surest road to tedium. The less experienced a writer is, and therefore on the whole the less well read he is also, the more he is tempted to this error. The experienced knows he had better avoid it; and the well-read, aware that he could quote if he would, is not afraid that readers will think he cannot.

There! Now, did our long quotation of Fowler's words—carefully chosen, artfully turned, and written by the greatest of authorities —quicken the pace of our chapter, or even enlighten you more than our humbler but personally preferred constructions? What's more, if we have not already convinced you not to misuse quotations, would our borrowing from Fowler really weigh the odds in our favor?

Here are some guidelines for using quotations so they support your writing, not get in its way.

FOR AUTHORITY
Use a quote when you need the voice of authority—and when that voice can't be incorporated into an anecdote or said more clearly and more interestingly as a paraphrase.

Earlier (Ill. 6.7) we reprinted one page from our CAT scanner article in *Family Health*. In Ill. 8.1, we mark the anecdotes which make up much of the following page, but we also mark with a Q three places where we needed an authoritative voice to make a generalization or offer an opinion. For example, it would not have been very convincing for two journalists to have concluded what Dr. Marvin E. Haskin concluded in the first quote: "The head scanner brings medicine out of the dark ages."

Later, on the controversial question of who should own CAT scanners, we wanted to share Haskin's expert assessment and make it clear that it was only his opinion, not fact. Again we put his words between quotes: "My experience has convinced me that every hospital with a patient load of over 100 should have a head scanner." Notice how we incorporated clearly into his quote the basis of his opinion: his experience.

Our third Haskin quote in the article was used as shorthand to cite our authority for some exciting data we wanted the reader to know: ". . . the CT scanner's record of 95 percent accuracy makes it 25 percent better than any other radiologic instrument!"

We quoted Haskin one more time on the reproduced page, this time on the subject of when CAT scans should be the preferred diagnostic tool. This is a recommendation better made by doctors than by writers, especially if the publication is *Family Health*. Notice, however, that we didn't put quotation marks around what Haskin says.

That's because it often takes doctors—and Haskin proved to be no exception—a lot of words to offer advice like this. They use half a dozen qualifiers before every noun and half a dozen more after every verb. We attributed the recommendation, giving him credit for the basic idea. But because he would have said it differently, we omitted the quotation marks. (Another example of that is in Figure 7.1, Judi's article on female alcoholics. She credited Ruth Maxwell as the authority for her information, but calculatingly paraphrased because quoting Ms. Maxwell's preferred way of offering the information would have slowed the story.)

FOR TONE OF VOICE
Use a quote when someone's exact way of saying something is important to the point or the coloration of your article.

Judi tape-recorded her interview (Ill. 6.4) with actress Lynn Redgrave because she knew in advance she wanted to capture Lynn's British speech inflections in her article. But when she used Lynn's quotes—and she used them extensively—it was *not only* to show off Ms. Redgrave's inflections. The quoted material had to contribute to the flow of the article. In addition to *flavor,* it had to add *information* about Lynn's weight problem. Examples, from an unreproduced portion of the article: "I assumed that if I got thin, I wouldn't be funny anymore. It was a lot of rubbish, but it was a great cop-out." "I had three complete wardrobes—and then my last resort, a shifty dress that covered all of me when nothing else would."

Judi seized the chance to point out the actress's flair for storytelling by incorporating one long quote: "We would sit on this beach in Majorca and we'd eat ice creams and such, and whenever I'd get depressed and say, 'Listen, girls, I've got to lose weight because I've got a job next month,' they'd say, 'Ah, darling, you're having such a good time—and you look lovely in that suntan.' Well, I wanted to believe it. And it's really true what they say about Spanish guys being more likely to pinch your bottom if you're fat. . . ." But did this *just* tell a story and show Britishisms? No, it also added pathos, humor, and a telling glimpse at Lynn's self-evaluation.

Judi chose her quotes for this article to make *its* point. She had so many leftover quotes that made *other* points that she was able to sell an entirely different article about Lynn to Canada's *Chatelaine* magazine. Her choices for *Weight Watchers,* out of the hour of taped interview, included many *picture words,* as you can see in the excerpted sentences—thin, three wardrobes, eating ice cream on a beach in Majorca, lovely suntan—so her readers had something to look at, not simply to listen to.

One of our students interviewed a local judge, a woman whom she very much admired. But an early draft of her profile rendered the jurist an injustice:

> *Judge B————is an accessible person: "I think it is very important that the people who come into these courts feel that this is not an aloof, distant, impatient or crabby person who doesn't care about their case, because their case to them is the most important thing at that moment in their lives, or they wouldn't be there. So it is very important to me that they feel they have got a judge listening to them and is trying to figure out why their case is unique and really willing to hear why it is unique. Whether or not they win or lose, they feel if they have had that kind of a hearing, most people, even if they lose, go out satisfied with the process and the system."*

Clearly, the student should have cleaned up the judge's way of speaking; we cover that topic more extensively in Chapter 13. The important point is that she should have left out most or all of this quotation. It *rambles* and *reiterates,* and doesn't make an *authoritative* statement, but shows only the judge's own biased *estimation* of her accessibility, and of whether people in the courtroom get a fair hearing. Moreover, her words—at least as quoted—aren't colorful or memorable, and give us no clue to what she's *really like.* The *way* the quote is used only *weakens* the writer's argument. We told our student to sit in the courtroom and see for herself what people did there that would lead readers to conclude what she wanted them to, and then go back to her typewriter to paint a picture of what she saw.

OUT OF NECESSITY

Use a quote if that's the only way there is to present the information.

When Metropolitan Sunday Newspaper Group assigned Frank to do an article entitled "The Nightmare of Nuclear Blackmail," he had to keep his own viewpoint on the controversial subject meticulously out of the way. In addition, due to the highly technical nature of the subject and the fact that much of the useful information was classified, Frank was obliged to let the ten experts he queried speak in their own words. Most answered in writing. A few insisted that not a single word of what they'd written, not even a punctuation mark, be changed.

What could be done to save the article from the inevitable boredom created by unliterary people giving dry facts about technical matters? First of all, Frank asked each of the ten experts ten identical questions. Next he sorted the answers, choosing the most significant responses for each. From those he singled out the one or two answers for each question that could be presented in the liveliest fashion. Finally, Frank organized the story to incorporate *every* expert and to answer *every* question. In all, he used *barely 4 percent* of the total wordage of written replies. He made the best of one of the worst possible ways to have to write an article.

Frank's result, part of which is reproduced (Ill. 8.2), is far from the world's most titillating article. But it is a highly authoritative look at a timely subject, and provides a working example for our classes of the effective use of quotes.

Ill. 8.2 ───────────────────────────────────────

The Nightmare of Nuclear Blackmail

Anybody who's seen a TV crime show could make up a likely scenario about a band of criminals, terrorists or crackpots who put together their own A-bomb and threaten to use it for whatever kind of blackmail they have in mind.

Already, students at MIT and the University of Iowa have talked about A-bombs they designed themselves. And the FBI admits it has investigated several nuclear threats, which to date have all been proven hoaxes.

But around the globe, the haunting question remains: Will homemade or stolen nuclear devices become the terror weapons of the future?

The possibility of this happening drew strong opinions from a panel of experts whose divergent views ranged from alarming to comforting. Some even felt that any publicity on the subject would excite sick minds. All, however, agreed that enough technical literature about A-bombs has been de-classified so that there are no secrets left about how to build a simple one, in theory at least. (An H-bomb is considered too far-fetched to worry about for several reasons including the fact that you'd have to start with a workable A-bomb.)

For instance, it's public knowledge that there were about 132 pounds of uranium in the bomb dropped on Hiroshima and it exploded with the force of 13,000 tons of TNT! Almost nothing is left to the imagination, too, in how it was put together and how its mechanisms worked.

As to the difficulties involved, veteran A-bomb designer Theodore B. Taylor feels uncomfortably certain that a clandestine A-bomb small enough to fit into the trunk of a compact could be built today.

Taylor, who worked at Los Alamos from 1949 to 1956 designing both baby and super-bombs and has been a consultant to the U.S. Air Force, thinks that anybody who's very knowledgeable in physics could blueprint an A-bomb from what he could learn in libraries.

Obtaining proper materials, Taylor believes, is the hard part.

After that, says he, "It is possible for an extra-ordinary individual or a few people to construct a workable nuclear device in a modestly equipped basement workshop. No exotic tools are required, but certain manual skills are necessary. Many nuclear physicists I know couldn't even fix a plugged sink, so they'd probably need help from skilled craftsmen."

Once the bomb is made, Taylor adds, "It's relatively easy to detonate a homemade nuclear device. Ordinary high explosives are required. But if somebody got just a little clumsy in working on the thing—a very real possibility for beginners—they'd probably end up very dead."

Gen. Edward B. Giller (U.S.A.F. Ret.) is deputy assistant administrator for national security at the Energy Research and Development Administration (ERDA), one of the two agencies formed out of the old Atomic Energy Commission. Previously, he worked for the AEC and he's one of the most widely known authorities in the field of nuclear security. We asked him, "Do you think a small group could assemble all the needed ingredients and then build an A-bomb?"

Gen. Giller said, "I'm under the impression that the detonators and wires and things that people use in hard rock mining would be the easiest to use in detonating the high explosives you need in any atomic bomb. But it's a very risky business. If the high explosives go off by mistake, there's going to be one hell of a hole in the ground, much bigger than some of the explosions today's terrorists have had.

"It's much different than the pipe bomb business. The amount of high explosives used in pipe bombs is peanuts compared to the amount of explosives you'd have to play with in building a nuclear device. You've got to man-handle a lot of explosives in a way that I for one would never care to do.

"Our agency's position is that we do recognize it's within the capabilities of dedicated, fearless, technical people to conceive a bomb design and survive to the point where they've fabricated it. But both we and they would be unsure whether it would actually give a nuclear explosion if they detonated their bomb. A lot would depend on their background, their dedication and their facilities.

"We can't say it can't be done. We can't say it can be done. So we address ourselves to protecting against the loss of nuclear material. I don't want to lose any of the stuff, now or ever. I couldn't take any comfort in trying to evaluate somebody's machine shop expertise or educational level in trying to help me with the problem I might face if somebody does acquire nuclear material illegally."

George Day is editor of the Bulletin of the Atomic Scientists which for many years has provided a forum for top people in nuclear research. We asked him, "Where would terrorists or criminals be likely to obtain enough uranium or plutonium to build an A-bomb?"

Day replied, "In the process of producing electric power in nuclear generators, plutonium is formed as a by-product inside the nuclear reactor's fuel rods. But in that form, it's so radioactive that you'd be dead before you got it home. So that part of the plutonium life cycle is not particularly vulnerable to groups eager to build a bomb.

"However, used-up fuel rods are hauled to reprocessing plants. There the plutonium is chemically separated out. It ends up as a relatively stable powder. It's not even dangerously radioactive right then. And that's when plutonium is most vulnerable to theft.

8·3 Exposition

The only other technique available to magazine writers, in addition to quotes and anecdotes, is *exposition,* which is the presentation of your thoughts with the data that back them up. The thoughts are offered in *generalizations* of fact and opinion, about which we'll have more to say in Chapter 9. The backups are all the *specifics*—dates and statistics, definitions and concrete examples—that prove the generalizations without the need to call on other people's experiences (anecdotes) or authority (quotes).

Most of our students come to us knowing all the fundamentals of expository writing that they have to know (except how to really make it colorful). It's the only nonfiction writing they've been taught in college and high school. All those "compare and contrast" essays have prepared them to find facts and figures and to pepper their papers with lots of convincing examples. Mostly, our job is to make students *avoid* exposition wherever possible, substituting anecdotes and lively, pertinent quotes.

Some articles, especially how-to's don't lend themselves to anecdotes and quotes. They become entirely exposition. One easy way to keep the reader interested is to speak to him directly. (See Ill. 6.1, our plastic-furniture article, for the use of *you.*) In addition, keep in mind that when you use expository writing, it can—and *should*—be as vivid as your quotes and anecdotes. Vivid exposition seems so difficult for beginners to achieve that all of Chapter 14 shows how to make words work for you. A small portion of our long cancer-immunology article illustrates what we always strive for—and sometimes achieve:

> . . . *Why do people get cancer at all?*
> *Stated most simply, it is for approximately the same reason that, when a flu epidemic hits, some people contract flu but most others don't. No one has been able to calculate how many mutated cells a normal body destroys* before

they develop into cancer, but the odds appear to be very, very much in favor of your staying healthy.

Working with American Cancer Society figures, we have extrapolated that on the average, the odds actually are 350 to 1 that you are immune to cancer at this moment. And if you are under 55 years old and are a non-smoker, the odds are more like 650 to 1 in your favor.

A number of factors enable cancer occasionally to outwit the immune-surveillance network. One factor is that a certain amount of time is needed to mount a strong defense. Even though, as one experimenter found, in 15 days your body could make 1000 different cells from one cell through consecutive mutations, what happens if none of those 1000 new antigen codes is the right one? The cancer would itself keep growing, of course.

All we had to work with, in writing the above, was a stack of statistics and dull research reports. By using the devices we'll explain later on, we were able to convert them into a salable article.

Chapter Nine

The Five Commandments No Pro Forgets

NOVICES WHO THINK THAT THE LOGIC OF PUT-
ting together a complete magazine article is self-evident ought
to read the Constitution of the United States of America. Its
copywriters, the likes of Benjamin Franklin, Alexander Hamilton, and
Thomas Jefferson, didn't notice until it was already enacted that they'd
left out all the important guarantees of personal freedom which led
them to found the United States in the first place.

They had the luxury of quickly drafting ten amendments. If
you're that far off the mark, no editor will allow you a rewrite.

There are five commandments that every pro makes part of his
consciousness so that he avoids a blooper like the one our foundering
fathers made. They are:

> Make your point and prove it.
> Offer generalizations but avoid generalities.
> Separate fact from opinion.
> Locate universal images and experiences.
> Above all, entertain.

9·1 Make Your Point—and Prove It.

We can't tell you how often we've polished off a first draft, beaming at
how cleverly we'd uncovered an unknown fact and sketched in a
breathtaking anecdote, only to be pulled up short, maybe days later, to
realize that in our excitement we'd *missed making the point* of our article.

Missing the point can kill article ideas as well as finished
manuscripts. If you don't clearly identify what you want to write about
when you first outline your article for an editor, you'll probably miss
getting the assignment. If you do get it, you may discover after weeks
of work that the story won't hold together. Or, having found a point,
you may turn it in—and have it tossed back because the editor thought
you had a different point in mind.

The main point of your article is usually in your topic sentence. It
includes your focus and your slant. When you've finished writing the

first draft of your article, check back to that topic sentence and make sure that what you've written after it backs up what you started out to write. Your ending, of course, must be about your main point. But that's not all. All your evidence—your quotes, anecdotes, and exposition—must keep building up the validity of your main point as your article progresses through its body. And your slant must never veer from its original point of view.

For some subjects, you will have to consider both the point and its counterpoint. But editors expect you to present a well-established case favoring one side or the other. The only exception is when you are specifically assigned to explore a controversial issue while remaining neutral. (This, by the way, is one of the trickiest pieces a pro can undertake. If you think it's easy to remain neutral while researching a controversy, just try it.)

Let's look again at our CAT scanner story for *Family Health.* We were assigned to research the controversy over whether hospitals really needed CATs. The question, it turned out, had two aspects: medical value and cost. The only opposition we found to the CATs' medical value came from a lightweight. A technician trained in traditional x-ray methods told us dozens of things wrong with the scanners, but it turned out she worked at the other end of the hospital from its scanner and knew less about it than we did. On a hunch that she was probably afraid of being displaced by the CAT, we left her opinion out of the finished article. We did present both sides as to whether the CATs cost too much, because both opinions were expressed by experts. However, our digging turned up information that convinced us that, in most instances, CATs were worth the cost. We weren't able to present all our technical backup data; as it was, the article ran longer than the assignment called for. But we did let readers know the decision we'd reached. And we designed the article to thrust home that positive viewpoint from beginning to end.

On the other hand, Frank's article "The Nightmare of Nuclear Blackmail" (Ill. 8.2) specifically avoided taking a stand on whether it was easy to fabricate a clandestine A-bomb. His main point was simply that the threat of such an occurrence represented a genuine nightmare to nuclear security people and to concerned scientists. That was his assigned title; that was his lead; and his selection and placement of data and opinion relentlessly led the reader to that conclusion.

Let's look back at the beginning of that article. First Frank presented a former A-bomb designer's opinion that it is easy to *design* a bomb (but tough—although possible—to assemble one). Next, one of the people responsible for U.S. nuclear security vacillated on whether it is possible for terrorists to assemble a bomb. His statement, meant to be a denial of Frank's premise, actually *supported* the article's contention that the "nightmare" isn't farfetched. Strengthening the premise was the authority's concern about keeping plutonium out of the hands of would-be bomb makers. By following with a quote from the editor of the *Bulletin of the Atomic Scientists,* who said that the nuclear reactor industry soon will produce easy-to-get plutonium, he made nightmare into plausible reality.

At first it might seem that Frank should have chosen the more dramatic slant that terrorists *can* build a clandestine A-bomb, no doubt about it. But if he had, fairness would have obliged him to give substantial space to the opposing viewpoint, whose representatives are solid and respected. The same resource people who were willing to say that bomb building is *possible* would have argued that it would never happen—and he would have been forced to give their opinions full weight. Then, if Frank had concluded that terrorists *can* build the bomb, his arbitrary stand would have been suspect. By choosing a less dramatic point to make, Frank was able to make it unequivocably —and because he proved it solidly, he actually produced a more dramatic article.

9·2 Generalize, but Don't Use Generalities

We don't often rely on dictionary definitions, since most words have several subtly different meanings and depend on context for complete definition. But the two words *generalize* and *generalities* throw so many would-be writers we'll call on all the ammunition we can find:

> Generalize: *active verb*; to derive or induce a general conception or principle from particulars; to draw a general conclusion from; to give general applicability to.
> Generality: *noun;* total applicability; a vague or inadequate statement.

It is the good writer's primary job to find interesting situations, study them, evaluate them, and finally draw general conclusions about them. In the most successful articles, the situational data are presented to the reader, and most of the generalizations are left for the reader to make. Sometimes, however, a generalization is necessary. In that case, it should always have, directly preceding or following, the specifics that back it up. The writer who makes *generalities* instead of leading the reader to *generalizations* is not doing his job.

Here is a generality:

> *We studied the Jones, Smith, Watson, Johnson, Olson, and Rogers families and concluded that residents of Shaker Haunts Houses are pretty decent poker players, lousy backgammon players, and let their kids throw Frisbees on the front lawn.*

Now here is a generalization, followed by the situational specifics that support it:

The Watsons are typical of families residing in Shaker Haunts Houses. They manage to win a few dollars at Friday-night nickel-stakes neighborhood poker games, but lose it all at Saturday-night backgammon club. Sundays, they try to mow the lawn. It isn't easy, since Shaker Haunts is the local Frisbee-tossing arena.

The first example is dry and devoid of humanity. The second example is vivid and personal. There's no doubt which will more quickly catch the reader's attention and remain longer in the memory.

Let's take an example from a student's article. His premise was that a guerrilla war is being fought between smokers and nonsmokers. At one point in the article, he wrote:

In public accommodations, nonsmokers are less and less being discriminated against as greater numbers of nonsmoking sections are being established.

There's a generality for you! *How much* less discrimination? *How many* greater numbers? *Which* public accommodations? Instead of relying on weak generalities, he should have created a line or two of expository specifics and let the readers make the generalization. We'll assume his research was deep enough to get the facts that led him to this conclusion. (The poor writer solidifies his conclusions *before* he checks them out, and then arms himself with backup data.) Let's use hypothetical data to show how the writer might have more effectively convinced the reader.

In public places such as restaurants, retail stores, elevators, buses, and airplanes, nonsmokers are breathing easier. So far, twenty-seven states have enacted laws that require nonsmoking sections in specific public areas; and in 1979, federal laws outlawed smoking on interstate buses, trains, and planes.

(This is a good place to point out that the good writer *always* chooses his words carefully to mean what he wants to say. The student used "public accommodations," a term limited mainly to hotels and restaurants, when he meant "public places." And his article nowhere proved, with evidence, that nonsmokers were ever *discriminated against* as that term is properly used.)

Look at another paragraph from the same article. See how many generalities you can spot and how many misuses of the language. (There are a lot of trite phrases, too.)

Smoking did in fact for a period of time become such an emotional issue that children and parents would have bitter quarrels over the smoking habits of parents. Husbands and wives at times would become angered beyond despair at the disagreements generated in households where one person was a militant nonsmoker and the other a militant smoker.

Intended here was the generalization that *families were torn apart by the smoking issue.* Instead, generality was piled upon generality:

"children and parents" and "husbands and wives" apply to nearly everybody on earth. There are two likely reasons for this: first, he hadn't done enough research to back up his hunches; second, he hadn't yet learned the power of using anecdotes, quotes, facts, and figures to bolster his generalization. We'd rewrite the above paragraph so it limits the generalization just to families housing nonsmokers and smokers, and use specific examples to make our points. But our rewrite is a generalization, not a generality, for another reason: because it paints a *general* principle derived from *particular* examples.

> *When a smoker lived with a nonsmoker, the living wasn't easy. Ned and Ellie, for example, had smoked all their lives. Suddenly their two teenaged children began to harass them like angry parents every time Ned or Ellie would light up. They began a guerrilla war, too, soaking cigarettes in soapy water, putting chalk in the filters, dumping unopened packs in the toilet tank. The tension became so keen that Ned and Ellie's smoking practically doubled. In the case of Ernie the smoker and his wife Susan the militant nonsmoker, the attacks were more subtle. Susan would only make nasty remarks in front of friends. Ernie retaliated by refusing to entertain or go visiting, and the couple only saved their marriage by etc., etc., etc.*

When in doubt, the safest way to be sure your writing makes meaningful generalizations, not merely meaningless generalities, is to examine your qualifiers. Do you use lots of *for example*s? That's good. Do you use lots of *most*s and *many*s, *some*s and *all*s? That's bad.

9·3 Separate Fact From Opinion

The necessity for separating fact and opinion ought to be self-evident. Unfortunately, we've seen many fine stories fall apart when their authors attempted to substantiate their generalizations with opinions instead of facts.

If an economist tells you that the gross national product is $47 billion, and you or he verifies the figure, that's a fact. (If he says it's $47 billion and it isn't verified, it may be an *incorrect* fact.) But if the economist says it *ought* to be $47 billion, no matter how many others concur, it's still an opinion, not a fact. You may overlook that important difference as you rush toward a deadline, but your editors and readers will know it's opinion. And if you treat it as a fact, they'll mistrust your credibility throughout the rest of the article.

The easiest way to signal opinion is with qualifiers—such words as *most, some, possibly, probably, can,* and *may.* But carefully selected nouns and verbs can also do the job. When we wrote about cancer immunology for *Science Digest,* credibility was a big factor since the article's point of view was at odds with the public's. One section of the article answered the question, "Are viruses a cause of cancer?" There, it was especially important to separate fact from opinion. For opinion, we selected nouns and verbs, as well as qualifiers, that signal opinion. (We'll underline them throughout the following extracts.)

> You _may_ have _heard_ that viruses cause cancer. _Suggested_ by researchers as a _question_—not an answer—some years ago—this _theory_ quickly was _espoused_ by physicians, patients, and especially the popular press. It was a pleasant _theory_ to believe; if a virus caused cancer, an innoculation that _would_ prevent or cure it _had to be_ just around the corner.

For matters of fact, we used words that left no doubt as to their factuality. Later in the virus section we wrote:

> A virus has the ability to sneak in beside a normal cell's DNA and unite with it at a point or two where the DNA is particularly vulnerable. Aided by enzymes, the virus then alters the composition of the normal cell's DNA.

An author has to make the point she sets out to make. Our point was the opinion, based on our research, that viruses probably don't cause cancer. So we proceeded to lay out the facts behind our opinions, but we took care to label every tentative conclusion with a qualifier:

> Many private physicians _still support_ the viruses-cause-cancer _theory_. And some clinical researchers are _still searching_ for viruses they can _link_ to human cancer. But _almost_ without exception, the basic scientists we interviewed and those whose papers we studied _doubt_ that viruses are (or will ever be found to be) _significant_ cause of human cancer. Dr. Temin states simply, "_Most_ human cancers _appear to_ result from genetic changes that are not a result of viral infection."

Incidentally, we'd earlier identified Dr. Temin as a Nobel laureate for his work on viruses in cancer. So it was not chance that led to our choosing *his* quote to settle the argument we fastidiously composed from irrefutable facts laced with strong, authoritatively held opinions.

Try doing the following to the above paragraph:

a. Add a summary statement of Temin's conclusion without qualifying it.

b. Change the quote to state the same conclusion without qualification.

Note how, if we try to color the opinions of our experts, or state opinion as fact, we lose credibility and, in doing so, lose our argument.

9·4 Locate Universal Images and Experiences

Many beginning writers fail to use universal images or single out universal experiences. They choose examples they understand, forgetting that it's the *reader's* comprehension they need. When a student wanted to put down a much-touted tourist attraction, she wrote:

> *The beautiful oriental dolls were so out of place I wondered if one might not mistake them for Bucky Badger dolls.*

Bucky Badger dolls? Many residents of Wisconsin know what she meant, since Bucky is the University of Wisconsin's mascot. But the image makes no sense to readers in the other forty-nine states. If she hopes to sell nationally, this writer had better keep *all* her potential readers in mind.

Another student set out to write an angry article on the lack of rights for women in Brazil. For her lead, she deliberately chose to use the images most Americans see when one mentions that country:

> *When one speaks of Brazil, the mind's eye sees Carnaval, samba, and sandy beaches filled with beautiful women.*

Then she introduced her topic:

> *Next to the beaches, women are the second biggest tourist resource, making Carnaval a mammoth and X-rated version of New Orleans' Mardi Gras.*

She called forth pictures stored in the heads of most readers, and based her *new* information and conclusions on those familiar old images.

"How do you know," we're often asked, "what is and what isn't a common experience?" Our best answer is, either write for the people you associate with, or associate with the people you want to write for. And read a lot. Learn the same things your readers learn. Even beginning writers know that, when communicating with third-graders, words like "philistine" and "plebeian" are out, and concepts like euthanasia and adultery are probably beyond the readers' imagination. The fact that good writing must be based on universal images leads us to recommend that beginning writers write for magazines they like to read—and on subjects they like to read about. If you do that, you'll start out with a useful set of images in your head that closely matches the set in your readers' heads.

We could now compose for you a list of 600 universal concepts common to the majority of *Popular Mechanics* readers, and another list for *Playgirl* readers. But our lists would do you no good, because 300 of those images will change as the trends change, becoming outmoded within a few years. Half the fun of vivid writing is spotting the changes in readers' image banks. The other half is using the old images to create new ones that may become commonly accepted. We found two clever examples of that in a 1930 issue of *National Geographic*. The author,

Frederick Simpich, obviously had a lot of fun orchestrating these images about one of New York City's most mundane statistics:

> *Can you imagine a man nearly a mile tall, with a mouth a hundred feet wide? A man who could wade across Lake Superior, which is 1,000 feet deep, and get wet only up to his knees? Such a monster, drinking night and day, could just about consume New York's water supply. On a hot day the city uses one billion gallons. There are less than two billion people on earth; so that is more than half a gallon for every person.*

Simpich, in his New York City opus, even played word games to help his readers grasp monumental quantities:

> *But how much food of all kinds does New York eat—it and its environs served by delivery wagons?*
>
> *Nobody knows exactly. Experts have estimated it at about 10,000,000,000 pounds a year. "How much is that?" you ask? Well, 5,000,000 tons. Neither does that mean anything.*
>
> *More then, than is consumed each year by all the standing armies of the world.*

9·5 Entertain!

After just reprinting those entertaining excerpts fifty years old, it seems redundant to mention that good writing has to entertain. But we stress it since this is one of the major shortcomings of beginners. In fact, we'll add that the most accurate way to perceive magazine writing is as entertainment.

If you're a magazine writer, you're in show biz. This doesn't mean you can't be a journalist. It doesn't mean you can't write informative, useful, exploratory, inciting, or touching articles. In fact, you *ought* to write informative, useful, exploratory, inciting, and touching articles, and use journalistic techniques in doing so. But your articles must also be lively, fast-paced, and to the point. You must never bore. You must always keep your reader begging for more until your very last line.

In order to entertain readers, you don't have to keep 'em laughing, or even chuckling. If you've watched a TV soap opera, you know that people also derive entertainment from having their emotions stroked and their tear glands exercised. If you've seen a TV documentary, you're aware that they do not document at all but dramatize, even sensationalize, contemporary matters. Even the TV news entertains with its short, chatty, heavily illustrated segments. People aren't used to thinking of the daily newspaper as entertainment, but even the once-staid *New York Times* has conceded that its business is entertainment and has changed its style accordingly. The underpinning of the magazine business, too, is entertainment, short and simple.

Not even the business trade journals are read for serious knowledge. Take, for example, the journal *Physician's Management,* for which we wrote a regular monthly feature, "PhoneScan,"® for several years. It was read by 200,000 successful doctors each month—read closely enough that advertisers kept renewing their contracts. If our articles had run in a newspaper, they might have been called gossip. They informed about trends, but used lively quotes and anecdotes from fifty randomly-chosen physicians each month to do it. If we had begun to turn in "PhoneScans"® that informed with statistics and medical jargon, instead of with the most entertaining quotes and stories we could find, we'd have been tossed out of the magazine instead of winning awards for it.

When we wrote our long, technical article on cancer for *Science Digest,* we had to take into account the readers' biases. The widespread fear of cancer made any levity on the subject taboo. How did we entertain in this tricky subject area? Here's the picture we created for the cell-by-cell dramas we discovered:

> *It's dark. Somewhere deep inside your body a T-cell is on patrol, outfoxing the darkness with hundreds of sensitive tentacles that instantly identify the shape of every cell it encounters. As long as the T-cells patrol, every other cell can go about its individual job without worry.*
>
> *Suddenly the T-cell tenses because its stubby tentacles brush against a strangely shaped cell. It doesn't belong there. It's a runaway cell that, left to its selfish devices, would become a tumor crowding nearby cells and robbing them of nourishment.*
>
> *Instantly the T-cell patrol sends out an alarm, a special bit of protein excreted only in emergencies. That alerts the body's soldiers, the Killer-cells, and their not-so-smart but hard-working helpers, the macrophage cells. Yet, even before help arrives, the T-cell attacks, attaching itself to the tumor cell.*
>
> *The T-cell is no match for the young giant. But within three minutes, several Killer-cells and macrophages have sped to the scene. Together they unite into an anti-body. Plunging against the tumor cell, the warriors rip at the invader's protective cell membrane.*
>
> *Ten minutes later, the barrier is breached, the tumor cell disintegrates, and the triumphant cells slowly move away.*

How to
Sell Your
Article Ideas

Chapter Ten

How to Write
a Dynamite Query Letter

I N CASE ONE OF OUR MORE IMPORTANT MESSAGES has somehow eluded you, we'll repeat it: If you want to be a magazine writer you have to face the fact that you are in the business of selling. The query letter (short for letter of inquiry) is the usual way in which authors sell their products—articles—to their customers —editors.

Like the magazine article itself, the query letter has evolved its own standard format. Many authors have worked out their personal variations in format, and no doubt you'll come up with your own touches, but if you want to appear to be a professional writer, you'd better include certain uniform information that editors expect to see. The best query letters are sales letters with everything presented deliberately in the way most likely to sell the idea.

Many beginning writers in our classes fooled editors into thinking they'd had long experience in article writing, and therefore could be trusted with hefty assignments, simply by learning to write professional-quality query letters. Then their only concern was to avoid suggesting articles too difficult for a novice to deliver. Judi herself learned how to write a selling query letter before she'd fully mastered the art of article writing. Her first sale was to *Good Housekeeping,* which had to pay her a $300 kill fee for an unusable article on school counselors that, years later, she realized sounded more like a term paper than a magazine piece. When she got over her embarrassment, she picked up the pieces and aimed her next batch of queries at magazines that demanded less professionalism of their writers.

10·1 Format

We use the term *query letter* because writers these days send their queries in the form of single-spaced business letters (with double spaces between paragraphs). In times past, queries were often called outlines and written as double-spaced synopses. You may still hear somebody using the term *story outline,* which originated in that period of magazine writing history. The story outline was useful when there were at least half a dozen very similar general interest magazines around (for example, *Life, Look,* the original *Saturday Evening Post, Coronet,* and the old *Pageant*). You could send the same outline to each of them in turn. Now every magazine is targeted to a slightly different audience, and each editor likes to feel that the author has taken the trouble to tailor a suggested story to her own magazine's peculiarities. By writing your query in letter format, you will give her the warm feeling that the idea has been especially developed with her magazine in mind.

If one query is turned down, the wily writer, of course, copies applicable segments in typing a new version for a different editor. But we've found that, even when copying, we make changes as we sharpen the focus or find better ways to express ourselves.

Unless it is utterly, honestly, journalistically impossible, limit your query letter to *one single-spaced page.* ONE PAGE! Editors are very busy people and hate to read long letters. They don't give long ones any more time than short ones, only less attention. Worse, they assume that—barring any obvious extenuating circumstances—if you can't say what's important in one page, you probably don't have a clear enough handle on the idea. Our experience supports the assumption.

If you have 8½ × 11-inch stationery with your name and address on it, use it. (White is preferred.) But it's not necessary. A few old pros have zealously resisted adding that touch to their repertoires. Judi did without until she teamed up with Frank, who'd always used printed stationery as a badge of professionalism—in fact, at least two years before his writing and story ideas were as professional as his letterhead.

Center your query (top to bottom) and make it look as attractive and businesslike as possible. Leave wide left- and right-hand margins. Make sure your type looks sharp and dark; in other words, change your ribbon and clean your type periodically. Keep a carbon copy, because you may not get back the original.

10·2 Salutation

Address your query letter to a real, living, breathing, working, thinking, buying editor at the magazine you've singled out. Otherwise your idea will probably be relegated to the lowest person on the totem pole. (Chapter 4 dealt with how to pick both magazines and editors.) Just as writing magazine articles is a highly personal endeavor, so is editing magazines. Like writers, editors have egos, and you should not risk offending an editor by misspelling her name, using the wrong form of address, or getting the name of her magazine incorrect.

Your salutation should be "Dear Mr. So-and-So," or "Dear Ms. So-and-So," unless you know that the editor prefers to be addressed as

Ill. 10.1 ————————————————————————————

Mr. Ernest Baxter
VIVA
909 Third Avenue
New York, NY 10022

Dear Mr. Baxter,

HOW TO KEEP RAPISTS FROM GETTING OFF SCOT FREE

If you like, this can be an as-told-to bylined by
the attorney whose plan it is. He's Neil Comer,
ex-professor of law at the U. of Minnesota and now in
private practice in New York. If so, we could call it:

YOU'RE HELPING ME FREE YOUR OWN RAPIST

Neil has gotten rapists off. He'd rather not, but
these people have come to him for defense, and the women
in the cases have, through their ignorance of the law, made
his job easy. We'll document these cases, and then we'll
present Neil's plan for preventing the freeing of rapists.
In essence, it calls for calling a lawyer <u>before</u> you talk
to the police. Get the lawyer to escort you through the
station house, the hospital, the D.A. and courtroom maze.
Have the lawyer make sure the cops take down your statement
showing how much force was used (usually they jot down only
the personally titillating elements of your case). Have
the lawyer insure that <u>your</u> rights are protected; you
can be sure the rapist has a lawyer protecting <u>his</u> rights.

Besides being well-credentialed and articulate, Neil
is young (not over 40, I think) and <u>very</u> good looking.
We could shoot some photos of the attorney in court
if you like.

I enclose Xeroxes of articles of mine which ran in
Playgirl. The <u>Divorce</u> article was reprinted by Educational
TV's Consumer Survival Kit (expurgated, of course). I
also write for Seventeen, Parade, Family Weekly, Modern
Maturity, the New York Times, Chatelaine, Barrister,
Change....

I look forward to hearing from you.

Sincerely,

Judi R. Kesselman

Successful query letter.

Mrs. or Miss. Using first names, unless you're genuinely on a first-name basis, is as taboo as addressing by first name the personnel director you've never met at a company where you're applying for a job. It's possible to develop a first-name relationship by mail. In fact, there are many editors we've never met personally whom we address "Dear Bob," or "Dear Sally," and who write to us as "Dear Judi," and "Dear Frank." Our rule is to wait until the editor has used our first names before we use his.

10·3 Title, Topic, Slant

Editors like to think about ideas in terms of titles. If you have what you consider a super title, or even a good catchy short title, it's great to start off with a bang by giving the title first:

Re: "How to Make Dynamite in a Backyard Barbecue."

Some writers prefer to work the title into the letter's opening paragraph.

If your title doesn't completely spell out your suggested article's focus and slant (see Chapter 7), you should try to work them into the first paragraph. In the classic query letter, therefore, by the end of the first paragraph the editor should have a concise but sharp understanding of the *specific* idea you are proposing, the *slant* you propose to take and, if you have one, a suggested title.

10·4 Why the Reader Wants to Read About It; Why the Editor Wants to Print It

Using everything you learned about marketing in Part II, your second paragraph should concisely tell the editor why his audience wants to read about the idea you're proposing. If you can't come up with a selling answer, you're trying to sell to the wrong magazine. It's not enough to simply say—as so many students do—"This is something your readers will really want to read about." Here's where you have to tailor the idea to your market. You must convince the editor that you know the specific interests of his audience and, knowing them, are sure your idea will cater to them. For example, if you're suggesting an article on job hunting to *Seventeen* and you have authoritative evidence that teenage females are terrified of looking for their first jobs because they're afraid to have anyone know they don't know the first thing about it, cite your fact and the evidence. Since *Seventeen* caters to young females likely to be looking for first jobs, it will be obvious to the editor that you know his magazine and your idea are tailor-made for each other.

Ill. 10.2

```
Mr. Don Feitel, Editor
Metropolitan Sunday Newspaper Group
260 Madison Avenue
New York, New York 10016

Dear Don:

            QUERY:  Don't Catch the Bad Food Flu!

    One half of all cases of flu and those minor but distressing ail-
ments we chalk up as a "virus" are probably cases of food poisoning.
That's the word from Dr. Howard Bauman, a respected bacteriologist and
vice president for science and technology at the Pillsbury Company in
Minneapolis.

    Bauman's 50 percent figure isn't something developed from a recent
survey of minor illnesses that will soon appear in print all over.
Doctors just don't take time out to study ordinary "flu" and ordinary
"virus."  Bauman bases his conclusion on a rule of thumb which a lot of
experienced MDs and food scientists have developed over the years.  It's
a figure we can make stick.  And if anything, the incidence of food
poisoning is on the increase.

    To supplement Bauman's expertise, we'll work in facts, opinions,
guidelines, and anecdotes from MDs and food scientists as well as pro-
fessors of home economics who are themselves starting to pay attention
to this problem.

    Today's homemaker just doesn't know how to handle food the way
Grandma did!  A few chief culprits are....

        ...cooking food at too low a temperature (we'll give guidelines)
        ...keeping frozen foods on hand too long (guidelines)
        ...canning without knowing how (guides here too)
        ...not chilling bit pots of food before storing them
        ...not covering food (the air is full of potentially harmful
                            bacteria and spores)
        ...cutting boards absorb bacteria from one food and pass them on
                            to others
        ...fish and chicken are particularly dangerous due to salmonella
        ...microwave ovens require special attention

    We can cover, as pleasantly as possible, symptoms of major forms of
food poisoning and how they differ from real flu and real virus infec-
tions.  We'll leave readers with the pleasant food for thought that,
after a few changes in kitchen routine, they can cut their family's flu
and virus rate in half.  How's that for a service piece?

                                        Very Cordially,



                                        Franklynn Peterson
```

Successful query letter.

If you're writing to David Williams, executive editor of *Kiwanis Magazine,* and one of the principals of your story is a VIP in a local Kiwanis club, say so. But don't let tangential facts provide your only rationale for querying that magazine. Williams would be more receptive to hearing about a new home-maintenance wrinkle with no ties to Kiwanis (since 82 percent of his readers own homes) than about a Kiwanis member who has done nothing more interesting to readers than undergo fourteen ingrown-toenail operations.

Aside from showing the editor why her readers will want to read your suggested article, your second, third, and maybe even fourth paragraphs should show why she needs to publish it. Convince her by answering the following questions:

WHAT'S BEEN WRITTEN ON THE TOPIC BEFORE?

Many editors feel it is your responsibility to tell them whether competing or major noncompeting magazines have run similar ideas within the past several years—and how the printed articles differ in general terms from what you are suggesting. *Reader's Guide to Periodical Literature (RGPL)* is the standard way of finding out, although it doesn't list every major publication. Be sure to check the latest supplements and make a note of how current the most recent data really are.

Just because a similar idea *has* appeared in print, it won't rule out yours, especially if you can demonstrate a new handle. But it's important that you let the editor know you're aware of what's in print, and explain why you still feel certain your idea is right for her magazine at this time. If you've done your homework and aren't afraid to admit that the subject has been tackled before, your genuine confidence that the idea is still right for her publication can be contagious. On the other hand, if you say *Reader's Guide* shows nothing has ever been written in widely read magazines about left-handed mousetraps, and the editor has read all about them in *Newsweek* six months ago, no matter how hard you pitch your idea, she may be wary of your research ability—with good reason.

WHAT'S NEW ABOUT THE SUBJECT?

While many editors feel obliged to run Thanksgiving pieces every November and Christmas pieces every December, they still want to know *what's new* about your Christmas-tree or turkey story idea. Have you found previously suppressed evidence that St. Nicholas was really a dirty old man? Or can you show how to make fifty different and original tree decorations from soda pop bottle caps? Addressed to the right editor, these are salable ideas. Taking a new focus or a new slant on an old topic is a favorite device of many old pros.

Ill. 10.3

MADEMOISELLE

350 Madison Avenue, New York, N.Y. 10017

3006 Gregory Street
Madison, WI 53711
608-231-1335

Ms. Mary Cantwell
Senior Editor, Mademoiselle
350 Madison Avenue, NY 10017

Our many thanks for your
inquiry. Although
the idea is not quite right
for us, we appreciate your
thinking of MADEMOISELLE.

Features Editor

Dear Ms. Cantwell,

Can you use an article we title:

ARE YOU SETTING YOURSELF UP FOR RAPE?

Males in social situations are almost always on the make -- and they
insist on making the assumption that the women who flirt with them are,
too. We have quotes to that effect by a male judge in California, a
male lecturer on the psychology of the sex offender, and a male reporter.

More women are raped by men they know than by men they don't know. We
have statistics and quotes to that effect from researchers and women in
crisis centers.

By trusting casual male acquaintances, women sometimes put themselves
in situations where they seem to be inviting rape -- and often enough,
the "invitation" is acted on. We have anecdotes that are poignant
revelations by women who have learned that lesson.

The article we propose to write for you makes the above points and ends
by giving 5 Rules to Avoid Rapes by Acquaintances:

    1- In every male-female situation, do what's best, wisest,
       and most comfortable for you.

    2- Don't accept any favors from males without first finding
       out what favors they want in return -- or making it clear
       there'll be no favors given.

    3- Learn to recognize the situations males consider to be
       sexual and stay out of them unless you want sex.

            etc.

We have published in PLAYGIRL, McCALL'S, VIVA, SEVENTEEN, and many others.
A sample of our writing is enclosed.

Sincerely,

Judi R. Kesselman and Franklynn Peterson

Even pros get printed rejection slips in answer to query letters.

Even on a highly topical subject, editors look for the feel of something new. For instance, just when everybody assumed there wasn't a single new wrinkle left to report on Jackie Onassis, a bunch of enterprising writers noticed she'd be turning fifty in 1979. They all suggested to their favorite editors, whose readers, they knew, were still eager for anything new about Jackie, stories on what it was like to be Jackie O. and turning fifty. They added yet another dozen Jackie stories to the thousands already published.

ARE PICTURES AVAILABLE?

Many magazines rely heavily on graphics. Editors at big-ticket magazines—the ones paying well over $1,000 for a story—let their art directors worry about getting pictures and paying for them. Editors elsewhere often consider picture possibilities at the time they consider article assignments. So if pictures are likely to be an important aspect of your story, and if you know they're readily available or you can provide *professional-quality* ones yourself (see 6.11), it can't hurt to say so. But don't send photos or any other artwork with your query letter.

10·5 Who Are the Authorities?

Aside from wanting to know the uniqueness of your suggested idea, the editor wants to be sure you're genuinely able to produce a usable article if he assigns it. Unless he knows you by reputation, he needs to be convinced that you're enough of a hard-nosed researcher to come up with the kind of authoritative information that most magazines demand. Therefore, the classic query letter—even from well-established pros—outlines where the suggested article's facts, figures, and opinions will come from.

If *you're* the principal source of information, you'd better come up with impressive personal credentials on the suggested topic. If you're pitching yourself as the authority for information that usually requires *professional* expertise (for example, medical, financial, child psychology, or employment advice), you'd better be a pro in that field. But if it's a craft idea, simply having made successfully the project is usually credential enough.

In Ill. 10.4, a corrected query letter by a former student, notice that she didn't claim to be an expert on how to make banners. She didn't have to. The editors who were interested in her idea—and she's sold it several times since—were convinced that if her local church hung her banners, it was proof enough that they were up to snuff.

This was a fine query letter for a beginner, but there were weak spots that could benefit from revision. We pointed them out to our

Ill. 10.4 ────────────────────────────────────

September 28, 1981

Ms. Doloris Kanten
Lutheran Brotherhood Bond
701 2nd Ave. So.
Minneapolis, MN 55402

Dear Ms. Kanten,

1   Could you use an article like this?

2   HOW TO CREATE A GREAT NEW BANNER FOR EVERY OCCASION

3   Most churches are accumulating a supply of
4   banners. The only trouble is, once you have banners
5   on hand you are stuck with them. The same banners
6   are used week after week and year after year.
7   Bright and bold decorations become "same old stuff."

8   I think your readers would like to know how to
9   make throw-away banners using permanent backs with
10   disposable designs in front. This would be a step
11   by step explanation of the throw-away idea. It
12   could include any or all of the following: size;
13   where and how to hang; how to finish off the back;
14   material to use for backs and fronts; idea sources;
15   how to apply designs and the advantages of these
16   throw-aways. I could arrange for photos of our
17   banner collection and the banner makers at work.

18   My only credentials are a desire to share a
19   good idea and lots of experience in making such
20   banners.

21   Hope you like the idea.

Sincerely,

(sig.)

Mrs. Connie Scharlau
Route X
Arcadia, Wisconsin 54612

Corrected query letter brought sale for student.

student, and with our suggested revisions, her query sold. We've numbered the lines so you can follow our suggestions.

Line 2: Change "great" to "cheap." That's your selling point. *Do* put it in the title. Also, say "banners." You're suggesting *many* designs.

Line 3: Change "are" to "keep." Stronger verb. Delete "a supply of." Extraneous words.

Line 4: Unless you mean "only", don't say it. There may be other troubles too. Change "have" to "buy expensive." Isn't *that* your point?

Line 5: Delete "on hand." Extraneous.

Line 6: Change "are used" to "are dragged out." Stronger verb.

Line 8: Delete "I think" and "would like to know," and substitute "Let's tell your readers," etc. Notice how much stronger a positive statement is. Avoid "I think" at all costs.

Line 9: Change "using" to "that combine," for a clearer statement.

Line 10: Delete "This would be": sounds extraneous and unsure.

Line 11: Delete "It" and period to make one sentence.

Line 12: Change "could" to "will" for a stronger statement. Don't say "any or all of". The editor wants to know now what you plan to deliver. Don't seem to vacillate or hedge. "Size": do you mean "sizes you can make them in" or what? Say it with enough words so the editor doesn't have to guess.

Line 13: "Where and how to hang": is this an important point? Are these banners hung differently from others? Do they need special care? Your inclusion of this phrase, without explanation and in a position of priority in terms of order, would make me wary if I were the editor. It probably should be mentioned last, and with an explanation.

Line 14: "Idea sources": this is also unclear and needs more words.

Line 15: "The advantages": this should come first or second in your listing, as it's very important.

Lines 16 and 17: Good!

Lines 18, 19, and 20: Be sure of yourself, not self-negating. I would say instead: "I have had lots of experience in making such banners, and would like to share it with your readers."

Line 21: Not really needed. If you run out of space on one page after your changes are made, you can leave it out.

When it comes to being expert enough in some field to be the sole authority behind an article, most of our students, we find, can offer national magazines only marginal personal qualifications. Even lower-paying national magazines do want some voice of authority—several voices, if the idea is important or controversial or if the magazine is

Ill. 10.5

---

barbara gibbons

Arthur M. Hettich, Editor
Family Circle
488 Madison Avenue
New York, New York

Dear Mr. Hettich:

I'm a former newspaper editor and fashion copywriter who has been teaching a very unusual group of adult classes for the past several months. The subject is "Creative Low Calorie Cooking."

This course was born out of my own experience with dieting. (I can't.) It wasn't until I started to "de-calorize" all my family's favorite foods that I succeeded in bringing my weight from 208 to 125 . . . where it's been for the past six years, without dieting!

These classes have been unbelievably successful, far beyond my wildest hopes. Each averages around 45 women . . . all ages, sizes and backgrounds. Before beginning these classes the sum total of my public speaking was getting a word in edgewise at dinner, but I guess my enthusiasm carries me through because my students really love it. I have a long waiting list, plus stacks of letters from women begging me to make room for them.

Which brings me to the point of this letter. I think that a regular monthly column on low-calorie cooking ideas would be a very popular feature in Family Circle . . . and I would like to write it. I don't mean yet another diet or nutrition column but one that takes a positive approach, with lots of recipes that only seem fattening!

I'm sure that your first thought for such a column would be to have it staff written or by-lined by a name cookbook author. Let me explain why I sincerely believe that I would do a far better job. I know this subject better than anybody. Anybody. Because I don't just write about low-calorie cooking, I cook this way. For myself and my family, everyday for the past six years. I've read just about everything in print on the subject . . . all the great imaginative ideas, plus the so-called low-calorie recipes that are simply slick translations of standard recipes with some skim milk and saccharin thrown in. And I've taught this topic to hundreds of women. I know what they'll accept and what they won't . . priceless experience you don't get behind the typewriter.

Beyond possessing the skill and subject knowledge to write this column, I also have the energy and enthusiasm to promote it . . . to speak to women's groups or make TV or radio appearances. I've got a good story to tell and women want to hear it.

I do hope you'll share my eagerness. I'm enclosing some columns I wrote for local newspapers for my course plus some clippings and my resume. I'd like very much to talk with Family Circle about it.

Thank you,

Barbara Gibbons

Barbara Gibbons' "letter that launched my professional career" after deciding to specialize in the subject matter she knew best.

paying what it considers a good fee. When in doubt, bring in backup authorities.

An authority, of course, is someone who is defined as an authority. Anybody who is the first to do something new, whether it's using alcohol as auto power or baking mixless cakes, is automatically an authority. Anyone who has studied under the primary authority is usually considered an authority, as is anyone paid to make decisions based on his authority. Volunteers can also be authorities, provided they have been given titles (such as Governor's Adviser on Women's Affairs) or won awards (such as First Prize for Rose Raising at the Dane County Fair). For some stories, a local authority is perfectly acceptable. For other stories, you will need to choose people whose expertise, unlike our rose expert's, is not limited to a particular locale.

Authorities are not difficult to find, even if you live away from the East Coast centers of intellectual swarm. Look for them in:

colleges
junior colleges
trade schools
local corporations
local hospitals
local trade or professional associations
government agencies

Also look for authorities in scholarly journals in your library. These days it isn't hard or even expensive to interview authorities in distant locations by telephone. (In Chapter 12 we discuss such research techniques in detail.)

10·6 Why You're Qualified to Write the Article

Writers, not just their authorities, need credentials. The editor reading your query letter will look for signs of your writing professionalism. There are three ways you can illustrate a substantial degree of professionalism *even in your first query letter.*

The first way is to write a dynamite query letter—the hallmark of a real pro. If you offer an exciting article idea, if you clearly delineate exactly what it is you'll concentrate on (focus and slant), if you spell out why the idea matches the editor's audience, if you single out qualified experts, and if you accomplish this all within the confines of a single page, your letter will stand out from among the flood of second-rate queries and the editor will assume you're a pro.

The second way is to play up, near the end of your letter, any writing credentials you've accumulated. For instance, if you're proposing an article about teenage stress to *Seventeen,* and you've written about teenage problems and mental health for markets such as your local newspaper's Sunday magazine, we suggest saying, "I've written about teen problems and mental health for regional magazines." If, instead, you've sold articles on gardening to *Elks* and on house plants to *Lady's Circle,* you could type, "I've written for such national magazines as *Lady's Circle* and *Elks.*"

There's something about writers—even those who can turn somebody else's rusty tin lean-to into a palace in print—that freezes their typewriters when it comes to shedding a line of light on themselves. Don't let it happen to you, even if you have to go through twenty-seven drafts until you finally arrive at a suitable, accurate, but sufficiently laudatory sentence or two of credentials. It's important. If you get stuck, ask somebody else to draft the honors for you.

On the other hand, if you don't have any credentials to speak of, don't make them up. Don't mention, either, that you write a mimeographed PTA newsletter or once had a letter to the editor printed in the *Wisconsin Rapids Daily Tribune.* It's better to say nothing than to list among your credentials a market that's obviously amateur. And never, ever mention college or adult ed writing courses, or relatives who write or edit.

You may laugh at this list of don'ts, but we've found examples of every item in one or another student's first query letter.

The third way to demonstrate your writing credentials to a queried editor is to enclose Xerox copies of a published article or two. This device is becoming standard, and is quite an important asset in making a sale. We've been at this exciting business for a couple of decades now, and we still maintain a file of Xeroxed articles for submitting with query letters to editors who haven't bought from us before (or recently). You may have something similar in subject or style to what you're suggesting. If not, send along the best you have, even if your only credit is a newspaper article. It proves, as nothing else can, that you really can write an article. If your by-line isn't on the article (as sometimes happens with our students who write first for local publications), send it anyway. No editor will doubt a piece is yours if you say it is. Rare is the writer with so little vanity he'll take credit for something he hasn't written. If you're so unethical as to send an unby-lined article that was really written by Al Toffler, you'd better be able to deliver an article as fine as Al would turn in.

If you have never had an article professionally printed in a newspaper or magazine, do not send Xeroxes of articles from amateur club newsletters, college papers, or the like. It's better to send nothing but a high-powered query letter.

10·7 Self-addressed Stamped Envelope

Another courtesy that writers traditionally show editors is the self-addressed stamped envelope (SASE) enclosed with every query. But it's not just for courtesy alone that we enclose ours. We hope the SASE will encourage the editor to respond as quickly as possible, since he can simply jot down a quick "thanks but no thanks" on our original letter or on notepaper and slip the reply into our SASE. (Yes, we get rejections. Most pros average about one sale out of every ten to twenty queries.) Having been editors working our way through tottering stacks of mail, with the concern most editors have for getting to all the queries as quickly and thoughtfully as possible, we can attest to how much extra time it seems to take to type out and put a stamp on a reply envelope.

Incidentally, when the editor has good news—an assignment —generally he'll stop to write an assignment letter. More about *that* in the next chapter.

Among established writers, one school of opinion contends that enclosing an SASE brands one a beginner. The genesis of that notion seems to be in the relationship between editors and writers who've already worked together on stories. Most editors do not expect frequent contributors to attach SASEs to queries. Some editors don't expect them from anyone who's sold anything to them, even one short piece. From that, some established writers (and some not so established) have extrapolated the notion that every editor ought to recognize their by-lines and give them these courtesies. Trouble is, it's hard to know in advance which editors go along with the notion. When in doubt —which is much of the time—*we* stick in an SASE. It doesn't hurt our pride a bit, and it does seem to get a quicker response.

10·8 Marks of an Amateur

There's some mysterious force that urges fledgling writers to stamp "Beware! Amateur writer at play!" all over their query letters. Aside from the points we've already covered, here is a list of some of the more obvious giveaways to avoid:

Colored paper. White 8½×11-inch paper is standard, everything else suspect.

Colored typewriter ribbons. Black is standard, the blacker the better.

School. Editors don't want to know where you've gone to school or even *if* you've gone. (The major exception is if you're suggesting an article for a scholarly publication.)

Appraisals of your writing skills by other editors, teachers, or your mother.

Ultimatums. If your idea is clearly timely—that is, if long delay makes it unsalable—a fast answer is essential. In that case, an editor won't mind if you ask for response by a certain date. We've recently discovered that a better way is to ensure exclusivity until that certain date. It means the same thing, but it sounds much nicer. (In the next chapter we'll discuss timing of queries and requeries.)

Pictures. Unless you're suggesting an idea that demands a photo story, don't send photos. If you want to write about something but don't trust yourself to describe it excitingly enough in your query letter, enclosing a snapshot may only convince the editor not to trust you with the article assignment.

Chapter Eleven

Sales Tactics

SOME OF US CAN SELL SHOES OR VACUUM CLEAN-
ers or encyclopedias or cosmetics for a living. Others of us can't.
But almost without exception, every full-time free-lance magazine
writer has to be a salesman for his article ideas, or he won't be able to
write for magazines.

Back in the good old days, agents would handle magazine
writers, making submissions to the likes of *Life, Reader's Digest, Liberty,
American Mercury,* and *Look.* In those days, postage stamps cost three
cents and the *Digest* paid $2,200. Now postage has more than sep-
tupled, but the *Digest* stopped climbing at about $3,000 and it's still
among the best-paying markets.

Few agents bother to try to sell magazine articles these days, even
for writers whose books they handle. But this new arrangement is really
preferable to the old because magazines are a fast-paced communication
medium. If editors and writers work out story ideas directly, with no
agent to slow things down, the process moves along more smoothly.

The idea that the writer must be a salesman first of all is
anathema to some of the more idealistic novices we've met. But article
selling is a more genteel endeavor than the high-pressure, low-
sincerity, memorized patter of a foot-in-the-door encyclopedia peddler.
Editors don't expect, or even want, patter. (Their doors won't slam,
having been propped permanently open years ago by stacks of old
magazines.) Besides, if your ideas are sound and your presentation to
the point, you're in a seller's market. Editors will welcome the chance
to buy from you.

This doesn't mean that if you simply zip off a bunch of query
letters you'll be deluged by prompt answers. Editors, as we've said
before, are busy people. Sometimes their replies are excruciatingly
slow. And when they reject perfectly fine ideas, they rarely take time to
explain why. All of these problems in communication raise immediate
questions for people breaking into the field. We'll answer some of the
most frequent.

11·1 Will Editors Steal my Ideas?

No!

Well, hardly ever. It's only happened to us once that we know for sure, and that was in the 1960s by one of those flamboyant new radical magazines out to conquer exploitation. We suspect it happened two other times. With more than three decades of experience between us, that makes one in a thousand purloined ideas. Those are better risks than in most professions.

Editors learn very quickly that it rarely pays to steal an idea. No matter how large or small a magazine, what its editor pays its writers is a tiny part of the overall budget. The comptrollers won't even notice the savings earned by stealing one idea a month and having it staff-written. If the editor steals it to give to a writer friend, he stands to gain almost nothing but headaches. First, there's the chance of getting a reputation for absconding with ideas, and that's dangerous in a small, gossipy profession like this. More to the point, it's very tough for one writer to do justice to somebody else's idea. The driving excitement, commitment, and basic knowledge of the subject are all missing, and it shows in the manuscript. Editors quickly learn that the best article comes from the writer who suggested the idea.

There's another reason editors don't steal ideas. Beginning writers think ideas are hard to come by because they haven't learned to recognize them quickly. Pros have more ideas than they can handle; we have several folders full of ideas we can't get to. Editors generate more ideas than *they* can get to. On top of that, they're bombarded every day with still more ideas.

Editors tell us that most good ideas seem to have their *time*. Several writers will offer the same—or very similar—ideas almost concurrently. What leads an editor to choose one writer from among the several who offer similar ideas? If she's worked with one of them before, she knows he can deliver. If another's query is the most exciting, she might choose him.

Why do we even bother to include this question of idea stealing under sales tactics? Because we've seen so many beginning writers paralyze themselves through misbegotten fear that their ideas will be stolen. They hold back information in their query letters, trying to make it tough for an unscrupulous editor to learn enough so he can misappropriate the story; in doing so, they only ensure the editor's not getting enough of a feel for the idea. They hide away their most precious ideas in filing drawers to await the day when they've made it and their brainchildren become unsnatchable. By the time they've made it, if they ever do, those well-hidden ideas are sure to be stale and unexciting.

Writers who hide away their best ideas have small chance of making it. It's tough enough to make a living in this field even when you push your very best ideas.

11·2 How Long Should I Wait for a Reply to My Query?

How patient are you?

Many editors say it takes up to six weeks before they can get replies back. Some of our faster-paced colleagues allow them much less time. Vic Cox, for example, politely mentions in his query letters that in approximately two weeks the idea will be sent to another editor. He tells us, "I've been an editor. I know that if an editor likes the idea, he'll be back within that time anyway."

There is no hard-and-fast rule about how long to wait for a reply. Different editors take different lengths of time; even the same editor takes varying lengths of time depending on time of the year (summer vacation and Christmas party times are very slow) or time of the month (going-to-press time is slow). From our own experience, and having picked the brains of friends, we've concluded that a month's wait is typical.

However, there's no law that says you have to wait for a reply to one query before you send out another. You too can set your lag time at two or three weeks if you like. If you've received no reply to a query letter by then, draft another one to an editor at another magazine.

You're not obliged to let the first editor know that you've decided to suggest the story idea to a second editor. Editors don't, as a rule, take kindly to notes that sound like ultimatums or the work of a dilettante. But, once in a while, with an editor we correspond with regularly, we tip her overflowing in basket by photocopying our carbon of the query letter and mailing it with a short, polite note asking if maybe it got lost somewhere along the way.

What happens, you're sure to ask, if queried editor number two agrees to buy your story, and then editor number one finally gets back to you with a go-ahead? Assuming you haven't already told editor number two you'll accept his assignment, you could take the best offer. If you must refuse editor number two's offer, explain that an editor who was offered the story earlier belatedly got back to you with a better offer. If you must refuse editor number one's offer, explain that he answered your query after you'd given up hearing from him, and someone else had accepted it.

This kind of situation doesn't happen very often, but it did to us on one occasion. Editor number one, who lost out on the idea for having dallied so long, took the news graciously, as we expected he would. He has remained our friend to this day, and has never stopped buying stories from us. In fact, we're sure his answers to our queries now come back a little faster than they used to.

11·3 Can I Submit the Same Idea to Several Editors at One Time?

Yes and no.

There was a time when magazine writing was a slower-paced profession. Dozens of magazines were running general interest articles. They'd publish a story on darn near any subject as long as the writing was exciting. Now magazines are quite topical. Topics come and go—quickly, at times. So writers have to get their ideas into print while they're still timely.

In those slower-paced, less news-oriented days, magazine writers used to send queries to only one editor at a time. If the first editor didn't buy, an idea often would be equally timeless the day it landed on a second, third, or fourth editor's desk. Many editors in this business still prefer that old way. Many of that breed feel they're in fierce competition with magazines similar to theirs, and relish the hope that an exclusive on your ideas will give them an edge over the competition. Others like to feel they're the only editor you want to write for, forgetting that a year's writing fees from them won't cover more than maybe your rent.

Until literary agents recently introduced the book auction, book editors also expected one-at-a-time queries. Now multiple submissions are increasingly the rule. Magazine writers, too, are pushing toward multiple query submissions. Here are some guidelines based on the collective experience of our colleagues and ourselves:

1. If you have a very hot idea that can become dated easily, but you're not yet a well-established writer, your best bet probably is to draft a punchy, well-documented query letter. Then you have two options.

   One is to send individually typed versions of your basic query letter at the same time to every editor who might be interested in your story. (We prefer to let editors know that the idea is going to more than one office at a time; not all our colleagues agree, feeling it will weaken the chance of a sale if an editor's prejudiced against multiple submissions.) Somewhere prominent in each query letter, ask for a prompt response due to the topicality of your idea. You can even risk raising a few editorial hackles by suggesting a reasonable date by which you'd like a yes or no.

   The second option is to send your individually typed query letter to one editor at a time, starting at the top of your list and working downward to the lower-paying or less prestigious magazines. In that case, include a statement that you're sending a idea to just that editor, but that since it's a timely idea you can't wait more than a few weeks for a response. (We usually offer several weeks of exclusivity on the idea.) When your deadline arrives—assuming you haven't heard by then—simply mail out a new query to the next editor on your list.

Another way to handle a hot idea is by telephone. We'll cover that later in this chapter (see 11.4).

2. If you have an idea that's very exciting to you, but obviously won't become quickly dated, you can't so easily hurry editors into fast response, no matter how eager *you* may be to get started with research and writing. In this situation, many of our colleagues simply type individual query letters to several editors, not mentioning the multiple submission, and mail them all at once. One New York pro hires a secretarial service to type the bodies of his form query letters on an automatic typewriter. Beginners, so delightfully full of hope, fear that every editor on their list will offer an assignment. Take it from us old-timers: it just doesn't happen that way, alas!

In case more than one editor does give you an okay, simply take the best offer. It's true, you risk alienating an editor with this method, but in our experience it's a very small risk and well worth it. Editors are well aware of (and many even sympathetic to) the hustling required to make a living as a free-lance writer. Some of our best writer friends have been—and will again be—editors.

3. If you have an idea that appeals to several completely different groups of readers, you are legally and ethically free to send your idea simultaneously to the magazines that reach those readers. Your only constraint is to make sure the readers of those magazines don't overlap. Julian Block, who specializes in short tax-tip articles, often sells not just the same idea, but the same identical article, to publications like *Electrical Contractor, Dental Economics,* and *Successful Farming.* He makes it a practice to tell each editor that what's for sale is not *first publication rights* but *one-time serial rights exclusive in your special-audience area.* Most editors of special publications welcome these simultaneous submissions because they know that they can generally buy one-time rights for less than first rights.

11·4 Is It Okay to Phone an Editor?

Sure, if you have a good reason. By "good reason" we mean something *the editor* thinks is a good reason. Here are three common reasons writers use for calling editors that editors almost *never* see as good reason:

THE IDEA IS TOUGH TO EXPLAIN IN WRITING

Tell that to an editor, and you're sure to build up molehills of confidence in your ability to commit any assigned idea to paper.

I DON'T HAVE TIME TO WRITE A QUERY

That's your problem! Since you're selling and the editor's buying, you'd better keep *her* time problem in mind. It takes much more of her time to talk on the phone than to skim your query letter.

I WANT TO GET TO KNOW THE EDITOR BETTER

So do hundreds of other writers. He tries to avoid calls from them all, and often ends up hating the ones who do get through no matter how nice their phone voices are. Read the magazine and get to know the editor by his editorial tastes.

Here are what the typical editor generally considers *valid* reasons for accepting your call:

1. He asked you to phone.
2. You have corresponded with him for many months. He has definitely encouraged you to continue suggesting ideas (not simply been polite). You can, and will, query in writing with an idea you have, but your idea has six different slants, all perfectly salable. You want to get his input into which slant to take.
3. You have a genuinely hot topic that could vanish before your query letter makes the rounds. This can't be an idea that depends on today's headlines, because that will be old hat by the time most weekly and monthly magazines can whip it into print. But it may be a topic for which your access to a key resource is about to vanish. An example is if Sophia Loren is in town to visit a long-lost sister, you've been promised an interview, and she's leaving town tomorrow noon. Even in this situation, you'd better be prepared to outline some appropriate writing credentials for the editor to whom you pitch the story over the phone. Enough editors have been bamboozled into making assignments to nonwriters who talk an exciting game that all editors are cautious about this way of doing business.

11·5 Can I Drop in to See an Editor?

Sure, under the right conditions. But unless you're a well-known pro, there are probably only two right conditions. Don't be like our prima donna Wisconsin student who announced one evening she was going to New York to "see the editors." She thought that if she could talk her way into an editor's office, he'd hand her an assignment and she'd at last crack the national markets. But she'd never queried those editors, so they'd never seen her name or her credentials (a few local publications). And when she phoned for appointments, she had no firm story ideas in mind to offer them. The editors politely declined to see her. If they took time to chat with every would-be professional, they'd have no time to put out their magazines.

A lot of beginners also pick up the idea that in order to make it as a magazine writer, you've got to live in New York City. They must think there are lots of late-night discos where all the editors hang out

Ill. 11.1

seventeen

320 PARK AVENUE
NEW YORK, N.Y. 10022
212-759-8100

Judi R. Kesselman
16 Pont Street
Great Neck, New York 10021

Dear Judi:

Your outline looks good and we would like you to go ahead with the article HOW TO IMPROVE YOUR TEST SCORES.

We will pay $550 for a mutually satisfactory article of approximately 2,000 words. Our reject fee is one quarter of the total offered. Please let me know what sort of deadline would be agreeable to you.

We will pay receipted expenses up to $75, so keep a record of long distance calls, gas used when doing research, etc., for we will need an itemized accounting in order to reimburse you. If you exceed that amount, let me know.

This can be a very useful article for our audience and we'll look forward to seeing it.

Sincerely,

Annette Grant
General Features and Fiction
Editor

AG:ds

Assignment letter.

awarding four-figure assignments to the best dancers, flashiest dressers, and funniest storytellers. True, editors attend their share of literary cocktail parties and writers' club meetings, but they go to relax just like everybody else. It's considered gauche to buttonhole them to pitch article ideas.

Knowing that a face-to-face talk *can* help pinpoint an editor's exact interests more quickly than a trial-and-error succession of query letters, we have occasionally made efforts to see editors whose magazines we wanted to write for steadily. However, while we were living, working, and partying in New York City, and met lots of editors socially and at meetings of the ASJA, our business contacts with them were usually limited to the mails, with an occasional phone call. Not until after we moved out of New York City did editors suddenly become accessible. Once we were rare visitors—incapable of becoming nuisances—they shuffled appointments to see us on our infrequent trips back to the Big Apple.

So the first conclusion we'll pass along is that it is appropriate to suggest visiting an editor if you're traveling and plan to be in the city where the magazine is edited. But unless the editor knows you by reputation, write first to ask if you can visit, include a few brief sample article suggestions and, assuming you have some, mention writing credentials at magazines similar in stature.

The second normal occasion for seeing an editor in person is if he suggests it. Even if it isn't convenient, you should try to make the visit. Although most editors are accustomed to looking at the world through pica type, some enjoy face-to-face contact with writers who they feel can benefit from personal guidance. A request that you come in and talk is solid indication of interest in your writing. (Assuming it's your writing that's on the agenda. A student of ours had been querying an editor regularly and had finally sold a slightly salacious article. He asked her out to dinner and she went, envisioning the proposition of several assignments, maybe even a steady monthly column. What she got was another kind of proposition. But that's an atypical situation.)

11·6   What Does an Assignment Look Like?

Most of them look like a lot of red tape and deadlines.

We've reproduced a couple of our assignment letters and contracts so you can see what some of them look like. There are certain standard elements, but not all assignment letters contain them all. Also, some letters are brief but are attached to contracts that require the author's signature. The assignment, whether in letter or contract form, contains such clauses and conditions as:

Ill. 11.2 _____

13-30 Corporation
Assignment Confirmation and Agreement to Transfer
Publication Rights

TO: Judi Kesselman and Franklynn Peterson
        3006 Gregory St.
        Madison, Wisconsin 53711

FROM: Don Akchin
        Associate Editor

This agreement confirms your assignment, and defines the rights and duties of both you as author and 13-30 Corporation as publisher.

1. Confirmation of Assignment

You agree to research and write an article on __job hunting__
_____ for the upcoming edition of 18 Almanac
The article will run approximately 3,000 words and will be due in 13-30 Corporation's offices on June 11.   .

The fee for your article will be $1,000.00   . 13-30 Corporation makes every effort to pay writers within three weeks of submission of manuscripts in satisfactory form, and guarantees that writers will be paid no later than the last printer deadline for the magazine named above.

In the event that the draft first submitted to us is unsatisfactory, you agree to revise and rewrite the article as required. If the revised or rewritten draft of the article is unsatisfactory (as determined by the associate editor) 13-30 Corporation will pay you a kill fee of one-third the agreed-upon writer's fee.

In addition to your writer's fee, 13-30 Corporation agrees to reimburse you for reasonable travel and telephone expenses incurred in connection with this article. Such expenses are not to exceed $50.00   and you must provide us with copies of receipts or bills in order to be reimbursed.

Assignment contract.

2. Warranty of Material

You warrant that the article you submit to 13-30 Corporation is original, that you are the sole author and owner of the article and all rights to that article, that it has never before been published, and that it contains no unlawful or infringing matter. In the event that certain parts of the article have been previously published (including tables, charts or graphics), you guarantee that permission has been obtained for publication in 13-30 magazines, and you will submit to 13-30 Corporation a copy of the permission document and information for credit lines.

3. Transfer of Publication Rights

You grant to 13-30 Corporation exclusive First North American Serial Rights to the article described above for use in a 13-30 publication. In addition, you grant 13-30 Corporation the right to produce and distribute reprints of the article and the right to grant reprint permission to other publishers. In the event that 13-30 Corporation receives requests to reprint or translate your article, you will receive 50 percent of the permission fee charged, if any. In addition, you agree to grant, for a mutually satisfactory fee, 13-30 Corporation the right to use all or part of your article in other 13-30 publications. If at all possible, however, you will be given an opportunity to update and recheck your article for accuracy.

You retain all other rights of copyright to your work. (Note that you retain these rights to the original manuscript, not to the edited version.)

4. Editing and Publication Decisions

You agree that your article will be subject to editing by 13-30 Corporation, and that we cannot guarantee publication. However, in the event that your satisfactory manuscript is not published in the magazine named above, 13-30 Corporation will pay you the agreed-upon writer's fee, and retain First North American Serial Rights to publish that article for one year. After this time, you are free to market your manuscript elsewhere.

5. Signature and Personal Data

Please sign and date this agreement and return one copy to 13-30 Corporation immediately. If two authors are involved, both signatures are required on this agreement. In order to issue payment to you, we will also need your Social Security Number. This information will be considered strictly confidential.

If you have any questions about the terms of this agreement, please contact me.

PRICE

That's one of the more important things to tie down before beginning the assignment. If it isn't in the assignment letter, ask for it. If you agreed on a price over the phone but it isn't mentioned in the assignment letter, respond with your own letter accepting the assignment and stating the agreed-upon fee. If the editor doesn't write back saying, "Hey, that's not what we agreed on," then the price is as legally binding as if it were in the original assignment letter.

With most magazines, the fee quoted in the assignment letter is pretty well fixed in the editor's mind. But if it's negotiable, the only time you can negotiate is *before* you turn in the assignment. (We devote all of Chapter 17 to the economics of writing.)

DEADLINE

Many editors plan their assignments with specific issues in mind. Your editor may be counting on your story for the next issue he's putting together. Even if he isn't, he probably knows that most writers work best when they shoot for deadlines. Unless you've worked with a particular editor before, you won't know for sure which reason governs his assigned deadline. So *meet your deadlines.* If you find the deadline unrealistic for some reason, let the editor know *as soon as you can.* That's the professional way of doing business.

LENGTH

The editor suggests the length of your article to fit his magazine's needs. Some editors expect fairly strict adherence to this figure; they block out a certain amount of space for each article, and if it comes in much too long or too short, they have to do heavy editing, ask for a rewrite, or juggle space allocations. If they've got enough extra manuscripts on file, they may even reject your article.

Other editors are more casual. They give suggested lengths and accept the fact that most writers turn in three or four extra pages. There's really no way to tell how a particular editor feels until you've worked with him. The safest approach is to be sure, as you write your first draft, that you cover all important points with as much depth as each deserves. If the first draft you knock out looks as if it may be more than 25 percent above or 10 percent below the suggested length, warn by phone or letter. If you don't get specific instructions or negative feedback, assume your new length is acceptable.

CONTENT

The editor may point out certain elements she particularly wants to see in the article, as well as material she'd like excluded, and she may restructure your slant if she thinks her emphasis works better than

Ill. 11.3

PLAYGIRL INC.   1801 CENTURY PARK EAST, CENTURY CITY, SUITE 2300   LOS ANGELES, CALIFORNIA 90067   213 553-8006

Ms. Judi Kesselman
160 South Middle Neck Road
Great Neck, LI 11021

Dear Judi:

This is to confirm your assignment to do an article for <u>Playgirl</u>
about Hit-and-Run Lovers, the men who take you to bed and whom
you never hear from again. As we discussed they are a prolif-
erating breed, and every woman on the scene, unless she is
extremely cautious, will run into one or more of them. Most
women are left unhappy by this kind of man. And generally they
are left wondering "What did I do wrong?" "Did he find me
unattractive?" etc. etc. Probably she did nothing wrong. These
guys are that way for other reasons--and the reasons are what we
want to uncover in this article. From shrinks and men of this
kind, find out their motivations, hang-ups, etc. Of course, you
must have women talking about their experiences and reactions, and
you will supply the usual anecdotes. In the end the reader should
understand the warning signs in order to avoid or be prepared for
a man who is a hit-and-run lover. Also find out if there is any
behavior on a woman's part that encourages this, or attracts
this kind of man.

In passing you might mention the increase of women who hit and
run as well--but that most women still don't and are left saddened
by such encounters.

Payment will be $750. Deadline as we agreed is November 22.
The piece should be about 3,000 words. Kill fee is one-quarter.

My best to you as always.

Sincerely,

Carol Botwin
Articles Editor

CB:rg

Assignment letter with helpful guidelines to author from editor.

yours. This may be because she understands her readers better than you do, or because she's interested in only part of your overall idea, or because she wants more of an overview than you suggested. Most editors are sticklers in this area. If they say they want a topic covered in your story, they expect to see it covered. And if they say they don't want it covered, they don't.

Like other points in the assignment letter, content suggestions are negotiable. If you think the editor's approach may cause problems for you or your story, say so immediately. The smoothest way to raise the subject is by asking the editor for her thinking behind the approach that bothers you, and by then raising the problems you're having with it: "I see it a bit differently . . ." or "I don't think I can get access to information that will substantiate that." She may convince you that her approach will work, she may alter her approach, or she may have a report on her desk that hasn't been published yet. The best way to handle a question about content is by phone. It's one time an editor will be grateful you called.

RIGHTS

Under the copyright law you own your story, every last well-chosen word in it. The magazine is obliged to buy from you the right to publish it. We'll devote considerable space in Chapter 16 to which rights you should sell and which rights the magazine's publisher wants to buy. For now, keep in mind that this aspect of the assignment is also negotiable.

KILL FEE

This is writers' jargon for *a money guarantee.* The better magazines guarantee professional writers that they'll be paid something, no matter what may go wrong between getting the assignment and seeing the story in print. And hundreds of things can go wrong. The profile's subject may die or be sent to jail in disgrace, the magazine's competition may come out with a story on the same topic before you turn yours in, promises of information may fail to materialize, the FDA may discover that the face cream you planned to write about causes stuttering, or all of the above.

It never ceases to amaze us how poorly communications professionals communicate with each other. On occasion, the editor who assigns the story may have a prose picture in mind that's totally different from the one in your head. In such a situation, your assigned story will be turned down—with regret, to be sure, but turned down nonetheless. It's happened to us with more frequency than any of the foregoing occurrences.

If your letter of assignment contains provisions for a kill fee or guarantee, you'll be paid something for your efforts even if the editor can't run your piece. Kill fees vary from about one fifth to one third, sometimes even one half, of the fee you would have been paid if everything went as hoped. Usually the killed article reverts to you, and you can attempt to place it elsewhere. We were able to turn around an article killed by *Parade* and sell it to the short-lived *Vital*. Most articles, however, are written with a specific readership in mind and can't be resold so easily.

Frankly, writers are not eager to accept a kill fee. Not only is it poor pay for the time and energy spent, but regardless of the reason for rejection it makes writers feel they have failed to deliver. Still, we like to get assignments that contain guarantees, because they are concrete assurances of the editor's seriousness about wanting the story, and of the likelihood he'll help patch up an article that falls outside the niche he's set for it. When an editor pays a kill fee, he has nothing tangible to show for the money. Rather than explain the kill fee to the bookkeeper, he'd prefer to work a bit to save the article.

You're not likely to be given guarantees for your early assignments, although Judi got one her very first time out. But keep them in mind, because as you build your reputation, you'll not only get them but find they're often negotiable. There's very little in the field of writing that's not negotiable except for strict compliance with the highest professional standards.

How to Write
Your Article

Chapter Twelve

Research, Research, Research

W HEN *READER'S DIGEST* WAS GIVEN AN ARTICLE stating that George Washington stood six feet three and a half inches in his size thirteen boots, editorial researcher Nina Georges-Picot wondered if old George really owned boots that big. But how to find out? First she pored over the New York Public Library's sixteen volumes about Washington. Nothing. Next she studied books, letters, and diaries of Washington's associates. None of them cared a whit about George's shoe size. The ardent fact finder called Mount Vernon to see if somebody there knew about a statue of George made entirely from plaster casts of his body. The likeness was standing in the Richmond, Virginia, state capitol building. Ms. Georges-Picot called Richmond and prevailed on the building's superintendent to measure George's feet. With boots on, the right foot was ten and seven eighths inches long, the left eleven inches—a man's size eight boot. If one is to believe the accuracy of the measurement, that's not size thirteen.

George Washington's boot size may seem entirely too trivial to have been worth so much of the *Reader's Digest* researcher's time. But the writer who evidently was caught with the wrong information in his article probably doesn't think so. We hope he went back and double-checked because, if the researcher was right, the tiny foot on such a big man could make a peg for another George Washington article.

A good magazine article must entertain. Some of the entertainment is dished out from a service of catchy facts, figures, and formulations. As our anecdote about Washington's boot size illustrates, they'd better come from authoritative sources, sources that can be trusted to be accurate and precise.

The facts should be not only accurate but plentiful. When we were editors, some of the dreariest stories we rejected were ones in which the authors tried to stretch too little research across too many pages. Many writers we know spend as much time at their local libraries as they do at their typewriters. We make it a rule always to collect more information than we think we're going to use, so we can choose the best and the most apropos in making our points. We think

153

of ourselves not as composers, but as arrangers who assemble somebody else's themes and counterpoints until they match the available instruments.

12·1   A Fact Is Only as Good as Its Source

There are at least three practical reasons why writers should stick to dependable sources and keep track of what they are:

IT'S MORE EFFICIENT
Let's say that you're researching a railroad crossing story. From a chart of statistics, you extrapolate that 3,392 people are killed or injured at crossings every year. Then, while organizing or writing the article, you decide it will be more effective to separate the number killed from the number injured. You'll waste a lot of time relocating your information unless you also made note of your source: the U.S. Federal Railroad Administration's *Accident Bulletin* reprinted in the 1973 *U.S. Statistical Abstract,* p. 561. (We also jot down the name of the library unless we used only one for the article, and the reference book's call number as well.)

IT'S MORE BELIEVABLE
One author writes, "3,392 people are killed or hurt at railroad crossings every year." Another writes, "Last year, the Federal Railroad Administration tallied 3,392 railroad crossing deaths and injuries." Which sounds more like a fact? Which sounds more dramatic? If the source of your fact is authoritative, its mention lends credibility.

IT'S SAFER
If you say that 3,392 people a year are killed or hurt at railroad crossings, without attributing the number to anyone else, in effect you're personally standing behind the statement's accuracy. If, instead, you include the source of your data, you are *reporting* it. Aside from being more authoritative, it also leaves you practically in the clear if somebody else got the numbers wrong. As we saw in the example about George Washington's boots, a fact is no better than its source.

There are two basic kinds of sources. If you get your information directly from the expert's mouth, that's a *primary source.* If, instead, you take information from a newspaper story, article, book, or movie, you're using a *secondary source.* This distinction is not merely academic, as all too many writers have learned the hard way.

One day in 1971, for example, Purdue University professor Dick Kerckhoff was piqued by a startling "fact" in *Today's Child*: "In a recent survey to determine the amount of time fathers spent with their fifth grade sons each week, the average time was found to be 7¼ minutes, reported the psychologist." That sounds authentic, doesn't it? Still, Kerckhoff wanted to verify the statement's accuracy from its primary source. The article attributed it to a psychologist at Florida College, who told Dick that she'd taken it from *The Father's Book* by Ted Klein.

Kerckhoff checked Klein's book, published in 1968, and found that the "fact" referred to the time seventh- and eighth-graders (not fifth-graders) spent *alone* with their fathers. Its source: a speech by a psychologist reported in *Vital Speeches of the Day,* September 1, 1961. Reading the speech itself, Kerckhoff found it was seven and a half minutes, not seven and a quarter. Its source: an article by Philip Wylie, "American Men are Loving Fathers," which appeared first in *The American Weekly* and was condensed in the March 1956 *Reader's Digest.* There, in a sidebar to the article, were those pesty boys and their minutes per week with dear old Dad. The source was listed: Gordon H. Schroeder, writing in the *Christian Herald.* Dick tracked the Reverend Schroeder to his church in Lincoln, Nebraska, only to learn that the preacher wasn't the primary source either, and didn't even remember where the "fact" had come from: he'd read it somewhere.

After arduous backtracking, Kerckhoff had established that the 1971 article that sent him on such a chase, had missed on every one of the four details he'd checked: (1) there was no recent survey, since the whole mess had begun at least sixteen years earlier; (2) it wasn't fifth-grade boys, but seventh- or eighth-graders—maybe; (3) the time wasn't seven and a quarter but seven and a half minutes—or maybe neither; and (4) no authoritative source could establish that there was ever a survey in the first place.

At this point, you're probably expecting a repeat of a rather standard lecture: Get Your Facts Straight. But we assume that every nonfiction writer starts with that premise. What isn't so obvious to a beginner—and unfortunately to some more advanced writers, too—is that we can't accomplish that goal 100 percent of the time. We don't all have staff positions at high-minded publications that let us spend hours verifying the size of Washington's feet. We can't all afford the time it would take to check the primary source of every statement we encounter. (Not even the *Reader's Digest* checks everything. *They* missed verifying the source of the kids' seven and a half minutes when it ran in their magazine.) But we do follow these three guidelines:

> Whenever possible, we start right at the primary source.
> When we're using a secondary source, we try to double-check with an *independent* secondary source.
> We always report our information accurately and, unless there's an overriding reason, identify our source.

There are five reliability checks against which you can measure the facts you research. At least one of them can be used to assess every piece of information you encounter.

ACCURACY

If you see an event happen and report it carefully, you and your readers *assume* you've also reported it accurately. Since six eyewitnesses to any accident may in reality render six conflicting reports, an "accurate report" may not always reflect precisely what happened. Since total accuracy is so seldom achieved, this criterion is the least useful of the five.

AUTHENTICITY

Not to be confused with accuracy, authenticity is what you get automatically from a primary source. It comes from the horse's mouth—the logical, natural origin for the chosen information. If you can't confirm your data, you must be careful to present them as authentic statements and not verified facts.

The best case for showing the distinction between authenticity and accuracy is that of the Pentagon. It's about the only team in town that has *authentic* information about U.S. missile strength. When it's asking for money, it claims there aren't enough missiles; when it brags about the good job it's doing, there are suddenly more than enough missiles planted in the ground. That's why sharp writers report that missile-strength statements coming from the Pentagon are authentic, but inevitably leave in doubt their accuracy.

CREDIBILITY

The source's *way* of telling his facts and backing them up, or his proven track record, may lead you to the subjective conclusion that the source is credible and his facts can be believed. *That's* how to present the information to your readers.

PLAUSIBILITY

You may conclude that, subjectively, the fact makes sense to you and presumably to other people. That's how you'll write it—not as verified fact but as plausible consideration.

CORROBORATION

You may obtain information from a separate, also believable source that substantiates the first source's facts. Then you will have objectively demonstrated, if not the accuracy, at least the honesty of your source. In reporting the fact you will probably tell the reader of the corroboration, although that is not always necessary.

12·2 The Library

Every year or so we teach a short course in research techniques for professionals in many fields, and the session we spend at the reference room of the University of Wisconsin Memorial Library boggles most of our students' minds. The amazed response is, "We never dreamed there were all these tools to meet our specific needs."

The library is the major depository of *secondary sources,* and a useful lead to primary data as well. Surprisingly, we've found that its untariffed wealth is sadly untapped by beginning writers. A typical nonfiction novice enters the local public library, heads for the card catalog, looks up the subject, checks out the available books, and calls it a day. But books are rarely useful to any magazine writer other than a history buff. By the time a book is written, printed, and tucked away on a library shelf, its information is usually at least a couple of years old. The more enterprising beginner adds *Reader's Guide to Periodical Literature* (RGPL) to the search. But by the time a magazine writer gets an assignment, does her research, turns in the completed story, the editors find space for it, it's published, *RGPL* indexers index it, and their printers print *RGPL, that* information is likely to be half a year to a year old.

Books and general interest magazine articles *can* be useful for providing an overview of the subject you're researching, especially if it's one you're not terribly familiar with. If you're doing a low-budget research job for a magazine that knows it can't pay for (and therefore can't demand) exhaustive research, books and popular magazines are a quick route to information, examples, and maybe anecdotes too. But even in that situation, your editor will expect more than just a rehash of what his readers have already read. Here's how to get it from the library.

THE LIBRARIAN

Right after God created the angels, She made the librarians. Your first contact after you take off your coat should be with a reference librarian. Tell him precisely what it is you're looking for, and why.

Not: "Something on cars."

Instead: "Something very current about pollution-control systems on diesel cars for a *Popular Auto Magazine* article that I'm researching."

Not: "A book about protein."

Instead: "Whatever is very new about high-protein diets and especially their hazards. I'd like to do an exposé on them for *Fat Prevention Magazine.*"

Great Neck, New York, librarian Elsa Resnick told us about the man who came in one morning and asked for "information about the old West." At the end of the day he was still searching through mountains of books and magazines. Starting a conversation, she found out all he wanted was an early map. Within five minutes she'd found what he was looking for.

As you become more familiar with your own library, you'll learn where all useful volumes are kept. But in some libraries, the most useful ones are *behind* the reference librarian's desk. As the librarians become more familiar with you, they'll probably feed you tips about what's back there—and about new reference tools as they come in.

THE REFERENCE COLLECTION

In most libraries, the tools designed for researchers are set aside as reference collections. In some libraries they are centrally located, sometimes filling entire rooms. In others, each division maintains its own collection. Some libraries allow a few of these books to be checked out; others insist that all must be used on the library grounds. (The Great Neck library where Judi researched her book *Stopping Out* had a marvelous system of permitting overnight check-outs—from after 5 P.M. to 9 A.M. the next morning. That way, the books were always there for researchers while the library was open, but could be taken home by late owls and deadline beaters.)

How does the professional magazine writer use the reference collection? Let's say you're looking for current information on the ancient art of enameling. Your library might have a book or two that covers the topic. You might also find a popular article or two by using *RGPL* and some of the other useful guides to current periodicals. But you still might not have all the information you'd like, and you might want to interview experts for livelier material. If your reference room has, for instance, A *Directory for Information Resources in the United States: Social Sciences,* published by the National Referral Center of the Library of Congress, that volume's index will steer you to entry number 1877, the Department of Industries of the National Museum of History and Technology, which is an unbiased, authoritative source of information on, among other things, "use of enamels from ancient times to the present." The entry gives its address and phone number; to obtain additional information you need only write or phone.

No matter how abstruse the subject, it's rare that a well-stocked library reference collection doesn't have, if not information, at least a solid lead to information sources. As we said before, the keeper of these nuggets is the librarian. We've found that the tougher the questions, the happier most librarians are to work on them for you.

PERIODICALS

Many libraries maintain their periodical collections in their reference departments. Others keep them separate. In addition to the popular periodicals—the ones indexed in *RGPL* and such—are professional and scholarly periodicals. For the free-lance magazine writer, these offer keys to current thinking and the latest research. Some libraries' collections of both general and technical periodicals are extensive, others are inadequate for our needs. But most now have interloan facilities for getting needed periodicals within a week or two, and many libraries maintain periodical subscription lists of the holdings of other libraries in the state. (We'll explain interloan further at the end of this section.)

INDEXES AND ABSTRACTS

These readers' guides to professional journals are published by professional societies and by companies catering to the needs of the various professions. One of those needs is quick access to research data. Therefore, a great many professional journals and their matching abstracts or indexes are on library shelves within a few months after the scientists have completed their research papers. For the magazine writer, timeliness is assured.

Aside from new, undog-eared facts and figures, the journals are also useful for providing leads to the papers' authors, people doing current research, whom you can reach by mail or telephone for the most up-to-date information, interpretation, and opinion. The journals usually note their professional addresses.

An *index* is simply a categorized listing of article titles or topics plus authors' names. You can find journal articles on your topic by first locating the general subject in the index and then singling out the titles that seem most appropriate. With your list of article titles, journal names, and page numbers, you can skim the journals in your library's periodical collection (or through interloan) to pick out what you need.

An *abstract* does everything that an index does. In addition, it includes a thumbnail summation of the salient points covered by each indexed article. The summations generally save having to skim dozens of articles to locate the two or three that are right on target. Sometimes the abstracts are comprehensive enough that, depending on how much detail you require, you can work from them and not have to read the articles at all.

SEARCH SERVICES

More and more libraries are linking up to computers that store and sort out information for researchers. For a fee of from about five to seventy-five dollars, depending on the service you need, your library may be able to provide you with a computerized index or collection of abstracts to journal articles on the topic of your research. The information available on computers is growing all the time. With luck, you may even be able to find a library hooked into *The New York Times* computerized index—a writer's dream research tool which indexes many periodicals besides the *Times.* (We've reproduced a page from Medline, a national, partly government subsidized computer search service. (We used it in researching our book *Eat Anything Exercise Diet.*)

INTERLIBRARY LOANS

Years ago librarians realized that even the best-budgeted libraries were not going to be able to purchase every book published. Eager to provide users with complete facilities, they developed interlibrary loan systems. Depending on which locality or state you live in, you may have easy access to almost any nonrare book and periodical in almost any public or academic library in the United States. Many states maintain special central collections of books that are mailed to smaller libraries on request. Even part of the Library of Congress's collection is kept busy circulating to libraries across the country. When you get into a major research project—better still, *before* you get into it—ask your librarian about interlibrary loan procedures.

Most people are aware of the local public library or, in the case of larger cities, the library system that serves them. But there are a great many other kinds of libraries available to serious magazine researchers. Many specialized libraries are indexed in directories such as the ones compiled by the Special Libraries Association.

COLLEGE LIBRARIES

Your nearest college or university no doubt has a library. The larger the institution, the larger its collection, as a rule. Most publicly run colleges permit citizens of the state or city free use of library facilities, although a nominal deposit may be required if you want to check out books. Many private colleges allow outsiders to use libraries, although there's sometimes a fee for the privilege. You won't know unless you ask.

Most colleges have more than one library, a fact that we've seen too many writers overlook. At the University of Wisconsin, for example, Memorial Library is the major library. But the School of Engineering, the School of Medicine, and the School of Agriculture have their own large libraries as well. A number of individual departments such as geology and Afro-American studies, maintain smaller, specialized libraries whose administrators know their respective fields intimately and can be very valuable guides to resources and to authoritative people.

CORPORATION LIBRARIES

American Metal Climax, Inc., in New York City, maintains a library of 10,000 books, 1,000 journals, sundry reports, and other backup

Ill. 12.1

```
00015009                                                    PAGE
                        ASPECTS OF OBESITY
----------------------------------------------------------------------


1  AU  - Durnin JV
   TI  - Energy--requirements, intake and balance.
   SO  - Proc Nutr Soc 27(2):188-91, Sep 68

2  AU  - Bloom WL
   TI  - To fast or exercise.
   SO  - Am J Clin Nutr 21(12):1475-9, Dec 68

3  AU  - Karlsson J ; Saltin B
   TI  - Diet, muscle glycogen, and endurance performance.
   SO  - J Appl Physiol 31(2):203-6, Aug 71

4  AU  - Mol'e PA ; Johnson RE
   TI  - Disclosure by dietary modification of an exercise-induced protein
         catabolism in man.
   SO  - J Appl Physiol 31(2):185-90, Aug 71

5  TI  - Diet and athletics.
   SO  - Br Med J 3(719):361, 15 Aug 70

6  AU  - Booyens J ; Frank M de V ; Waal VM de ; Campbell GD ; Goldberg MD
   TI  - The food intake and activity patterns of offspring of connubial
         Indian diabetics.
   SO  - S Afr Med J 44(10);271-8, 7 Mar 70

7  AU  - Campbell DE
   TI  - Recovery heart rates of two groups of subjects with distinct body
         weight differences.
   SO  - Am Correct Ther J 23(6):180-4, Nov-Dec 69

8  AU  - Celejowa I ; Homa M
   TI  - Food intake, nitrogen and energy balance in Polish weight
         lifters, during a training camp.
   SO  - Nutr Metab 12(5):259-74, 1970

9  AU  - Gwinup G ; Chelvam R ; Steinberg T
   TI  - Thickness of subcutaneous fat and activity of underlying muscles.
   SO  - Ann Intern Med 74(3):408-11, Mar 71

10 AU  - Pa˘r'izkov'a J
   TI  - Activity, obesity, and growth.
   SO  - Monogr Soc Res Child Dev 35(7):28-32, Oct 70

11 AU  - Johnson RH ; Walton JL
   TI  - Fitness, fatness, and post-exercise ketosis.
   SO  - Lancet 1(699):566-8, 20 Mar 71
```

Page from Medline computerized search service.

information for its staff. But the company makes its facilities on copper, vanadium, zinc, lead, molybdenum, aluminum, potash, coal mining, and Zambia available to all serious researchers and is even willing to make interlibrary loans. The Zator Company in Cambridge, Massachusetts, holds 4,000 technical reports, 400 books, 350 volumes of journals, and other data on artificial intelligence, computer-programming languages, information storage and retrieval, and so forth. It, too, welcomes serious researchers. In fact, a great many corporations maintain in-house libraries for staff purposes, and most of them permit limited access to researchers of magazine articles on their special interests.

TRADE ASSOCIATIONS

Darn near every association of professionals, businesses, and activists, from the Administrative Management Society in Pennsylvania to Zero Population Growth, Inc., in California, maintains a library. Most of them feel it is part of their mandate to help you research articles in their fields of interest. Your public library has indexes to these special libraries.

NEWSPAPER MORGUES

Ever dramatic, newspapers have always called their libraries *morgues*. Invariably crammed between the boiler room and the coal bin, a typical morgue includes 143 filing cabinets, two shopworn tables, and four intelligent and eager employees. Morgue employees clip and file their newspapers by topic and name. If you want to find out how many different businesses a local hustler has defrauded, your newspaper morgue should have whatever information has made the papers, filed under the hustler's name. If you're researching how many times a particular company has been defrauded, ask for the company's clip file.

There are very few newspapers that refuse access to morgue files to magazine writers. Most also handle short questions by phone, and some answer mailed requests by photocopying shorter files, usually for a fee.

12·3 How to Locate and Work with Primary-Resource People

Although plenty of fine stories have been written from secondary sources located in local libraries, the *big* stories, the *better-paying* ones, and the vast majority of the ones pegged on *new* data hinge on writers' using primary sources—getting facts, figures, anecdotes, and quotes right from the experts.

Most novices have little trouble locating primary sources. Their biggest slip-ups come from using only sources that can be reached with local phone calls. It's important to realize that if you're writing for a national publication, editors look for a national distribution of experts. We're now living in Madison, Wisconsin, and we could locate dozens of experts on almost anything at the University of Wisconsin. But we're forever quoting experts in Minnesota, Michigan, Illinois, Indiana, Texas, Pennsylvania, New York, and California, to make the editorial point that the subjects of our articles are national in scope.

The most convenient way to get information from distant sources is by telephone. It's not cheap, but it is cheaper than many writers realize. For proof, let's examine one of our recent telephone bills. To research one article we called:

New York City, 9 minutes	$3.22
Macon, Georgia, 2 minutes	.84
Anchorage, Alaska, 8 minutes	5.14
Washington, D.C., 7 minutes	2.54
Phoenix, Arizona, 4 minutes	1.50
Total	$13.24

With good interview techniques, you can elicit a lot of facts and figures in 2 minutes, and 9 minutes on the phone is equivalent to 20 or 30 minutes face to face. (We'll discuss interview techniques in the next chapter. Nearly all of them apply to telephone interviews as well as in-person ones.)

Results you get by mail may not arrive as fast nor always be as quotable, but for lengthy projects it's often the preferred way. Jack Harrison Pollack, former Senate committee investigator, author of best-selling books such as *Earl Warren: The Judge Who Changed America*, *Dr. Sam.* and *Croiset the Clairvoyant*, and prolific magazine writer, tries to reduce his by-mail research requests to a form letter for each project. But to *every* copy he appends a short handwritten note, such as the one attached to the letter for researching his Earl Warren book: "My apologies for this form letter. I'm trying to meet a deadline." People these days understand deadlines. Jack had no trouble eliciting replies. "Even Haldeman and Ehrlichman wrote from jail," he told us. "Supreme Court judges, college professors, presidents' wives, all answered promptly."

When Judi was researching her first book, *Stopping Out*, she needed to know the attitudes of members of law- and medical-school admissions committees toward applicants who'd taken time out from college. She wrote to committee chairmen at forty-seven representative schools, describing the purpose of her project and listing the four specific questions for which she needed answers. She enclosed a stamped, self-addressed envelope with each letter, and was rewarded with twenty-one responses, including several good quotes she could use verbatim in the book.

To be successful at researching by mail:

Address the letter to a real, live person.

Tell why you need the information.

Tell how the information will be used. (Is it background? Are you asking permission to quote it?)

Ask specific questions. If there's more than one, number the questions. Don't expect more than a few words for each answer, though you may be pleasantly surprised.

Refer to your deadline. Allow at least a week after the letter is received for reply.

Keep it typed, businesslike, and short—no more than one page.

Enclose a stamped self-addressed envelope.

Where do professional writers get the names, addresses, and phone numbers of primary sources? Here are just a few of our own favorite aids:

WHO'S WHO AND OTHER BIOGRAPHICAL DIRECTORIES

Almost every field of endeavor—science, medicine, psychology, even journalism—has its own biographical directory. Often addresses and phone numbers are included along with achievements. Many libraries maintain at least small collections of these tools in their reference sections. Even home addresses of the movie stars are listed in some (though the best way to get to celebrities is through their public relations representatives).

COLLEGE CATALOGS

These are shelved in most college libraries, and they tell us who's teaching the subjects of our articles. It's a good bet that these people are authoritative and up to date. (Public relations departments of the larger colleges prepare directories of experts and mail them free to writers who request them. They are even better than college catalogs.)

JOURNAL ARTICLES

After reading the article on our subject, we get in touch with its author at the institution listed (along with his name and title) at the beginning or end of the article.

SOURCES FROM PREVIOUS ARTICLES

Even if an expert used in a previous article isn't exactly right for our new project, she often has friends where she works who are. It takes only a one- or two-minute phone call to find the new source. (This is a particularly valuable way to sneak past red tape when using sources employed by the government or by large, careful companies.)

TRADE ASSOCIATIONS

Most of them know which member companies have experts; many volunteer to contact the companies and ask the experts to call us. Often, they phone at their own expense.

PUBLIC RELATIONS OFFICES

Manufacturers and sellers of everything from nuts to education, hospital care, and peace are all out to promote their products. Many produce packets of information for writers (press kits and press releases) and for the general public (pamphlets, booklets, and such). They are often useful in researching articles, and are usually yours for the asking. In addition, every fair-sized company, association, and university —even some professionals such as doctors and dentists—hire public relations specialists whose job is to make your research task easier if it will conceivably get their products' or organizations' names into print. Sometimes these people are staff members; often they are in outside agencies.

Simply call (or write) an organization's public relations office, public information officer, community relations person, promotions director, corporate communications office, or the agency that handles its public relations (the organization's switchboard usually has the name and phone number), and say, "We need an expert on . . . for an article we're preparing." The P.R. department usually asks the best authority it can find to call you back at its expense.

It is important that you pay particular attention to evaluating the credibility of information provided by public relations people. Keep in mind that they are hired to promote the images of their employers. It would be unrealistic to expect a P.R. employee to volunteer data that reflect badly on his boss or client. You can often get information from him that is not entirely favorable to the employer, but you'll probably have to ask or even, in some cases, demand it.

Because of the credibility gap, editors are not fond of having writers quote public relations people.

There are public relations subtleties even some pros don't know. Writers learned a new wrinkle at a recent meeting of the American Society of Journalists and Authors, where a public relations representative told the group that his firm employs writers to shill for manufacturers on radio and TV. As an example, he mentioned a woman who had written a book on toys. "She has been touring for us for four years. We pay her *per diem,* and we pay all her expenses. We smooth the way and book stations for her . . . as an author and an authority on toys. Of course, she happens to be traveling with our toys. When she talks about a good or a bad toy, the *good* toy is our toy."

FEDERAL, STATE, AND LOCAL GOVERNMENTS

One of the largest sources of primary (as well as secondary) information is the feds. The *U.S. Government Manual,* an annual guide to the expensive bureaucratic morass that we call the federal government, is available at most libraries, or you can buy it for under ten dollars. Detailed though it is, it just touches the tip of the information iceberg. The names listed in the manual tend to be department heads and subheads who will refer you to knowledgeable subalterns.

For quotable facts and figures, no library (except the Library of Congress) contains as much up-to-date and often practical data as the huge library of publications that's ground out by the U.S. Government Printing Office and stored in pamphlets and in microfiche by depositories in selected libraries in every state. Novices quickly learn that most of this material is uncopyrighted and can be lifted whole; what most don't realize is that every once in a while, the preparer of the pamphlet or chart has received permission to use something that has already been copyrighted. Unless you are sure that the government is the author, you cannot safely assume that everything emanating from the GPO is in the public domain.

State governments inevitably have matrices of informed individuals tucked into their political superstructures. If you can locate them—generally via public information officers of the various government departments—they're ready sources of up-to-date information and leads to other sources. Larger local governments have good resource people too.

In using government sources, keep in mind your readership as well as the scope of your subject. Quotes from a federal official have fairly universal applicability, so if a Department of Agriculture expert on green potatoes talks about green potatoes, you're safe using his quotes and data to make nationwide generalizations. However, if you opt for a state agriculture official as your authority, her comments on green potatoes may not carry much universality.

Nowadays, readers don't entirely trust government sources. When it comes to potatoes, weather, and census figures, you're on sure footing. But start to build an argument in an area such as employment, taxes, or housing that relies for its documentation on government figures and government officials' opinions, and you may be in big trouble. To play it safe, answer in advance whether, if you were *reading* instead of *writing* the article, you'd have much confidence in the information's bearer. If not, maybe you need to turn to the private or academic sector for input. This is just one more situation where the sharp writer has to be careful not to think *for* his readers, but to think *like* them.

Chapter Thirteen

Power Interviewing

T HE INTERVIEW IS ONE OF THE WRITER'S MOST effective research techniques. Yet the rookie writer seldom interviews well or makes sharp use of the results of the interview. Much of this ineffectiveness, we're convinced, comes from not appreciating the six different kinds of objective and subjective things to look for during even a short interview.

13·1 Six Article Ingredients to Get from Any Interview

Don't waste your interviews. In every interview, go after as many of these six ingredients as you can. (We've annotated part of an article by Frank (Ill. 13.1) so you can see where the six kinds of input his interviews gave him fit into place.)

Ill. 13.1 ————————————————————————————

The Arm Bone's Connected
to the Microphone

Inventors and hobbyists who spend years perfecting the proverbial better mousetrap have a staunch ally in the new but highly respected field of biomedical engineering. Its specialists look over the paraphernalia and techniques of medical procedures and seek to develop better tools for doing things. A leading research center in this field is at Vanderbilt University in Nashville, where Paul King, a Ph.D. in engineering, runs a special biomedical engineering program in cooperation with university medics. His students are both graduate engineers and undergraduates bent on continuing in this field or specializing in medicine.

Of late, Vandy's biomedics have come up with some fascinating cures for longstanding bottlenecks in medical technology. When physicians at the Vanderbilt hospital described to Prof. King how difficult it was to pinpoint the precise location of a brain tumor, he eagerly set his engineers to tackle the problem. With X-rays, it's often hard to differentiate between a tumor and healthy brain tissue, so for many years doctors injected patients with a radioactive substance which is absorbed by the tumor. However, all the various X-ray machines proved too imprecise to come closer than an inch or so away from the actual site of the buried growth. Finding the exact position of a brain tumor can be a clear-cut matter of life or death since the brain cannot tolerate much exploratory surgery.

Prof. King and colleagues designed a type of camera which can zero in on the radioactive substance that has been imbedded deep inside the brain, via the circulatory system. The result is a picture of the tumor's location, accurate to within ¼ of an inch. This newly developed camera is called a Tomographic Scanner, a special form of X-ray device which gives a more precise picture by bringing the area under examination into focus while leaving the adjoining tissues fuzzy. "The first version of our Tomo Scanner is like a Model-T Ford," says Prof. King, pointing to a new, more sophisticated version being erected by his students.

The new Vanderbilt Tomo Scanner uses 12 lead cylinders, plus steel and aluminum hardware. It all adds up to a 500-pound device which, despite its size, can be easily positioned around a patient's head. In two minutes, a patient can have his condition diagnosed at a cost that is considerably cheaper than X-ray analysis.

These days, Vanderbilt's graduate students in biomedical engineering, Leslie Hightower and Norton Busby, are inviting friends into their lab to be hit on the elbow with an electrified version of a doctor's rubber hammer. The engineers want to determine how fast sound can travel thru a healthy bone. Prof. King explains that the project was requested by Dr. John Connolly, an assistant professor of orthopedic surgery at Vanderbilt, who often takes engineers with him when making hospital rounds.

Dr. Connolly, and other orthopedists, want to know how well a bone is knitting, information X-rays cannot give adequately. Prof. King and Busby and Hightower tried various ways of finding measurable differences between bones that are healed and those still in the healing process, and the progress of healing, as well as determining if a bone is broken at all. Their solution involves a new use of sound waves. For instance, a patient with a broken arm bone is fitted with a microphone at the wrist. A doctor, outfitted with an electrified version of an orthopedic rubber hammer, taps the patient on the elbow and watches the results on a TV-type screen. The screen instantly displays three types of data which will vary, depending upon how completely the fracture has healed. Sound waves travel faster in a solid bone than in a broken bone, and that's one of the three measurements. A broken bone vibrates at a higher frequency than a fully mended one, so frequency is another measurement shown on the screen. But the vibrations of the broken bone are less regular than a solid or well healed bone, which is the third quality displayed instantly on the screen.

Once Prof. King's sound wave device is perfected, a physician will be able to assess accurately the state of a broken bone in under a minute, a process which now can involve hours of clinical diagnosis.

Another branch of medicine to benefit from Vanderbilt's engineers is ophthalmology. Doctors, engineers, and even two psychologists have gathered in the basement biomedical engineering lab to design new ways to study the eyes. Vision may be our most important sense, but laymen would be shocked to find out how little basic information actually is known about the eyes and why they function. For instance, from two to five per cent of all people suffer from a condition called amblyopia ("lazy eye") which can cause many physical and psychological problems if not corrected early in life. But ophthalmologists have been stymied in positively diagnosing the condition in children too young to cooperate with a complicated examination. Vanderbilt's engineers have developed a workshop full of devices which can analyze eyes without a subject's need to cooperate. Among the devices is a set of glasses with two tiny lights and two tiny photoelectric sensors attached, all of which are so miniaturized that a patient would hardly notice them. The photoelectric information is fed by electricity to a computer which then gives the appropriate diagnosis.

Dr. Robert Fox, a psychologist, and Dr. John Bourne, an electrical engineer—both of them under thirty years old—have had this project funded by grants from the National Science Foundation, the National Institute of Health and other organizations concerned not only with eyes but also kidneys, cancer, nerves, and arthritis.

"The challenge of the space age is not lost on the medical profession," says Dr. Connolly. "It has created, however, an interstiture of learning for which the field of biomedical engineering has had to be developed. The end result is that medicine with its new technological aids will rapidly fill a lot of old knowledge gaps."

INFORMATION

Books and magazines are okay for looking up facts and figures, but by the time they're in print, they're dated. Few editors buy a story from somebody who turns in stale facts. On the other hand, most editors place great stock in writers who consistently submit information that has never been published anywhere before.

Facts, figures, observations, guidelines, and similar data can't be more current than when they're gleaned directly from a person who's doing vital research or making important decisions on the topic of your projected article. In Frank's article for Metropolitan Sunday Newspapers (Ill. 13.1), *every* fact and *every* figure came from an interview.

Frank had to do it that way because most of the medical hardware he was writing about was too new to have been written about anywhere else.

ANECDOTES
Exciting writing is built on exciting anecdotes, so the good interviewer is always listening for them. A really sharp interviewer also listens for *clues* to experiences that could make lively anecdotes. Then he directs his subject to "Give me an example" or "Tell me about a time when that actually happened."

In the interview leading to the marked examples in our illustration, at first Professor King simply described the results of his work, a piece of metal, not how he achieved those results. Only when Frank prodded the inventor to recap what had transpired along the way did he offer an anecdote about why the machine had been needed, how it had been invented, and what it did. True, it's not the world's most exciting anecdote, but it is more interesting to read than just a description of the end product.

DESCRIPTION
You can't interview in a vacuum. We all want to view the subject —whether machine or person—in some kind of real-life setting that magazine readers can relate to. If the article you're researching through interviews is about a person, you may want to point out the special things about his office or apartment that reflect his personality. If the article is about a technological breakthrough, as in the case of Frank's reprinted piece, it helps readers visualize your points if you tell them what the equipment and labs look like.

During his interviews for "The Arm Bone's Connected to the Microphone," Frank jotted down notes so he could later re-create the following descriptions: 1) the size and complexity of the Tomographic Scanner, 2) the fact that the lab is in a basement at Vanderbilt University, 3) the youth of the behavioral and physical scientists cooperating on those projects.

AMBIENCE
Is the subject you're interviewing entirely on the level, or is this person puffing up her accomplishments? Does the office look like that of a corporation that's really earning $27 million in profits a year? Do these researchers take themselves superseriously, or do they paste intemperate cartoons onto expensive lab equipment? All these and dozens of other subjective clues and hunches make up the atmosphere that colors a writer's viewpoint. They will color yours. If you go into an interview consciously prepared to jot down clues to ambience instead of

permitting yourself to pick up unconscious "feelings" you can't substantiate, you'll be a better writer for it. You'll have something tangible to pass on to the readers.

You have to look closely to find clues to the ambience Frank felt at the Vanderbilt University biomedical engineering lab, but they're there. One clue is that nobody smiles as he speaks. Frank is telling readers that these fellows take themselves seriously. Even Professor King isn't painted with a grin as he says that an early version of his Tomographic Scanner is "like a Model-T Ford."

Frank rated the biomedical engineers highly. How do you know that for sure? Because he connects practically no qualifiers to the information they gave him. If, for example, he had thought the engineer was being overly enthusiastic in saying, "In two minutes, a patient can have his condition diagnosed at a cost that is considerably cheaper than X-ray analysis," Frank could have either put quotes around the sentence and added . . . *the engineer believes,* or displayed doubt by reporting, *"Usually* in *about* two minutes a patient can have his condition diagnosed for *somewhat less* than common X-ray analysis."

LEADS TO ADDITIONAL RESOURCE PEOPLE

Who should know better than one expert on your topic who the other major experts are? Make it a habit, during interviews, not only to find out *what* your interviewee knows on the topic of the day, but *who* he knows who can offer additional information. Also ask him to recommend important books or journals on your topic.

At Vanderbilt University, for instance, the public information office steered Frank to Dr. King and Dr. Fox. By asking them for more leads, Frank found Dr. Connolly and Dr. Bourne.

When our friend Terry Morris was preparing an important *McCall's* story about the romantic life of Stalin's daughter Svetlana, she convinced the magazine that the real story lay in India. (Svetlana's husband had come from India.) When Terry stepped off the plane in New Delhi, she had leads to only two resource people in the entire subcontinent. She parlayed her two contacts by asking each interviewee to suggest at least one more person for her to see. When she boarded the plane for New York, her attaché case was bulging. *McCall's* felt amply rewarded for its investment when Terry turned in an article bulging with information and anecdotes that no other writer had been able to get.

Hal Higdon told us that when he was in a number of small towns researching the Leopold-and-Loeb murder case, he made it a point to interview the towns' librarians. First of all, many of them personally knew the people involved. Second, they provided easy access to people who could offer insight into the men and their doings.

QUOTES

The least important purpose for most interviews is to gather passages to repeat verbatim in your articles. The overuse of quotes is a common error of beginning writers.

There are three major situations in which interview material should end up as quotations in your article:

1. When the interviewee's use of language is particularly picturesque, and sharing it with your readers will add to the point of the story. *Both* criteria must be present. Picturesque language alone is not enough. Dr. King's "Model-T" quote in "The Arm Bone's Connected to the Microphone" is an example of such use.

2. When it is important for written information—especially interpretive information—to come from an obviously authoritative voice. Remember that this works only if your reader *knows* the voice is authoritative. You've got to make your authority's credentials clear to the reader. Dr. Connolly's quote at the end of Frank's article shows this second purpose for quotes.

3. When you want to insert an opinion or point of view that the reader may quibble with if it's merely your unauthoritative opinion. This is particularly useful if the opinion is not a popular one. When they see the quotation mark, readers get a clear and quick signal that your viewpoint has been interrupted and another, perhaps contradictory, viewpoint has temporarily taken over.

13·2 What Exactly Is a Quote?

Here's a situation we invented to discuss quotes with our classes:

> *John Dean was told that President Nixon was about to bug his inner office. Two writers heard Dean's reaction. One of them sent in the story this way: ". . . Dean said eagerly, 'I'd like to see him do it.'" The other wrote, ". . . Dean said challengingly, 'I'd like to see him do it.'"*

Both writers reproduced Dean's quote exactly. But it's obvious that at least one of them was misrepresenting what Dean said.

The fact that exact quotes don't always quote exact *meaning* is one major flaw in the definition of *quote* advanced by journalism professors and high school English teachers. At the risk of their undying enmity, we'll share with you the pragmatic definition used by most of the working writers we know:

> A quote is a well-written passage placed between quotation marks to indicate that the information or opinions contained therein—if not the precise language—came from someone other than the article's author.

It's the insertion of the phrase "if not the precise language" that gives some of our academic friends apoplexy. Let's risk upsetting them further by adding to the working writer's definition:

> A quote is not necessarily the words a person *did* say, but the words a person *would* say if asked to retell his ideas within the context of the article in which the quote is going to be written.

This addition meets head on a situation that's faced time and time again by almost every experienced writer: You interview a person with one article idea firmly in mind. After more research, the theme or point of view shifts slightly so that the interviewee's responses are no longer precisely in context. Alternatively, the same responses also fit into another article you're writing. In both cases, if you quote the persons exact *words*, you find you're no longer representing his exact *ideas*.

We teach that it is dishonest to quote an interviewee's precise words if you know that they give a false impression of what he really meant to say. A good writer reports accurately the *sense* of his interviewee's words, but not necessarily their *exact language*. The same holds true in a situation in which note-taking gets the gist, but not all the words, of a person's thought. If, in reviewing notes, the writer wants to use the quote, it is common—and perfectly permissible—to bridge the gap with words the interviewee would have said in the appropriate time and place.

Only once in our decades of writing has an interviewee later claimed, "I didn't say that." In that instance, we'd transferred *his exact words* from our notes to our story. People recall their own exact words as rarely as interviewers remember them. It's their exact *ideas* that you'd better get right.

Academics troubled by our earlier two-part definition of *quote,* which forces writers to think at least as much as their interview subjects, will find little comfort in our third installment:

> A quote may be the words a subject *wishes* he said.

Very few people *speak* in a style that *reads* in an exciting or precise fashion. Most tend to be tentative, internally contradictory, ungrammatical, and either too choppy or too long-winded. One of the fastest ways to make your interviewee appear illiterate is to quote his exact spoken words. (Section 8.2 has a good example of this.)

Sometimes a writer does want to make the point that the interviewee's speech patterns are illiterate, picturesque, or disjointed. Then he copies the words exactly and quotes them without cosmetic improvement. But in most cases, the essence of a thought, not the manner in which it is delivered, is what's important to a story. A good writer cleans up mistakes in grammar and word usage, and the interviewee is always grateful for the courtesy. In fact, people who are frequently interviewed *expect* writers to make them sound good and are indignant at anybody who quotes them too candidly.

What if you interview someone who has trouble saying what she really means? The ideas may all be present, but the presentation so poor you can't extract a good quote even by cleaning up the fuzzy language. In a case like that, the experienced interviewer listens for quotable *ideas*. When we hear one that's good—but not expressed well enough to make exciting reading—we prompt the interviewee with, "Do you mean to say . . ." and, on the spot, rephrase the material so it can be used in our article. If the interviewee answers, "Yes, that's it!" we feel we have received permission to write the quote the way *we* said it and attribute our restatement to the source of the idea.

Frankly, were not all of the foregoing working definitions of the quote vital to tenderfoot writers, we might not have expressed them so candidly. By revealing what's not commonly shared with the public, we invite caustic comments not only from critics of the press, but from folks who were taught in journalism school (and may be teaching it there now) that "integrity of the press" means copying down exact words, just the way they're said. We want to stress, especially for those people, that we cannot condone writers who invent quotations from whole cloth, who put words into unwilling mouths, or who in any substantive manner alter the true meaning of what a person has to say. Ethics aside, such perversions invite libel suits, and justly so. But the opposite is equally unethical and equally libelous, as our little John Dean parable at the beginning of this section shows.

13·3 Should I Use a Tape Recorder?

The hardware of our profession is much less important than the skills writers wield. Unfortunately, one of the very first questions beginning writers ask us is whether or not they ought to use tape recorders for interviews. So, even though the topic deserves only parenthetical mention near the end of this chapter, we'll deal with it right now.

No, you should not use a tape recorder unless you are convinced that it is the best way to get the job done. We've interviewed hundreds of people during our careers. Yet we've used tape recorders no more than a dozen times or two. In fact, it's been over two years since either of our recorders has gone along on an interview.

In deciding whether or not to tape-record, keep in mind that, earlier in this chapter, we pointed out at least six kinds of input to go after in almost every interview. Only two of them—quotes and anecdotes—can be captured on tape. Even then, you can't capture a quote's context, only its words. Ambience is tough to capture on tape. So are scene descriptions. You can tape facts and figures, as well as leads to more resource people, but then you'll have to wait until your tape is transcribed before you have easy access to the data.

If you do use a recorder, here are some technical tips based on sad, sad experiences, ours and other writers':

Be sure you know how to work the recorder.
Be sure the recorder is functioning and the batteries are fresh.
Be sure you have enough tape to last the entire interview, even if it takes twice as long as expected.
Set up some foolproof gimmick for knowing when the tape has run out (unless your recorder features a built-in signal).
Set the recorder's microphone as close to your subject as practical so you avoid as much voice-muddling room noise and echo as possible.

Even if you've verified all of the above, cross your fingers. During the most important taped interview of your life, your recorder is sure to give you trouble. We can't help but remember the young California writer who was practically a neighbor of Alex Haley, and used that connection to get an assignment from us when we were editing a national magazine. Murphy's Law prevailed, of course, and his second reel of tape turned out stone-blank. Having relied entirely on his recorder, all the young writer could do was drop an SOS into Haley's mailbox and pray. His prayers were answered when Haley phoned to say, "Come on over, and this time use *my* recorder." Early in his writing career, Haley had done several of the *Playboy* interviews; he remembered a few horror tales himself about when he'd trusted his tape recorder. You might not be interviewing as simpatico a subject when your recorder dies on you.

Technical matters aside, there are plenty of practical questions to ask yourself when you're considering the use of recorders. Here are a few:

WILL THE SUBJECT BE AT EASE?
Most people in this era of electronic journalism are perfectly comfortable with recorders. Many of the tape-recording writers we know simply turn theirs on at the start of interviews without even asking permission. Others consider permission to be a professional courtesy that writers ought to extend to their subjects. You'll have to let your own instincts decide these matters.

WILL *YOU* BE AT EASE?
If you're forever fiddling with the tape machine, you'll end up nervous and so will your subject. Since the recorder can capture only a small part of what you probably hope to find out during an interview, you may miss out on ambience, descriptions, and such, while worrying about whether or not the exact words are going directly onto the tape.

WILL YOUR MIND WANDER?
Some writers tend to be less alert to answers when they know that the recorder is "getting it all down." They miss important afterthoughts that might otherwise clue them into asking new questions they hadn't thought of in preparing for the interview.

WILL TRANSCRIBING THE TAPE BE A TERRIBLE CHORE?
Once the interview is recorded, successful or independently wealthy writers have it typed out. Most of us have to transcribe it ourselves. And can *that* kill time! A few writers work with the tape, not the transcription, to pick up the nuances that get lost in transcribing. Those writers have good memories they know they can trust. In any case, if you interview a subject who rambles, or if you tend to invite rambling, relying on a tape recorder ensures a monumental job even before you can get to the actual writing.

ARE YOU PRONE TO EDIT INSTEAD OF WRITE?
So many articles based on interviews read as if they're simply edited transcripts. That's because they are. The creative input—the interpretation—by the writer just isn't there. If you find yourself cutting and pasting transcripts and inserting transitions that merely edit them into articles, you should seriously consider working from notes instead of recordings.

AFRAID YOU CAN'T TRUST YOUR MEMORY?
Several years ago, Frank had a standing assignment: if he ever managed to interview the sometimes reclusive Professor Marshall McLuhan, he would be paid well for an article entitled "Marshall McLuhan, What're You Doing Now?" On one trip to Toronto, he managed finally to wangle an hour with the media guru. But McLuhan specified right up front: No recorders! Not even any note taking allowed! After chatting with the wizardly McLuhan for an hour, Frank had to hop a cab to the airport and then a plane back to New York. All the while, his feverish pen was re-creating the interview from memory. By the time the 727 touched down, his first draft was finished, crammed with fresh, accurate, witty McLuhanisms.

Ill. 13.2

Marshall McLuhan Is Still A-Doin'

When the Guru of Media was spreading his message to an audience at Princeton recently, a streaker ran through the hall yelling the once familiar intellectual query—"Marshall McLuhan, what are you doing?"

Chuckling as he relates the story, McLuhan says, "That streaker knows best what I'm doing. I'm trying to strip away the facade of life in America and see what the ground beneath actually looks like."

This observation is remarkably clear in comparison to McLuhan's usual pronouncements. Several dozen articles, a few books, at least two films and endless debates have attempted to interpret what McLuhan really meant.

Even the public relations director at the University of Toronto, with which McLuhan is affiliated, says: "He doesn't tell us what he's doing. It's just as well. We wouldn't understand it anyway."

McLuhan, one of the most prominent names on the cocktail party circuit of the 1960s, has almost vanished from the discussion scene. His ideas, however, have been entombed in millions of copies of books in which, among other things, he talks about the imminent demise of books at the hand of television.

Those who remember McLuhan at all recall him as "the-medium-is-the-message" man. That was from the first chapter of his epic "Understanding Media" and the basis for a pun, another book, "The Medium is the Massage."

"I'm sorry I even used those terms," McLuhan says today. "That's all some people remember about those whole books. It singles out the media for special attention when they're really just one more institution working tirelessly at making everybody anonymous, just like government, big business and education.

"The streakers," says McLuhan, "were just a spontaneous cry for recognition in this individual-less age we live in. By removing his clothes, the streaker adds further to the illusion of anonymity. To make their point, they have to appear totally anonymous."

At 63, McLuhan is as fast as ever at drawing conclusions. "Nobody recognizes the individual today," he says. "But it's a strange anonymity. There is no privacy in our own homes. TV barges in day or night, friends call or come over, solicitors invade the home. Interruptions are the rule. People have to get out of their home to find privacy today. And that search for a moment's privacy outside our home leads to some terribly interesting phenomena," McLuhan notes, obviously warming to a new idea of his.

"We don't want waiters to talk to us in restaurants, because we go there to find privacy. People in the street shouldn't talk to us either. The car is about the biggest way people seek some privacy from their overly stimulating way of life. They get into their automobiles, where there's a lot of space around them, roll up the windows, turn on the music and air-conditioner. And at last they're alone. That's why the small, personalized, form-fitting European kind of car will never catch on in the U.S.A. or Canada. And that's why mass transit systems are doomed—there's not enough privacy there.

"People actually have to go to work to find privacy," McLuhan insists from his carriage house converted into offices on the edge of the University of Toronto. "Most people need only a telephone or a few tools for their work. They could communicate (sic) to work instead of transport themselves to work if they had enough privacy at home. But even that's breaking down now. The coffee break broke down the privacy of the office. It was a revolution and marked the end of the work system as it used to be."

Consistently, there is no sign of a coffee pot or water cooler in McLuhan's global headquarters. Nor TV. Not even a tiny transistor radio. To hear this self-admitted eccentric hold forth about revolution in social practices and rebellion of the mind might lead to the suspicion that McLuhan is another of those radicals hoping to tilt the government off its hinges. Yet during the red-tinged 1930s, when he taught at the University of Wisconsin, Herbert Marshall McLuhan opted to join the Roman Catholic Church while fellow intellectuals were joining the Communist Party.

Son of an actor-mother and in-surance salesman-father, McLuhan has mastered the dramatic art of selling his interpretations of social events to the intellectual community. He began by claiming to be an expert on the arcane works of Irish author James Joyce. Since nobody else really understood some of this stuff who could dispute McLuhan's claim to expertise?

"I'm still mainly a professor of English literature. All of my media studies began from that," says McLuhan. "At best, my medium and message research was a hobby."

It turned out to be quite a hobby. Book royalties have garnered over $250,000 for him, his lecture agent can command fees of around $1,500 for appearances at seats of learning, and tries to get $1,000 even for an interview with the prophet.

McLuhan claims that he writes very little about American society and the media because he's hot on the trail of new interpretations of James Joyce's "Finnegan's Wake." To friends or colleagues passing through town, however, he's still willing to spin a few yarns about the passing of American life as it used to be.

"This is the age of Acoustic Man," McLuhan declares. "While scholars and the media are busy talking about what they believe is a new thing—the Visual Man—they're too late as usual. Society has moved at the speed of light past Visual Man and into something new. It's just as well, really, because our visual environment has become overpolluted with atrocious houses, visually vicious ads and sensory-insulting industrialization.

"Rock and roll killed the visual electric media," McLuhan says quietly. "By the time most people realize intellectually that the Acoustic Man is hear—er, here—he'll be gone and something else will have taken its place."

It really isn't necessary to understand what an Acoustic Man is . . . McLuhan, however, does offer a partial explanation. "Acoustic Man harkens back to the tribalized age when people could only communicate orally. There wasn't any printing and certainly no electric media. It started as a language of grunts and groans, just like rock and roll. Moral standards in a tribal community are very high at a national level. But personally, they're very, very low. That's what we see all around us today.

"President Nixon is a Visual Man," says McLuhan. "He can't understand our Acoustic Age. That's why he's having so much trouble with this Watergate thing. He made the blunder of translating his acoustic materials (that's McLuhanese for "the tapes") into visual materials ("the transcripts," in other words). But visual materials are open to all kinds of interpretation, some of them favorable and some of them hostile.

"I think President Nixon is a sincere person doing only what all of his predecessors did. But now we're in an Acoustic Age, it's a tribalized sort of existence. Tribal Man won't allow a government leader to help his family or friends. He can help only the public at large, only the tribe, so to speak. But everybody else in the tribe is not only allowed to help family and friends, it's expected." McLuhan unfolds his morning paper to show that Canada, too, has a government leader in trouble because of the changing moral values of Acoustic Man. The Canadian, it seems, awarded government contracts to family members.

"The whole Watergate episode actually unfolded in a single Sunday evening," McLuhan insists. "All the rest of this is just writing footnotes to keep the government and media busy. I fully expect that President Nixon will be sacrificed. Tribal Acoustic Man demands it. He violated their new sense of national moral standards, even though at a personal level most Acoustic Men do the same things themselves as they criticize the President for doing."

McLuhan's tribe includes his son Eric, an artist, and a secretary who all share the quaint carriage house plastered with posters, cartoons and clippings from the newspapers and magazines which McLuhan says are extinct—they just don't know it yet! A former darling of the hot and cold media who popularized his wit and wisdom, McLuhan himself is risking extinction. His tomes are sold now mainly as textbooks in the history of communications, and reporters rarely use the well-worn path to his carriage house door.

Dressed with the studied casual air of a country gentleman in corduroy and tweed, McLuhan tops his slender frame with unruly, gray strands which he seldom cuts any more. But he does quickly push his hair back with one self-conscious hand whenever a camera appears. He obviously enjoyed his fling at muddying the media waters. But right now he's more intrigued with studying James Joyce anew, and perhaps getting back to literary scholarship, which is, after all, his admitted specialty.

As he shows a guest out the front door of the carriage house, he warns about the mud out front caused by a watermain break. It reminds him of a significant line from Joyce, "The mud is thickest from where it's thrown."

He smiles enigmatically, and you leave feeling sure he said something profound—until you try to decide just what he meant. . . .

Playboy interviewers have to tape-record; no assignment is given without that proviso. Still, the famous *Playboy* quote in which President Jimmy Carter admitted to having lusted was written from memory. Carter didn't make that particular remark until *after* the tape recorder had been turned off and the *Playboy* entourage was on its way out the door.

Given a chance (and a bit of on-the-job training), your memory will serve you better than you think. That and your eyes, your pen, and your pad are all the tools you'll need to successfully handle most interviews.

13·4   The Eleven Commandments of Power Interviewing

Too many beginning interviewers let their subjects wander off the track and, sometimes deliberately, miss the point of their questions. They don't know how to practice the craft of power interviewing.

Aside from doing tough interviews all our professional lives, we've taught courses and seminars especially on interviewing for writers and other professionals. During those years we've condensed some of the fundamental points of take-charge interviewing into eleven easy-to-remember commandments which, once adapted to your style and personality, will keep you in control of your interviews.

DEFINE THE PURPOSE OF YOUR INTERVIEW
You must know concretely why the interview is taking place before it takes place or you'll end up with a conversation instead of an interview. It helps if you run through the six article ingredients that interviews

offer, and figure out how much you can expect to get from a particular subject for each of those items. Usually it's helpful to let your subject know concretely, in advance, what you're looking for. Most people want to help. They may prepare charts or find papers that make their points better than their words. They may remember anecdotes at leisure that last-minute questioning doesn't call to mind. They may simply pull together some of their muddled thoughts.

Even if you're on a tough investigative assignment, tracking down a shady character, it's wise to let her know, once you've found her, why you want to interview her. It's a safe bet that she'll know, anyway, pretty much what you're looking for.

Draw up a list of questions that need answering. Use it as a guide, not a bible. Make sure to get them all answered, but be prepared to ask other questions that are suggested in the course of your interview.

DO SOME BACKGROUND RESEARCH

If you know something about the topic and the person before the interview begins, your prepared questions will display intelligence instead of ignorance and you'll elicit more thoughtful, less simplistic answers. An easy and useful place to do backgrounders is the library. (Chapter 12 is full of tips on library research.)

If your subject has written books or articles, be familiar enough with them so you don't ask questions they already answered—or if you deliberately ask some, let the person know you've seen an answer she's given to a similar question. Mentioning that you've read something by her may reward you with an easier interview. Knowing her title and the spelling of her name in advance is a must. (You can get them from the secretary.)

If you're researching a technical topic, become passingly familiar with the field's vocabulary before the interview. Nothing stymies an interview more than to have a professor finish a five-minute detailed discourse that perfectly explains his findings, only to have the interviewer say, "I lost you after the first minute. What's the meaning of *interface?*"

GET OFF TO A GOOD BEGINNING

Review your background notes and your questions in advance. List your questions in the order in which they can be most logically answered. Get to the interview on time. (We try to arrive five minutes ahead of time: it shows that we're there on business, not for a social call.) Look, and feel, like you're ready. Dress appropriately; jeans may give you credibility in one office and erase your credibility in another. When in doubt, dress conservatively. Take two pens so when the first one dries up, you'll still have one working. Take a pad, not scraps of loose paper.

Begin the interview in a cordial yet businesslike manner. We know there are a lot of old pros who suggest you start like a peddler, with talk about sports or the weather. But we believe it is more relaxing to a nervous subject (and novice interviewer) to get right to what you're there for than to meander through five minutes of aimless chatter and then make an abrupt switch into the *real* business.

GET TO THE POINT

Don't be vague. Don't let the interviewee be vague either. Be sure her answers are to the point or ask the question again, adding that the first answer wasn't quite specific enough. Be sure *you* stay on the point; few things make a busy subject more nervous than an interviewer who beats around the bush or can't keep to the topic at hand.

Don't ask complex, multifaceted questions. Most people think and speak one thought at a time.

BE SENSITIVE ABOUT RAPPORT WITH YOUR SUBJECT

Tune in to the interviewee. Don't take out a cigarette or stick of gum unless he smokes or chews first. He may hate smokers or gum chewers, and then where are you? On the other hand, if you're offered a cup of coffee or a smoke, it may be a clue that a break is needed.

It's okay to acknowledge that you know you're inflicting some strain. But don't ever think that you need to apologize for it. If you've done your job right, he's known in advance what you're after and has agreed to see you about it—even if reluctantly. If the strain is due to *information* you're bringing out (or struggling to bring out), it isn't your fault.

If the strain is due to your ineptness or impoliteness, that *is* your fault.

SAVE SENSITIVE OR EMBARRASSING QUESTIONS
FOR LATE IN THE INTERVIEW

There are two major reasons for adopting this stance. The first is practical: if you get booted out for asking impertinent questions, at least you've managed to get *some* information; moreover, it sometimes makes a dramatic point to say in an article that you interviewed the subject but got tossed out for inquiring about closeted skeletons. Second, during the early part of the interview you can assess whether you're getting candid answers; that's something you'll have to know during the tougher give-and-take.

However, don't shift gears consciously for incisive questions, or in other ways signal that you feel it's time for the really tough stuff.

The more matter-of-fact your questions, the more matter-of-factly the subject will answer.

Don't save tough questions for too late. If you do, your interviewee might do a quick "Oh, I'd love to answer that but our time is up. Isn't that a shame?"

Don't feel you have to be a nice guy and avoid touchy, controversial, embarrassing, nosy, or probing questions. If they're necessary in your pursuit of information for a story, it's your duty to ask them and unprofessional not to. Keep your fact-finding responsibility as a writer in mind and you'll be surprised at how easily even impertinent questions will be answered.

One *Playboy* interviewer was bothered by the fact that although every Barbra Streisand article sounded nice-nice, people who worked with her complained how difficult she was. So in his interview with her he fired off, point-blank, "Why are you such a bitch?" Stunned by his honesty, Barbra talked for six candid hours about how the media had misinterpreted her entirely. According to *Playboy*'s interview editor Barry Golson, "It was a great interview."

Terry Brunner, executive director of the Better Government Association, a citizen's watchdog organization in Chicago, says that his technique when dealing with a hostile subject is to accuse him of a dozen different foul deeds. "Sometimes he'll deny one or two, but not even attempt to deny the others." It's devices like that which enabled Terry to assist in convicting Mafia members and corrupt police officers. If you routinely interview shady characters, you might give Terry's device a try. But for most interviews, honest, straightforward, tireless questioning—whether it's "Where were you born?" or "Why did you disappear with the document?"—pays off most consistently.

VERIFY WHAT THE SUBJECT IS TELLING YOU

Investigative assignments require interviewers to check, wherever possible, the accuracy of everything they're told. Everyone knows that who has followed the exploits of Woodward and Bernstein. What beginners don't know is that every interviewer ought to at least spot-check that he's *hearing* the subject accurately and verify that the subject is telling the truth. Basically there are three ways to verify information obtained through interviews.

Corroboration is backup proof of the honesty or accuracy of your interview subject's statements. You can corroborate a statement by going independently to a separate resource person or by asking your subject to provide proof. Of course, corroboration is no more than corroboration: if everybody is lying or in error, you still may not have *the truth,* only corroborated statements.

Internal checks are simple to make if you think quickly enough. Ask questions, at two or more points during an interview, that should elicit identical information. If you get it, probably he's telling the truth and you're hearing it right. If answers differ, however, you'll have to find out—with more questioning or with corroboration—if you heard wrong or he told wrong. Or both. Or neither.

External checks are only a bit different. Ask one or more questions to which you already know the answer, probably through background research. If the subject's answer checks out, you've got verification of what he's saying and what you're hearing. If it doesn't, you're in the same spot as with internal checks.

LISTEN TO WHAT YOUR SUBJECT IS SAYING

If you work only from a list of prepared questions you may miss a lot of very valuable information. If you are lucky enough to be interviewing someone who plunges into new ground—or skillful enough to lead her there—follow up with more questions in that direction, or take up a pastime other than writing. We will never forget, as long as we live, the transcript of an interview one writer sent us (in our days as editors) in which controversial basketball great Kareem Abdul-Jabbar ended an answer about his youth by saying, "But that wasn't the worst of my problems then." The amateurish writer plunged right ahead with his next prepared question, "What about your eating habits now?" At that instant Abdul-Jabbar had been prepared to reveal something special to the interviewer about his childhood. He may never be in that expansive a mood again.

KEEP YOUR MOUTH SHUT

A subject cannot give you information while your own voice is in gear. Self-evident though this simple fact may be, it is overlooked by countless interviewers who monopolize interview time. A good interviewer is a great listener. There are so few good listeners around these days that if you can be one of them you'll be able to move quickly and effectively through most of your interviews.

On many occasions we've actually used silence as a device. We'd just sit quietly, not speaking, not asking another question, waiting to see what the subjects would spontaneously have to say. Often it's been a surprising elaboration on the last question we asked. That's because the subjects didn't know how much we knew, felt we could evaluate their answers better than we actually could, and—eager to stay clear of trouble—tried to explain their responses more fully.

Barry Golson says, in agreement, "The value of silence is something worth knowing about." His favorite example was when one *Playboy* interviewer asked Mel Brooks how he would describe himself. Brooks groaned and said, "How can I answer that?" There was a pause, Golson told us, and the interviewer knew enough to wait it out. "Then Brooks said: 'Well, I'm six-two, blond, blue-eyed and have a physique like Robert Redford. . . .' and he was off into one of the funniest answers we ever had."

END WITH AN OPEN-ENDED QUESTION

"Is there something I didn't ask that you think I should have?" and "Have we covered everything now?" are two of our favorite endings.

EASE OFF BEFORE LEAVING

If you feel obliged to chat, *this* is the time for it. First of all, it's nice to part on a cordial note. Then, too, some people react entirely differently when the pressure's off. It's not just Jimmy Carter who mumbled his most quotable words after the recorder was switched off. We've gotten some doozies after packing away our pens. It wasn't until after Frank stopped his interview and started taking photographs that Notre Dame's Father Hesburgh finally revealed his real feelings about President Nixon, who'd just fired him from the Civil Rights Commission. And while Frank was researching a twentieth-anniversary article about the Brown *v.* Board of Education of Topeka, Kansas, desegregation decision, the lawyer who'd originally argued the case for desegregation volunteered, as they were walking together to their cars after the interview, that he'd just filed a friend-of-the-court brief that supported separate but equal schools.

So, just because you've eased off your pressure on the subject near the end of your visit, don't lose your own alertness. Some valuable information often changes hands even when the interviewee has stopped noticing you and you're putting on your hat. Such as?

The subject nervously pulls out the file he slipped into a desk drawer so you wouldn't see it on his desk. What's it about?

The interviewee starts returning the urgent but possible compromising phone call she wouldn't take while you were on the job. Who's it to?

Getting back to work, the subject puts on the glasses he usually wears but was too vain to let you see. What can you make of it?

Leaving on a cordial note has another purpose too. You should try to leave the door open for a follow-up phone call in case you missed a few important points or need clarification of points already made. Other questions may not occur to you until you do more research or start writing.

13·5 The Telephone Interview

We can't hope to cover in one chapter all the bases that professional writers have to run when using interviews to research their stories.

We've concentrated mainly on pointers needed by writers early in their careers. One more pointer is, know how many different forms the interview can take.

Classically, the writer phones for an appointment, shows up at the appointed time and place to talk face to face with the subject, then goes back to his own office and incorporates the formal interview into his story. These days, however, interviews are commonly done on the telephone. With just an electronic connection between you and the subject, you won't be able to *see* her office setting, face, and clothes, but you can tell from her voice how seriously she treats the topic you're discussing, and whether she's hedging or sharing information straight out. Humor, anger, sarcasm, cynicism, wistfulness—all transmit well over telephone lines, giving busy interviewers the chance to gather factual material for stories in a minimum of time.

The telephone interview isn't always the first choice of writers. But it is often a necessary expedient. For instance, when Terry Morris was researching her *McCall's* scoop on Svetlana Stalin, she interviewed face to face most of the major personalities involved. Svetlana herself was kept off limits by lawyers for the publishers of her memoirs. Terry did entice Svetlana into making a social phone call, however, and she managed to extend the chat into a thirty-minute interview that not only answered many of her research questions but, equally important, lent enormous credibility to Terry's story in *McCall's*.

Chapter Fourteen

Writing the First Draft

W HEN ASKED AT A WRITERS' CONFERENCE WHAT she liked most about writing, Bonnie Remsberg quickly replied, "Having written." Those words have been said by many writers. There's no magic and very little glamour in sitting at a typewriter to write an article, only hard work that demands unrelieved concentration. Few writers work in sunny picture-windowed offices, simply because the distractions become overwhelming.

When small groups of professional writers gather, we inevitably share with each other the latest ploys for procrastinating when there's a manuscript to be written. Shopping for the family's groceries, reorganizing the files, writing personal letters, sharpening pencils, reading books, doing extraneous research . . . they've all been tried. The two of us write query letters as a form of procrastination, albeit an often profitable one. You'll have to find your own favorites—and your own way to discipline yourself into gluing the seat of your pants to a chair for as many hours as it takes to write what has to be written. Take heart; it's the first draft that's the hardest.

We've already taken a long, hard look at the elements and techniques that belong in that first draft. Now let's concentrate on the steps to take in braiding them together into a strong article.

14·1 Find the Point

One of a writer's trip-ups, in getting a story onto paper, is becoming so involved in orchestrating the wealth of statistics, anecdotes, and quotes he discovers in his research that he overlooks or drifts away from the story's purpose. In your query letter you promised the editor an article that presents a particular slant on a specific topic. If the editor is to okay your finished story, you must deliver substantially on your promise.

When your research is completed, go over it all with your article's original proposal in front of you. Does the information you found match what you expected to find? Do you have the kinds of experts you promised? Are your anecdotes and quotes strong enough to make the points you have to make? In short, do the extensive data in your files fulfill the sketchy picture given in your query? If they deviate markedly into a new slant, you'd better discuss your changed overview with the editor. If they're close enough, rivet the story's underlying purpose to your consciousness and plunge ahead.

14·2 Organize

You can jot down a formal outline, or make just a few notes. But whichever works best for you, you must begin with an unclouded perspective of exactly how your article's first draft is to be organized. That perspective may change once you've got your first draft typed. You may see relationships that weren't clear until you wrote down your ideas. You may discover that an anecdote fits better in a different place, or leads to a different conclusion than you thought it did. But unless you begin with a plan, you'll come out with a hodgepodge of long notes instead of a first draft.

Very often the subject matter itself dictates the most logical sequence for writing it up. Some articles beg chronological or step-by-step organization. Often you must impose logical order on your ideas, such as a point-by-point sequence or a succession of pros and cons. Many articles include several types of organization, but in those cases there is still, as a rule, one main organizational pattern that weaves from start to finish.

CHRONOLOGICAL ORGANIZATION

Just before the twentieth anniversary of the famed Brown *v.* Board of Education decision, Frank headed for Topeka to interview people who'd been involved in that landmark desegregation case. When he sat down to write his first draft, there was no doubt in his mind how the story would be organized. It fit neatly into one of the easiest formats to work with, chronology.

Judi's article "Miss Lynn Redgrave" (Ill. 6.4) is the story of growing up fat. Chronology was an obvious way to tell it. John Hirsh's article, "Food Greaser Loses 47 Pounds" (Ill. 6.11), talks about growing thin. It too lends itself to chronology. Judi's "It Costs Too Much to Go to a Museum" (Ill. 6.13) tucks a long chronology of events between its lead and its ending.

Do-it-yourself articles, too, are naturals for chronological organization: first you do that, then you do this, and finally you do something else. The exact order is dictated by the sequence readers must follow in duplicating the project. It helps, of course, if you've done the thing you're writing about (or a similar undertaking). Then you'll have no doubts as to the correct sequence.

Our "Build Your Own Luxurious Plastic Furniture" (Ill. 6.1) is organized in order of the jobs to be done: getting the materials, collecting the tools, cutting the plastic, making the holes, polishing the cuts and holes, gluing the pieces together, and so forth.

POINT-BY-POINT ORGANIZATION
Even when the various topics you plan to write about don't fall into chronological sequence, you still have to arrange them sensibly so that the reader follows easily from topic to topic. Some arrangements to consider are:

> from the general point to its specific aspects,
> from the easy concepts to the more difficult ones,
> from the least controversial to the most controversial,
> from the least complicated to the most complicated,
> from the theoretical to the practical.

Sometimes several techniques are combined. For example, you may decide to move from the least controversial to the most controversial points and, within each point, from the theoretical to the practical examples. The reader is able to follow much more easily if you stick to one pattern than if you sometimes reverse the pattern (going, for example, from the theoretical to the practical within one large topic and from the practical to the theoretical within the next).

In our article on house calls, reproduced from *Practical Psychology for Physicians,* the seven conclusions that governed our organization could have fit together in several ways. We laid them out so the article began with generalized conclusions arranged chronologically: "Most doctors develop guidelines for deciding when a house call is necessary" (decisions about *future* visits), and "Most doctors feel they can't practice good medicine on a house call" (on-the-scene decisions). Then we moved to conclusions that became more directive. Our conclusion number seven, "When care is taken to educate patients, they are actually surprised when you do suggest a house call," is a refinement of conclusion number six, "Patient education lessens the house call problem."

Ill. 14.1

Are House Calls Ever Necessary? A Survey of Current Practices

Among the arsenal of treatment techniques which the practicing physician has at his disposal, the house call creates perhaps the greatest dilemma. The AMA has no official position on its value or use. Medical schools generally don't counsel practitioners-in-training on its advisability, suggesting only that those who prefer not to make a house call should make *that* their policy right from their first day in practice.

The general feeling in the medical community seems to be that patients want house calls too often, and for no good medical reason. Patients, on the other hand, sometimes complain that doctors never make home visits, even when a person is dying.

To help determine just where the truth lies, this team of reporters surveyed 25 primary-care physicians randomly chosen from a geographic cross-section of large cities and small towns. From these interviews we were able to form seven general conclusions with regard to house call policy.

Conclusion One: *Most doctors develop guidelines for deciding when a house call is necessary.*

It's a rare doctor who *never* makes a house call. Every doctor in our survey said he would respond to a call from an elderly or severely disabled longstanding patient who had no easy means of transportation to the office or hospital. But the majority reported that they rarely make house calls, now that most people have cars to bring them to where services are available.

Each physician's house call guidelines are slightly different. Some doctors go out if, on phone evaluation, it seems like an emergency. Others visit the home only if it *isn't* a real emergency; for crisis situations, they feel, an ambulance or

rescue unit could bring the patient to the hospital much faster than they could get to the home. This is especially true if the symptoms suggest a heart attack, but the preponderant feeling is that for any emergency it's better to examine in a setting where testing and medicating resources are available.

Now that it is generally accepted that fresh air won't exacerbate even a fever of 105°, a good number of doctors said, they make house calls more for the patient's convenience than for rendering emergency care. "I cannot think of any medical indications for making a house call," one physician stated flatly. Others said they use the house call for follow-up after hospitalization, and for the critically ill who couldn't be placed in a hospital.

One doctor attempts to save his patients the expense of ambulance service by first calling at the house to decide if it is, in fact, "as serious as they thought." This physician told of one instance where he visited a patient to convince her that the hospital was indeed the best place for her. "An elderly woman, she had been convinced hospitals were only for dying," he said. On the other hand, several doctors feel the house call is abused by family members who are too lazy or reluctant to miss work to bring the patient in. After meeting a few such cases, these physicians tended to sharply limit their house call practices.

Conclusion Two; *Most doctors feel they can't practice good medicine on a house call.*

Quite a number of doctors feel, as one expressed it, "Too many things are missed when you're having to examine a patient under poor light, bending by a bedside that's too low to get at the patient, with all the. . .

In using a point-by-point organization, it isn't necessary to number the points as we did for *Practical Psychology for Physicians.* But it's a handy device. (See also Ill. 6.2, "12 Ways to Get More out of Studying," and Ill. 6.17, "10 Questions Patients Are Afraid to Ask About Cancer.") If the topic paragraph tells the reader to expect *x* points to follow, numbering them makes for fast and easy transition.

In our "Reasoned Strategy Prevails as You Battle the Odds" article for *Science Digest* (Ill. 14.2), we had only a casual organizational outline in mind before tackling the first draft: show why we're writing about war gaming; define it; tell who plays it, how it's played, and why. Since it was strictly an informative article, the journalistic who-what-why-when-where-how organization could be juggled for the smoothest flow of ideas. Articles like this one can be written without advance outlining once you find the knack. Others, like the house calls article, demand rigid planning. (It's a worthwhile exercise to read entirely through the original articles reproduced in part in Ills. 6.2, 6.5, 6.6, 6.8, 6.9, 6.10, and 6.17—all organized point by point—to see if you can uncover the outlines behind the finished products.)

Ill. 14.2

Reasoned Strategy Prevails as You Battle the Odds

Lee's infantry are hard on the heels of his cavalry that have just ridden through the streets of Gettysburg, swords flailing. Meade's infantry are dropping their muskets and fleeing. Union artillery are pointed the wrong way and Lincoln may have to surrender to the Confederacy at any minute.

Given some lucky rolls of the dice and smarter leadership than some of Lee's original generals dis-played, *it could happen today*—in any of today's war games that not only realistically restage battles such as the U.S. Civil War, but fight wars in space or Middle Earth.

Hobbyists of all ages are turning by the thousands to war gaming. War gaming companies put the number of hardcore war gamers in the U.S. at half a million—"and growing geo-metrically." The rate of increase in

Canada is believed to be at least as great. In England, 4 percent of the population plays war games, making it the largest indoor sport there. Those figures don't include the less fanatic war gamers who indulge occasionally in some battle that happened years ago—or hasn't yet taken place. The half a dozen war gaming companies sell some 2 million games a year, costing $8 million retail.

Don't let the name "war gaming" scare you off. Actually, the entire basis is the science of probabilities. The appellation is an old, unfortunate one that people who market war gaming equipment are trying to replace with "adventure gaming" or "fantasy gaming." Stendahl in his 1830 classic *The Red and the Black* told of an imperial general who passed time between battles playing war games. And H. G. Wells in his 1913 book, *Little Wars,* used war gaming in his plot.

Wars with soldiers and guns and battles—*strategy and tactics war games*—are still around, and preferred by many enthusiasts. But new since the 1960s are the *role playing, fantasy war games.* These include marches by elves and dwarves against dragons and giants, all straight out of Tolkien's *Lord of the Rings* and similar adult fairy tales. Or "Star Wars" characters struggling to outmaneuver each other at Warp-3 speeds. Or Earp and Holliday drawing to see who wins a trip to Boot Hill.

Reformed Computer Addicts

Nowadays, war games are the sport of many cured computer junkies. In short, war games are a humanized version of the computer-vs.-man strategy games. The players, making an algorithm of an entire war, first devise a set of parameters for their game, then a game board, and finally a comprehensive set of characteristics for the "men" involved in the game. Probability plays a key role in deciding moves, but instead of pushing computer buttons, the players use a set of dice with, variously, 4, 6, 8, 12, and 20 sides.

One of the most popular roleplaying war games today is "Dungeons and Dragons"—"D&D" to aficionados. In it, lovers of Tolkien and western mythology each actually choose a mythical character to portray —elf, dwarf, cleric, wizard, hobbit, thief. . . . But the characters have to be chosen after chance rolls of three 6-sided dice describe its strengths and weaknesses.

High *strength* ratings are helpful for fighters who take on giants and dragons. *Intelligence* and *wisdom* scores of 13 or more are needed by clerics and magic workers. Everybody can use hefty *constitution* ratings to endure damp dungeons and hot-breathed dragons. *Dexterity* upwards of 13 helps to dodge weapons and monsters. Not everybody needs high *charisma* points, but when an elf is defeated by a witch, if he has an 18 *charisma* rating she'll keep him around as a lover instead of turning him into a frog. As is true in most similar war games, "D&D" players roll dice at the start to determine how many *hit points* they have, or how severe a hit from a spear, stone, or magic spell they can withstand. Dice also decide how much wealth a character begins with.

Then, unlike "Monopoly" and

similar board games in which players compete against one another, in fantasy games the players compete against mathematical probabilities, using their own reasoning powers. The goal is to avoid point-losing pitfalls at the hands of dragons and evil wizards while trying to accumulate points through experience, finding treasure, and out-maneuvering the bad guys.

Science Digest, April 1978. Copyright © 1978, P/K Associates Inc.

PRO V. CON ORGANIZATION

An extension of point-by-point organization, this one could be called "point by counterpoint." It's especially useful when organizing material presenting both sides of several different topics.

In researching her article on how to select a divorce lawyer (written originally for *Playgirl* and reprinted as shown in Ill. 14.3 —with its lead hacked off and minor changes in language—in *Consumer Survival Kit*) Judi concluded that none of the lawyer types she found was all good or all bad. So she laid out her story to show both the pros and the cons. But she also used a point-by-point organization and, toward the end, a chronological one.

Ill. 14.3

The Divorce Game

There are over 260,000 lawyers in the U.S. and every lawyer is a general practitioner: in theory, he's supposed to be able to handle every type of legal work. In reality, the men who want to do corporate law start out employed by businesses, the men who want criminal law join the D.A.'s staff right from law school, and many of the people who open an office immediately drift into handling divorces.

Nobody has ever counted how many actual divorce lawyers there are. In small towns, matrimonials are merely one facet of almost every G.P.'s practice: it's only in large cities and densely populated suburbs that "divorce lawyers" per se are found.

Most divorce specialists have two things in common. First of all, they're combatants: they enjoy slugging it out with an opponent, although some like a courtroom battle whereas others prefer to fence toward an out-of-court settlement. "They're taught in school that divorce is an adversary contest and their entire stance is in terms of 'our side' and 'their side,'" one lawyer told me.

Second, most of them have an

extremely old-fashioned attitude toward women. They've hatched this attitude in law school, where there are few women among faculty or students. They've nurtured it in the course of their practice, because most male clients have already had some dealings with lawyers and appear smart and cool, while most women come in green, ask the wrong questions, and tend to "tell all" emotionally. The lawyers think in terms of "handling" these "frail nincompoops." Many lawyers "handle" them no more patronizingly than they've been "handled" for years by the banker and the plumber. **TR** But there are three types of tacticians to beware of.

TOPIC SENT. First there's the *Lover Boy*—the kind who uses words or sexual insinuations. Attorney Joan Goldberg, of New York, says: "A woman feels ambivalent about her divorce, and emotionally upset, and the lawyer is often the first person she's been able to trust in years. These male lawyers take advantage of the dependence."

Then there's *Big Daddy* lawyer, graying or balding on top, who says "call me counselor" and proceeds to counsel you on everything from your self-image ("You're young; go out, have a good time") to your image of your husband ("He's a sick, horrible, selfish man. How could you have lived with him for so long?"). Remember that most legal counselors have never taken a psychology course. In emotional areas, their advice is no better than your mother's.

Many men have the ability to change from Big Daddies to Lover Boys or vice versa: they're the *Chame-*

leons. Sometimes it takes several visits: somewhere along the way, they cross the line from fondness to fondling. Others are quick-change artists.

A *Chameleon* will often try to psych out a potential client and give her the father image or sexual overtones he thinks she's looking for. Even nonchameleons tend to assume that all women are emotional creeps while men are clear-headed and businesslike—even though William Gold has found, "Men frequently are just as hysterical as women are supposed to be, with just as much rejection and hurt coming through and just as many phone calls at three a.m."

TR In addition to how they relate to women, divorce lawyers can be understood in terms of how they do their job. There are two distinct types, the *Classy Character* and the *Lone Wolf*.

TOPIC SENT. The Classy Character is a partner in a middle-to-large-sized firm. He speaks well and smoothly, dresses with conservative elan, usually smokes a pipe, and has a clean, airy office. It's impressive, but keep in mind that appearances don't count: what counts is what he can do for you, and what it'll cost.

The Classy Character has lots of legal secretaries to do your paperwork, lots of clerks to read your files, and lots of young assistants to research applicable rulings and appear in court on routine matters. Since your fee is determined not only by the time spent on your case, but also by whether Mr. Class or his less expensive assistant puts in the time, your divorce may cost less than you'd settle out of court, so he'll tend to think. In addition, he usually likes to avoid antagonizing the opposition.

When you're dealing with nebulous subjects, it's important to make them as graphic and quickly distinguishable as possible for the reader (and editor). The names Judi gave to divorce lawyers were mostly her own invention, triggered by discovering a newspaper article that referred to one advocate as a "bomber." (The careful researcher picks up a lot more than just facts and figures.)

14·3 Pick Out and Write the Lead

In Chapter 7, we spend a great deal of time discussing what leads do, in theory, for your article. (You might want to review that section before you go on.) Now you've actually got to choose a lead. The most vital part of the story, it's also the place where beginning writers most often get bogged down. They try one approach after another, discard them all, and finally end up staring at the blank paper. They let the lead lead them instead of the other way around.

Once you really know what a lead is and does, it often jumps right off your notepad and hits you in the face. As you become more experienced, you find yourself recognizing a lead statistic, quote, or anecdote that appears during an interview, or one that pops up in your research. For instance, when Judi was interviewing actress Lynn Redgrave for her *Weight Watchers* article (Ill. 6.4), and Lynn said, "I was a food junky," Judi knew instantly that the quote would be her lead.

At other times, writers have to work a little harder to find the most exciting hook. Here are some questions pros ask themselves when hunting through their notes for the best possible lead.

CAN YOU STATE A PARADOX IN THE TOPIC?
That's what Judi did in her study article for *Seventeen* (Ill. 6.2): "Effective studying is the one element guaranteed to produce good grades in school. But it's ironic that the one thing almost never taught in school is how to study effectively."

That's what we did in our *Family Handyman* article about how to build plastic furniture (Ill. 6.1): "Wood has always been a favorite of do-it-yourselfers. Plastics, however, being relatively new, still frighten a great many people. But working with plastic is in many ways easier than . . ."

CAN YOU FIND AN EXCITING QUESTION ABOUT THE TOPIC
THAT'S GUARANTEED TO GRAB READERS' ATTENTION?

Judi opened her museum-for-pay essay in *The New York Times* (Ill. 6.13)
by asking, "So the museums are doing poorly, are they?" (See also Ills.
7.5, 7.6, and 7.7.)

IS SOME FACT ABOUT THE TOPIC DRAMATIC ENOUGH ALL
BY ITSELF TO SERVE AS A LEAD?

In his extension-cord exposé for the Sunday Newspapers (Ill. 6.10)
Frank began, "Every year hundreds of serious fires resulting in deaths
and millions of dollars of damage can be traced to faulty extension cords
or their improper use."

In her skateboard exposé for *Family Health* (Ill. 6.9) Judi opened
with, "Business is booming for orthopedists all over the country this
year. Broken wrists, splintered elbows and smashed ankles are just
three common hazards of the reborn skateboard craze."

IS THERE ONE ANECDOTE ABOUT THE TOPIC
SO DRAMATIC OR EXEMPLARY THAT IT MAKES AN EFFECTIVE LEAD?

Our tornado story for *Popular Science* (Ill. 6.6) began: "On April 3,
1974, one of the most ferocious tornado storms ever to hit the United
States screamed across the Midwest. By the time the winds died down,
more than 148 separate twisters had bulldozed a path through 13
states—killing at least 300, injuring thousands, and destroying several
billion dollars' worth of property."

In the CAT scanner article for *Family Health* (Ill. 6.7) we opened
with a long anecdote about a likable man who'd been spared pain
because of the new machine.

IS THERE SOME WAY TO OPEN BY IMMEDIATELY INVOLVING
THE READERS IN THE TOPIC?

That's what we did in our *Popular Science* article on painting (Ill.
6.19): "If you, like most home-owners, dread the next time your house
needs an exterior paint job, take heart!"

Mike Frome did likewise in his "Traveling Alone" piece for
Woman's Day (Ill. 7.10).

So many people with backgrounds in newspaper writing try to
make it in the world of magazines that we have to warn you: a good
lead for a newspaper article *almost never works* as a magazine lead.
Journalism schools teach newspaper reporters to tell the whole story in
miniature in the opening paragraph. In magazine writing, we want to
show only enough of our hand in the opening play to keep the reader in
the game. We give him a peek at our best card as a teaser and reveal the
rest, little by little, only after he's hooked.

14·4 Write the Body, Using Transitions and Subtopic Sentences

Once you have chosen your lead and written it, you'll follow it with a topic sentence (or phrase or paragraph) that's neatly dovetailed from it. (If you're stymied on the lead, choose any lead at all for the time being and move on. This is only your first draft, and as you write it the best lead will reveal itself.) We covered topic sentences fully in Chapter 7, so we'll plunge right into your next writing job—the body of the article.

It's important that you write the major portion of your article as quickly and in as straightforward a manner as possible. Arky (Arturo F.) Gonzalez puts it the best we've heard. He says that in the first draft, he's trying to get the Christmas tree up as quickly as possible, even if he knows it's not completely right the first time. Then, when the tree is up, it's easier and more satisfying to add the tinsel, lights, and baubles of good writing.

But even in your first draft, when you're finished dealing with your first point, you shouldn't abruptly begin point two. You must warn readers with a transition, and then mark each new point with its own subtopic sentence (or phrase or several sentences). If you've spent a page or two writing about the care and cultivation of apple trees, it may seem self-evident that you're switching to a page or two about pear trees. But that's only because *you* know how you've organized your notes. If you lose the readers while they try to figure out where your new point began and what it is, you may never get them back.

In general, the greater the shift in context, the more obvious your transitions and subtopic sentences have to be. If you're switching from Jonathan apple trees to MacIntosh, you might end the last Jonathan paragraph with ". . . that's why Jonathans are so easy to pick," and simply begin the next paragraph with "MacIntosh (the topic), on the other hand (the transition) . . ." Dozens of other short phrases also work as simple transitions: *however, but, in addition, unlike, at other times. . . .*

More radical changes in context demand more obvious transitions. Often they're contained in the last sentence of the previous subtopic combined with the sentence or two that introduce the next one. In the third column of the first page of the "House Calls" article (Ill. 14.1), we've marked with T a transition that introduces, at the end of one point (emergency care), the subject of the next point (hospital care). If you can find a noun or strong verb common to both subtopics, that's an effective shortcut transition.

On the second page of Judi's divorce lawyer article (Ill. 14.3), we've marked two transitions. The first, near the center of the first column, seems a simple one provided by the word *but* and directly followed by the next topic sentence, ". . . there are three types of tacticians to beware of." It's actually not as simple as it looks: the beginning writer might have made this sentence the beginning of a new paragraph. By tying it in at the end of the old one, Judi heightened the reader's sense of transition. She felt that was needed because the tie between the two points was really very tenuous. She could have written more of a transition and solved the problem that way. But she decided that the reader's interest was great enough to carry him along. What do you think?

In the middle of the second column, Judi uses a sentence to provide transition ("In addition to how they relate to women") as well as introduction to the new subtopic "divorce lawyers can be understood in terms of how they do their job"). But she immediately follows with another transition ("There are two distinct types") to move to her subsubtopic ("the Classy Character and the Lone Wolf."). Then she immediately begins elaborating on her first subsubtopic, the Classy Character.

For the war-gaming article (Ill. 14.2), we were obliged to pack a lot of information into a relatively short assigned length. So we worked with sparse transitions and subtopic phrases. At the end of our fifth paragraph, the transition phrase "But new since the 1960s" directs the reader's attention away from the historic aspects of war gaming and into the present. We offer two sentences' worth of what's new, and use the transition "Nowadays" to move through "computer junkies" to the mathematical basis of the pastime. Sparse though they are, our transitions lead readers through our organizational network.

14·5 Write with Subheads Wherever Possible

A great many magazines use subheads—bold type that breaks up articles into short units. These subheads are usually used as graphic devices, not editorial ones. Their approximate placement is suggested by the artist who lays out the page, often without having even read the article. Therefore, the subheads don't always divide subtopics exactly the way the writer might divide them.

Many writers include subheads in their finished manuscripts anyway. We generally do, except when writing for magazines that never use them. The subheads are a convenient way for editors, as well as writers, to quickly see the logical progression and locate the various subtopics in the typed manuscript. For beginners, they are as helpful as curve-speed signs are to drivers on strange roads. We suggest you insert them as regularly as you can.

But *never* use subheads to substitute for transitions and subtopic sentences. An article must be able to stand on its own without them. If the subheads get dropped onto the editing-room floor and leave you without transitions, some editor is going to have to compose some for you. He may not enjoy it a bit. In our years of experience, we've found that editors seldom mind crossing out, but usually resent taking the time to bridge your gaps.

14·6 End with a Bang

By now we assume you're all the way through your first draft, right up to the ending. But even if you've said it all, you can't just stop writing. You must bring the article to a definite conclusion that leaves the reader satisfied that you've delivered what your topic sentence promised.

Endings don't have to be long; they seldom are. But they do have to be included. Here, too, is where the magazine article differs greatly from the newspaper article, which often just tails off after the last point is made.

There are as many ways to create a good ending as there are ways to create a good lead. And there's some similarity between the two devices. Here are several of the more common ways to end.

SUM UP
Pick a line or two that neatly wraps up the entire subject with a note of finality for readers.

The *Practical Psychology for Physicians* article on "House Calls" (Ill. 14. 1) ends by summing up the seven conclusions—its seven subtopics —into one general rule: Have a fair and consistent policy.

> *Despite all of the public criticism of medicine today, the uselessness of most house calls is understood and accepted if your policy is consistent and fair.*

"The Miners" article (Ill. 6.5) ends by summing up the topic, stated as "the mine is their life," with statement and quote:

> *When employment at the mine opened again . . . he leaped at it. "I packed away all his white shirts and striped ties. . . . They're still in the closet. Guess we haven't even opened the box in years."*

HARKEN BACK TO THE LEAD
Judi begins her Lynn Redgrave interview for *Weight Watchers Magazine* (Ill. 6.4) with Lynn's line, "I was a food junky." In ending, she picks a matching quote: "It's not hard to be sensible about food . . . because I'm not hooked on it any more."

John Hirsh begins his article (Ill. 6.11) with the word "greaser." His ending picks up that word from the lead. (The editor liked it so much he put it in the title.)

I feel more awake than ever before. And I can jog almost 30 minutes at a clip which is pretty good for a greaser who couldn't walk one block without feeling totally exhausted.

Judi's "Museum" article (Ill. 6.13) echoes the "slammed door" image of her lead with "open doors" and "turnstiles" in her ending:

Can't the city's Cultural Affairs Bureau find some way to open the doors to these children again? Or are they planning to put turnstiles at the entrances to playgrounds next?

END ON AN IRONIC NOTE

After spending a few thousand words warning about the skateboard menace for *Family Health* (Ill. 6.9), Judi ends ironically:

And don't mention this consoling thought to anyone under 21: If the fad lasts as long as it did the last time around, it'll be gone by this time next year!

In our war-gaming article (Ill. 14.2), the concluding irony is aimed at one variation of the pastime:

One company, Flying Buffalo, Inc., has run computer war games by mail for years now, but they've stayed rather small. Without rolling a 12-sided die, the odds are strong that war-gamers who've tasted the kibbitzing and improvising that go on with living, breathing partners are not likely to wave a white flag after a frontal assault by some punch-card general.

OFFER SOURCES FOR MORE INFORMATION

In a way, this device doesn't end the story at all, but encourages readers to continue it on their own. In her study techniques article (Ill. 6.2) Judi ends:

For more information on studying, consult the following books: How to Study in College, *second edition, by . . . and* How to Study, *second edition, by. . . . Both, available in paperback.*

Our *Family Handyman* story on how to build plastic furniture (Ill. 6.1) ends in similar fashion:

For 75c, Rohm and Haas Company, Dept. FH, APO Box 9730, Philadelphia, Pa. 19140, will send you all of the following literature: 1) Do-It-Yourself with Plexiglas, 2) How to Install Plexiglas for Safety Glazing, 3) Project Plans Mail Order Catalog, 4) Approved Tools for Working with Plexiglas Mail Order Catalog, and 5) List of Approved Plexiglas Distributors.

Often, the writer or editor tacks this ending onto one of the other endings. At the end of John Hirsh's "Greaser" article (Ill. 6.11) the editor plugged an accompanying article:

Some of my recipes which have helped me drop my weight can be found on page 7 of this section.

If you don't like that ending, write one yourself. In fact, try writing new leads, topic sentences, transitions, and endings for some of the articles we've looked at, or for others. You'll soon find your own unique way of putting your ideas on paper—the way that works best for you.

You'll know you've succeeded the day someone finally says, on first meeting you, "I read your article in my favorite magazine and loved your style."

Chapter Fifteen

Good Writing = Rewriting

U NLESS YOU'RE A CLOSET SHAKESPEARE, YOUR words will *never* fall onto the paper just right on your first try. There are too many words in the language, too many shades of meaning, too many opportunities to be just a bit more precise or effective. Your first try can never be just retyped and shipped off to a waiting editor. Would-be writers who make that mistake become has-beens before they ever break into the field.

Magazine writing is in no way like writing for a newspaper, where a rewrite department is part of the staff. This field demands a honed and polished finished product. Of course, any good editor can edit drivel into finished prose. But *he won't*—that's not his job. If you want to make it as a magazine writer, you must learn to be your own editor.

We've been in this business for decades, with hundreds of published magazine articles plus seventeen published books. Yet we still go through a minimum of two or three heavily edited drafts on everything we write. In our earlier days, we needed four or five drafts to get an article right. We don't expect we'll ever be able to turn in unrevised manuscripts that give us the pride of ownership that makes all of writing's headaches worthwhile. Some of our professional friends prefer to do their editing on typewriters or word processors instead of with pens, but they still habitually churn out several drafts.

If you organize your article tightly before you begin, and cover almost every salient point on the first run-through, maybe you'll be able to carefully edit that draft, cut and paste, and make final corrections as you're typing a second draft. On the other hand, you might be one of those writers whose first drafts are little more than loosely organized notebooks of typed thoughts. In that case, you'll probably need a second draft that takes you down the plotted channel. Then, after meticulous pen editing of the bumps and dips, you may be able to type a fourth and final draft for your editor. Even then, we wager you'll be making corrections along the way.

If you are to successfully conquer the challenge of writing for magazines, you must develop the skill of recognizing good writing in other articles, and in your own. More important, you must develop the discipline required to turn in an article that represents the best writing you can do at the time. Every word need not be the best possible word. A few beginners put off submission by polishing past the point of shine. They rub away at each and every word, and end by wearing off the spontaneous flow of thought that is the real object of writing.

Perhaps if we share with you *our* thoughts as we edited the first draft of a manuscript with our red ballpoints, you can start thinking like editors as you study your own manuscripts.

15·1 Good Writing = Good Editing

Ill. 15.1, from our own files, is a page of a brief article we wrote for a regional magazine. It's the first of a series of restaurant reviews, and had to establish our credentials and objectivity. The first draft, reproduced here, is not bad—but it's not good enough. So, as you can see in Ill. 15.2, we used a pen to edit the rough draft. (We like to pen-edit instead of retyping because we believe it offers us the flexibility of changes, changes on changes, and even changes back when the original words prove to have been best after all.) The editing was slow and painstaking; usually it takes us more time than the quick run-through we do at full speed to get the first draft down on paper. When we felt the manuscript was sufficiently ready, we typed the final draft (Ill. 15.3). But even as that version flew through our fingers we were making improvements, as you can see by comparing it with the edited page. Never perfectly content, we penned in a few smoothing-out touches *after* we'd typed the final draft. When we decided the article said what we wanted it to (though we knew that if we fussed some more, we might have changed a bit of syntax here or there) we mailed it off.

Let's look first at the *purpose* for each paragraph in our example.

> *Paragraph 1* The primary purpose is to provide a lead. Since this is a local magazine, we've chosen to tease the readers into wanting to know how cosmopolitan big-timers rate their restaurants. A secondary purpose is to establish our credentials as big-timers. It fits easily into our lead, and we get it done in the very first sentence. A third, even more subtle, purpose—to establish objectivity without seeming snobbish—is handled in the next two sentences. The final sentence is a transition and the topic of the article: several restaurant reviews.
>
> *Paragraph 2* Our purpose here is to review one restaurant in particular without wasting any time. We use *specific examples* (see the second sentence) and *comparison* (the third sentence) to make the point—that this is a good restaurant—in the liveliest yet tersest way.

Ill. 15.1 ───────────────────────────────────

Since we travel so much as writers, we've

grown to appreciate Madison's unique position as

a homey place to live, where people of all sorts

are free to enjoy a very high standard of living

at a relatively low cost of living. Nowhere is

that reflected more dramatically than in Madison's

retsaurants.

While we were visiting Madison with an eye

to moving here, imagine our delight at discovering

L"Etoile where we were served like royalty a duck

lavished with orange sauce, sipped the finest wine

reasonable money could buy, overlooked the calories

in fresh torte, and nearly fell over when the bill

came to almost $20. Only a month earlier we'd

enjoyed truly comparable spendor at New York's

famed Algonquin where the tab ran up to almost 3

times E'Toile's!

Page of first draft.

In the first draft, we quickly set down our tentative words and phrases aimed at meeting these purposes. We knew they wouldn't survive intact into the final draft. But we knew that we'd never *get* to a final draft if we didn't start out with some approximation of our thoughts on paper. To take you through our editing thoughts line by line, we've numbered each line on our second draft so you can follow along.

Line 1 "As writers" is too general. "Free-lance writers in search of articles of national interest . . ." is more specific, more vivid, and more credible.

Lines 1 and 2 Since the purpose of the article is to discuss restaurant dining, which we do in more places and more often than most people by virtue of our traveling, not our writing, we switched around the two clauses so the "free-lance writers . . ." fits into an introductory phrase while the more important "we travel" becomes the sentence's subject and verb.

Line 1 Whoops! We'd forgotten to include the article's topic—the point of "we travel"—in our opening. We didn't want readers to be misled, even for a moment, into thinking the article had to do with writing or travel. We quickly edited in "and we eat out a lot."

Lines 2 and 3 We tied the third sentence to the second with the thought "appreciate." We could have made it more evident by saying, "We especially appreciate . . .," but didn't want to be top-heavy with "appreciation." Apple-polishing, we figured, was fine from us outsiders; bowing and scraping was not. We chose "pleased" instead.

Lines 3, 4, and 5 That we live in Madison—the region covered by the magazine—is important to help readers identify with us. But "homey place to live" is *off* the topic, so out it went. Also, comparing "high standard of living" to "low cost of living" is too clichéd for comfort. We chose more straightforward language.

Notice the progression, from sentence to sentence, from the general "many things" to the more specific "good living" to the most specific "restaurants."

Line 6 A noun's missing here—not a crucial oversight. Many magazine editors would not have paused to insert one, but it caught our attention because, as originally drafted, that sentence was arhythmic. Add "fact," and it's got rhythm. We could have chosen from many other nouns, any one of which would have been appropriate. However, if we'd selected a more noticeable one, such as "merger" or "amalgamation," it would have shifted some impact from the two more important parts of that sentence, "dramatically" and "Madison's restaurants."

Line 10 ". . . served like royalty a duck lavished with . . ." is too awkward to ignore. We knew it stuck out when we were typing the

Ill. 15.2

As free-lance writers in search of articles
(and eat out alot.)
of national interest,   a great deal Since we moved to Madison

1   ~~Since~~ we travel ^so much as writers~~,~~ we've

2   many things about this lovely city. We are especially
grown to appreciate ~~Madison's unique position as~~

3   pleased to find that people here
~~a homey place to live, where people of all sorts~~

4   ~~are free~~ to enjoy ~~a very high~~ good ~~standard of~~ living

5   at ~~a~~ relatively low cost. ~~of living.~~   Nowhere is

6   fact
that ^reflected more dramatically than in Madison's

7   res^taurants.

8   first   (like gastronomic kings)
~~In fact, one of the seasons~~ We knew we could live^
~~While we were visiting Madison with an eye~~

9   in Madison when, we on a visit from New York City, we
~~to moving here, imagine our delight at discovering~~

10   (In the little second-floor restaurant overlooking the Capitol,
L'Etoile, ~~where~~ we ~~were served~~ dined on ~~like royalty~~ a duck

11   lovingly   the best house
^lavished with orange sauce, ^sipped, ~~the finest~~ wine,

12   we consumed ~~the lovingly~~
~~reasonable money could buy, overlooked the calories~~

13   ~~prepared~~ baked
~~in~~ fresh ^tortes, ^and, we grinned from ear to ear at the less-than- ~~nearly fell over when the bill~~

14   $20 bill for two.
~~came to almost $20.~~   Only a month earlier we'd

15   feast
a   dining
enjoyed ~~truly~~ comparable ~~splendor~~ at New York's

16   only there   had run   SP
famed Algonquin, ~~where~~ the tab ~~ran up~~ to almost ③

17   L'Et
times ~~L'~~Toile's!

Page of edited first draft.

first draft, but at that point our emphasis was in getting the ideas down on paper. And it's good we didn't take the time to change it then. While editing this portion, we had more than mere clumsy writing in mind.

Lines 8, 9, and 10 In the first draft, we deliberately put in first position "While we were visiting Madison" to act as a transition between the last sentence of the paragraph past and this new paragraph. Then we saw a chance to neatly sew up our own personal transition from living in New York City to living in Madison by adding the phrase "with an eye to moving here." During editing, however, we decided that we really didn't have to include minutiae such as "with an eye to moving here" since obviously we *were* here; we'd said so in paragraph one. Out it went. We kept "Madison" in our rewritten sentence to act as transition via the "Madison" in the last part of the last sentence in the previous paragraph. But we also carefully laid out all the information we wanted in this sentence.

Most beginning writers would have cast that sentence this way:

We first knew we could live like gastronomic kings in Madison when we discovered L'Etoile on a visit from New York City.

Why did we make a complex sentence of it instead? Because we wanted to save our most dramatic revelation for the end. If you give away your punchline at the start of a story, why should your friends listen to the rest of the joke? The same applies, in general sense, to sentences and paragraphs as well as entire stories. We wanted "L'Etoile" to be our punch line. It's the topic we were about to discuss over the next several paragraphs. So we reversed the positions of "on a visit from New York City" and "L'Etoile."

Lines 8 and 10 The first draft hadn't taken time to set the scene at all. So we edited in a very short picture of what L'Etoile looks like. We also edited in "live like gastronomic kings" to underline the topic of our article, restaurants, providing a second bridge from paragraph 1.

Line 10 In the haste of getting the first draft onto paper, we'd cast this sentence with an inactive verb: "we were served." But to create exciting reading, you need *active* verbs. So we reworked the sentence so that, instead of passively watching the duck being served to us, we actively dined on it. Still later, if you compare that line to our final draft, we crossed out "dined" and substituted the more explicit, and point-making, "feasted." By using the simple expedient of a specific, active, exciting verb, we were able to eliminate adjectives and adverbs and still create the same mood as in our first draft. Contrary to what your English teachers told you, adjectives and adverbs often get in the way of exciting writing. If you link explicit, active verbs to

Ill. 15.3 ────────────────────────────

As free-lance writers in search of articles

of national interest, we travel a great deal and

eat out a lot. Since we moved to Madison we've grown

to appreciate many things about this lovely city. We

are especially pleased to find that people here

enjoy good living at relatively low cost. Nowhere is

that fact reflected more dramatically than in

Madison's restaurants.

We first knew we could live like gastronomic

kings in Madison when, on a visit from New York City,

we discovered L'Etoile. In the little second-floor

restaurant overlooking the Capitol, we ~~dined~~ feasted on duck

lovingly lavished with orange sauce, sipped the best

house wine, ~~consumed~~ ~~nibbled~~ tasted fresh-baked tortes -- and grinned

~~from ear to ear~~ with pleasure at the less-than-$20 ~~bill~~ tab for two.

Only a month earlier we'd enjoyed a comparable ~~feast~~ banquet

at New York's famed Algonquin -- ~~only~~ but there the ~~tab~~ bill

had run to almost three times L'Etoile's.

Final draft.

explicit, vivid nouns, you won't have to prop up weak sentences with extraneous modifiers.

Line 11 However, here we actually added a modifier, the adverb "lovingly" before "lavished." First of all, the alliteration is fun. Second, the word is anything but extraneous. It makes an entirely separate point on its own, showing the manner in which the whole staff at L'Etoile approaches food.

Line 13 Notice here how easy it is to cross out one cliché, "nearly fell over," only to substitute another, "grinned from ear to ear." Fortunately, we corrected that slipup in our final draft. Also notice our struggle over how to describe the wine and the reasonable price we paid for it. The first draft's elusive "sipped the finest wine reasonable money could buy" evolved to "sipped a wine as good as any." That wasn't at all accurate (if compared to a seventy-four-dollar bottle of Dom Pérignon, for example), so we struck it, too. Then we remembered that the *purpose* of the paragraph was to show the *overall* reasonable price we paid for an *overall* outstanding meal. We weren't setting out to criticize individual items on the menu, so we didn't have to deal with details about the wine at all. Simplicity prevailed over superlatives and we ended up with "sipped the best house wine."

Lines 16 and 17 Here we deliberately left in two far-from-extraneous adjectives. For accuracy, we had to say that what we'd eaten at the Algonquin Hotel's restaurant was "comparable" in quality, otherwise our price comparison wouldn't have held water. We kept "famed" before Algonquin so that Madison's readers—not, as a whole, nationwide travelers—would know immediately that the Algonquin is a good many notches above Howard Johnson's.

Lines 13 and 16 At the last minute, we switched around "tab" and "bill" so line 15 of the final draft gained a pleasant alliteration, "less-than-$20 tab for two," without in any way diminishing the overall impact of line 17.

Line 17 It took us until the very last minute to pick up Liquid Paper and take a swipe at that exclamation point. If the sentence itself didn't excite the reader, a tiny blob of ink wouldn't either.

As you may have noticed from other examples in the book, this article, so loaded with puffery, is unlike our usual writing style. That's because, in studying the magazine, we discovered that the readers expected a light, flighty, filigreed style. As we said in Chapter 3, write for the readers and you won't go wrong.

15·2 A Checklist for Editing Manuscripts

It's easier to learn good editing on somebody else's manuscripts. We suggest you practice editing your kids' school papers, your friends' articles or letters, your spouse's business reports. Then attack your own sloppy first drafts again. By the time you've become a bloodthirsty editor of your own writing, you will instinctively reach for a red pen every time your eyes spot something to read—even when you pick up a letter from the folks back home.

To start you thinking like an editor, we've selected unedited pages from three different manuscripts. When you think you've got them whipped into fine shape, compare your editing to ours, which we've reproduced at the end of this chapter. If your changes don't match ours, don't automatically assume that yours are wrong. Editing, like writing, it a personal art, and there are a hundred right ways of doing it. Did you fix a few things we didn't bother with? Did you pick up the same errors and clumsinesses we zeroed in on? See if your corrections are worse or better than ours.

Eventually you'll develop a mental checklist of problems to look for when editing your manuscripts. At risk of having you edit *this* book first, here's a condensation of our own long list. Most items can be summed up in one underlying principle: *good* writing *is simple writing*. It's not, as many beginners seem to think, the sorcery of taking simple notions and opaquing them with overly eloquent words and abstruse sentence structures. It is, instead, the art of taking eloquent ideas and making them readable, even enjoyable, through careful selection of everyday words and sentence constructions.

SELECT VIVID NOUNS

The subjects and objects of your sentences must paint pictures in readers' minds. Don't write about a *horse* if *stallion* is accurate. Don't choose *cat* when *Persian kitten* is what you have in mind. Given a choice, would you look first at a *picture* or a *tintype*? Pick explicit nouns that don't require adjectives to clarify their meanings.

CHOOSE ACTIVE, EXPLICIT VERBS

Make your subjects *do something* by choosing active verbs—*prance, dance, enhance, romance*. If you insert the passive voice too often—*was carried away, is being lifted, was improved, is being put to sleep*—your subjects will feel passive too. And so will your readers.

Choose, too, the verbs that most explicitly show the actions you're thinking of. Do you mean *grab, grip,* or *grapple with*? Do you say *like* when you mean to say *prefer, admire,* or *enjoy*?

STICK TO SIMPLE TENSES

Whenever possible, use the *simple present tense* unless the *simple past tense* is more accurate. The *future* and *conditional* tenses (such as "he would fly") tend to undermine the author's sense of authority; readers suspect people who forever hedge with *could*s and *should*s and constantly predict the future. And *has been*s and *had been*s are hard to follow.

Ill. 15.4

> At Christmas, every bdy wrote about toys. But we asked,
>
> what ~~xhsuxx~~ happens to all of those damned battery powered
>
> toys <u>after</u> Christmas. And ~~xxsxsxx~~ we wrote an expose about
>
> how batteries are marketed: "The caustic truth about
>
> batteries." ~~While all of our friends were~~ ~~/When/every/body/was/~~ encouraging people to get
>
> themselves ~~a~~ creative ~~hobby~~, we wrote "The Hazards of   ^hobbies
>
> Hobbies."
>
> Every magazine feels obliged to run some seasonal material.
>
> And after a few years on the job, editors find Christmas
>
> and similar editorial holiday issues to be more and more
>
> depressing as fresh ideas get harder and harder to find.
>
> Our newspaper group editor was no exception. One year
>
> we did the coldest spot ~~dn~~ the nation, the~~n~~ next the snowiest.
>
> What next? Well, there was a northern Wisconsin town
>
> that was red-light district from one end to the other all
>
> summer. What went on there in the depths of winter?
>
> "Where are the snows of nexteryear?" predicted
>
> with help from the federal government's/climate ~~xxd~~   ^weather and
>
> experts, how much colder the U.S. was becoming, and
>
> how fast, and ~~/where/~~ the big snows would fall, and so o~~n~~.   ^on which states
>
> Editors -- and there readers -- love predictions.
>
> Next year we predicted, thanks ~~xx~~the nation's
>
> #1 weahter wexpert, an M.I.T. professor, that we were about
>
> to have a record cold winter: "It's going to be a red
>
> flannel winter." We even sketched maps, based on the
>
> expert's prognotications, showing how much colder various
>
> parts of the country would be and where the heaviest
>
> snows would fall. It was a marvelóus story. ~~ixwsxx~~

Page of first draft for *you* to practice editing. (Later, compare to *our* editing in Ill. 15.8.)

Ill. 15.5 ─────────────────────

++Sometimes the person who lived the experience gets the entire by-line. Other times, the actual author is listed second: "As told to....." Rarely, usually only in articles involving celebrities, does the author get ᵗʰᵉtraditional by-line.

Riskingxupxthexeurrentx̶READER'S̶xDIGESTxwexfind

personalxexperiencesxxstories

How many of us can survive enough falls off 28
                                          near
storie buildings, or ᵏᵉᵉᵃx recover from enough/fatal

illnesses, to make a living at writing personal experience

articles? So, the pros who make at living at writing

personal experience stories write about some body else's

tragedies and triumphs. ++P̶r̶o̶b̶a̶b̶l̶y̶ the dean of personal
                                    must be
experience story tellers ᵢ̶s̶ Terry Morris, one-time

president of the American Society of Journalists and

Authors and p̶r̶o̶f̶i̶ p̶r̶o̶f̶i̶i̶ prolific pagazine writers.
           abandoned
She s̶w̶i̶t̶c̶h̶e̶d̶, about 1950, f̶r̶o̶m̶ writing short stories

in favor of human interest magazine articles about people

in crisis. But she never abandoned her gift for

telling a touching story, so she sold her first two

artgicles to COSMOPOLITAN and McCALL'S early in 1951.

Terry's all-time favorite was "Please don't lose faith
                              from the viewpoint of
in Me" an as-told-to article b̶y̶ the mother of a
                    son.
schizophrenic s̶o̶n̶n̶x̶t̶h̶a̶t̶ McCALL's ran it ᵢ̶n̶ July 1953;

we've reprinted the first page nearby̶x̶ so you can

study how a master handles somebody else's personal experience.

Page of first draft for *you* to practice editing. (Later, compare to *our* editing in Ill. 15.9.)

Ill. 15.6

6.11 The Photo story

      This is a bonus! The photo story ~~kan~~ technically

isn't a genre all by itself since it can be used

as a form of personality piece, a bit of an expose,

a graphic side to history, humor,... And in photo

stories, the writing is often less important than the
            although no editor will object to your writing.well.
photos // But so many writers these days pack a camera

alongside their typewriter, that we think writers ought

to keep the photo story in mind as part of their
            ing
market/armada.

      The photo story has to satisfy all of the requires
                              create
for a good story.~~xx~~ you must ~~have~~ a lead photo, that

gets the reader hooked on your photo story and seta a

tone for the rest. Your pictures have to be organized

~~chronoxaiiy~~logically or logically. The story has to

have an ending or conclusion. (In a later chapter we'll

discuss tehnical aspects such as size, presentation,

quality, etc.)

      When we suggested to POPULAR SCIENCE that we ~~km~~ could

do an article about how home owners can paint their

palace ~~x~~only once every 10 years, the ~~dix~~ editors liked the

idea. We knew they would~~x~~! But they suggested, instead
            giving
of ~~telling~~ the information once in words and again in

pictures, why not do it only once, through pictures with

comprehensive captions. The result was our first pictorial

how-to story.

Page of first draft for *you* to practice editing. (Later, compare to *our* editing in Ill. 15.10.)

WEIGH ADJECTIVES AND ADVERBS

Adverbs and adjectives slow down the pace of reading. They dilute the impact of nouns and verbs. They diminish the author's authority, since people are trained to suspect a string of modifiers that accompanies a fact.

Here's an example of adjective overuse, from a student's first draft:

> When my *four-year-old* daughter *gently* slipped her mother's cigarette from its *familiar* pack, placed it *jauntily* at the edge of her mouth, and said, "Hey, Dad, howya doin'?" I entered the final phase of a *long, too* drawn out *personal* battle against smoking.

All the italicized words are extraneous. Read the sentence without them and see for yourself.

Here's a fact that loses credence due to the author's timidity:

> *Entering college freshmen, on the whole, are often prone to develop homesickness.*

A confident writer simply says, "College freshmen often become homesick."

Some modifiers sneak in by force of habit. We've seen them so often with certain nouns we forget they don't always belong together: *golden* opportunity, the *right* answers, *pretty* close, *force of* habit. Here's our rule for determining whether a modifier is needed: If the word adds meaning to only one other word, such as an adjective making a noun more precise or vivid, we try to cross them *both* out and look for a more explicit word. However, if the modifier adds substantial meaning to the *entire sentence*—better still, to the entire paragraph—we leave it in.

CONSIDER CLICHÉS

Clichés are not all taboo. The proper time to use one is when you want to make your idea sound familiar, commonplace, or old hat. The improper time is when you should find a vivid way to make your point.

ALWAYS AVOID JARGON

If the readers for whom you are writing understood the jargon, it wouldn't be jargon.

We know that the inventors of these words (such as *interpersonal communication* for conversation, and *overachiever* for someone who's been underrated in the first place) claim that their coinages clarify meaning and express subtle nuances. But some would-be writers hide their insecurity or lack of research behind these words. And jargon merely makes their writing bad.

VARY SENTENCE LENGTH

Make sentences as long as you need to, as short as you want. But don't make them all the same length. Many teachers try to convince beginning writers that short sentences are required for clear writing. But the fact is, we can relate complex ideas to one another most clearly in complex sentences. Carefully written, they're no harder to read than short sentences.

DON'T HAMSTRING YOUR PARAGRAPHS

You already have a natural rhythm to your paragraphs. Some are long, some short, depending on how much you have to say within the paragraphs. Consciously trying to write only very short paragraphs, as some journalism teachers suggest, defeats the purpose of paragraphing, which is to organize ideas into readable compartments which are then linked together with transitions. If you arbitrarily chop up your articles, you'll either put transitions into miniparagraphs and end up with a longer and more complicated article, or else you'll omit transitions and leave readers wondering just when you've hopped from one idea to another and just how the respective ideas relate.

Nonetheless, it is important to recognize that magazine paragraphs are as a rule shorter than book paragraphs and longer than newspaper paragraphs, and that the educational level of the readers often determines a magazine paragraph's average length. If you don't want your paragraphs arbitrarily chopped up for you, study the market your article is aimed at.

ERADICATE CUTESINESS

We all have fun hammering out clever turns of phrase that show off our normally hidden genius. Unfortunately, anything that makes the reader notice *the writing* instead of *what is written about* is distracting. And that's bad writing.

Nearly every beginning writer has to find a personal way to cope with cutesiness. When Frank was getting started, he'd go through every manuscript and cross out ten of his choicest expressions. That way, unless he'd had a particularly trite day at the typewriter, the cutesiness was extracted. Most of it turned out to be irrelevant anyway.

CUT AND PASTE

Two of the writer's most useful tools are scissors and a roll of Scotch tape; we use them on occasion to cut up the first draft, subtopic by subtopic and paragraph by paragraph, and then tape it back together in more logical or more exciting sequence. Sometimes, where reorganization involves only a few sentences or paragraphs, we just put circles around the sentences and scribble, "Move to page x"; on page x, we remind ourselves at the appropriate place, "Insert from page z."

In cutting and pasting, it's often necessary to add or delete transitions between joined portions. That's all part of good writing.

15·3   A Reference Shelf of Writing Basics

Within the limited confines of a single chapter, we can't begin a thorough treatment of how to become a good writer. We must presume that you already know how to write correct English. If you need more help, we recommend our textbook, *Good Writing* (Franklin Watts, Inc., 1980), which has hundreds of illustrations and self-help exercises. For quick summations, keep Strunk and White's *Elements of Style* near at hand. A good, up-to-date dictionary is also a must, but use it mainly to spell correctly *every* word in your manuscripts and to find definitions of unfamiliar words.

When you're looking for exactly the right words to use in your articles, a dictionary is not much help. For the noun that shows precisely what you want the reader to see, or the active verb that's so on-target you don't need modifiers, a thesaurus is the preferred tool.

Let's assume you're writing an article involving a *not entirely savory* character, but you want to find a more explicit, shorter way of describing him. Look at the choices you'll find in *Roget's International Thesaurus:*

> § 735: *cunning:* crafty, artful, wily, guileful, sly, tricky, insidious, shifty, smooth, cunning as a serpent, slippery as an eel, too clever by half, sneaky, stealthy, slick, vulpine, feline, Machiavellian.
>
> § 740: *lawlessness:* licentious, unrestrained, rampant, unaccountable, headstrong, disorderly, nihilistic, insubordinate, mutinous.
>
> § 758: *laxness:* lax, slack, imprecise, slipshod, negligent, remiss, indifferent, unrestrained, unexacting.

We recommend that every writer purchase a hardbound or paperback thesaurus and use it until, like ours, it's dog-eared (§ 692.33: worn, well-worn, deep-worn, worn-down, the worse for wear, timeworn, shopworn, shelfworn, worn to the stump, worn to the bone, worn ragged, worn to rags, worn to threads, threadbare, bare, sere [archaic]).

Another book we suggest for our students is *How to Make Money Writing Magazine Articles,* edited by the late Beatrice Schapper for the Society of Magazine Writers (which later became the American Society of Journalists and Authors). It's published by Arco, and there isn't another book like it. Eight top professional writers contributed their files, each for a particularly memorable magazine article. For each, you'll find facsimiles of the query letter, notes, correspondence, first draft, editing, and final manuscript that went into making the chosen article. Each author shares his memories of the assignment, and the result is a highly instructive, if slightly out-of-date, look at eight different working styles.

15·4 How to Prepare Your Final Manuscript

Prepare your manuscript for submission the way nearly all other professional magazine writers prepare theirs. That way, the editor will assume that yours is from a professional, too.

Use only 8½ × 11 paper.

Use only white paper.

Use only quality twenty-pound bond paper.

Don't use obviously expensive paper (with inlaid pattern, gaudy watermark, or such).

Don't use erasable bond paper.

Use only black ribbons that are *new* or *still very dark.* (If you're penurious, use old ribbons for your first drafts.)

Double-space.

Pica type is preferred over elite, but not enough for you to scrap your workable elite machine.

Set your margins at about 20 and 75 (pica) so you get a left-hand margin of 1½ to 2 inches, and a right-hand margin of about 1 inch.

Leave a margin of about 1½ inches at the top of your page and 1 inch at the bottom, to get about twenty-six lines per manuscript page.

Type only on one side of the paper.

Indent paragraphs five spaces.

Don't footnote unless the magazine usually prints footnotes; don't indent for long quotations unless it's the magazine's normal style.

Even if you own a typewriter with changeable type (such as the IBM Selectric), don't use a fancy script or italic typeface for any manuscript. Don't change typefaces in the midst of a manuscript, either. Italics are indicated by <u>underlining</u>.

Clean your typewriter's type whenever the *e, o,* or *d* start filling up with lint.

Put a copyright notice (see Chapter 16) and your name, address, and telephone number in the upper-left-hand corner of your manuscript's first page. (A title page that contains nothing but your identification and your article's title is for books and classroom essays.)

Put the page number at the top of each page. Also type in the title (or an abbreviated version) so the editor can keep your story separate from every other one piled on his desk.

You can fold manuscripts that are no more than four pages long. Mail others flat. Cardboard isn't necessary unless you're mailing illustrations at the same time.

Ill. 15.7 ——————————————————————

Dome Sweet Home

by Franklynn Peterson and Judi R. Kesselman

It's been a quarter century since Buckminster

Fuller told a generally unappreciative American public

about goedesic domes. However, artists, experimenters,

and an entire counter-culture quickly adopted Bucky's

globular network of triangles that offered maximum floor

space but required minimum amounts of building materials.

But the dome of that generation was too kinky to appeal

to the masses of home buyers, too unproven to merit

mortgages from conservative bankers, too unorthodix to

satisfy zoning and building codes. All that's changing!

Bob Casey, energetic president of the National

Association of Dome Home Manufacturers reports, "We're

got about 65 members who manufacture domes. All in all,

members and non-members must sell 5,000 to 10,000 dome

domes / 2

homes a year, but that's just a good guess. That's up
from almost zero only 5 years ago."

Casey adds that his^own company, Domes America, has an
8-week backlog of orders. "But I can show you at least
a hundred domes in the Chicago area. And we're erecting
a 55-foot dome at the Rockford (Ill.) air terminal, and
another one nearby that'll house a beauty parlor, barber
shop, photo studio, and other stores. But only 5 percent
of our domes are for commercial buildings, and 3 percent
are vacation homes. The other 92 percent of the domes
we sell are for family homes."

Dome building

"I got interested in domes through <u>Popular Science</u>
over 5 years ago, but I couldn't cut 2x4s accurately
enough to even think about building my own dome house
from scratch," says Charles Romaine of Laramie, Wyoming.
"Then I found a man near here who sells dome kits. I
picked up a 39-foot kit in mid-October 1976, and moved
my family into it in March 1977 even though all the finishing
work wasn't done yet. Building the dome was sort of a
family affair; nobody involved had ever built one before.

Romaine, brakeman for the Union Pacific Railroad,
says, "We got 1,100 square feet in our dome. We put two
bedrooms one one side, the bathroom's kinda in the center
and we left the rest undivided for a big kitchen,dining
and living area.

First two pages of manuscript, final draft, in correct format.

Send assigned (even on-spec) stories by first-class mail. Mark "assigned manuscript" on the top of the first page and in the lower-right- or left-hand corner of your envelope. This is to keep your prodigy from accidentally ending up on the slush pile of unsolicited manuscripts.

We've reproduced the first two pages of one of our manuscripts (Ill. 15.7) so you can see for yourself what ours look like when we submit them. Frankly, we aren't near-perfect typists. We invest heavily in bottles of Liquid Paper and sheets of Ko-Rec-Type and suggest you do likewise. Not every editor insists on secretarial school manuscripts, but we assume that our professionalism is weighed by the care we take with our submissions.

We *do* always read and correct even our final drafts. Editors appreciate small signs of careful, thoughtful proofreading and infinitely prefer an occasional smudge or crossed-out word to misspellings and the misuse of grammar and punctuation.

15·5   Three Edited Manuscripts

On the following pages, fully edited, are the three manuscript pages that were reproduced for you a few pages ago. See if you can find the reason for every change we made. It's really true that every time you edit someone else's manuscript you polish your own writing just a little more.

15·6   A Few Words About Word Processors

It's almost impossible to talk to writers these days without getting into a discussion of word processing. If you're just starting out, our advice is to forget about them until you're sure you're going to write long enough and hard enough to make one pay for itself. But if you're a professional writer, or a serious amateur who can afford one, you may want to give the matter serious thought. The time and aggravation you may save by computerizing your efforts may actually recoup the investment within a few years.

Computers and word processors are so different from the old-fashioned electric typewriter that we'd be wasting our time and yours if we tried to write down a comprehensive description of all that these electronic packages can do for you. You've got to actually play with one yourself to know whether it's for you. First find friends or colleagues who've made the investment, and try out their machines. Then shop around in computer stores and try out their machines. We spent six months shopping for our system, comparing various features in competing equipment ("hardware") and in the programs ("software") for each manufacturer's products. We finally settled on an NEC outfit as the best for our needs. (And we do mean *outfit*; a computer

Ill. 15.8 _____

At Christmas, everybody wrote about toys. But we asked,

what ~~xhmmxx~~ happens to all ~~of~~ the ~~those damned~~ battery powered

toys <u>after</u> Christmas, And ~~wmmkmxx we~~ wrote an expose about

how batteries are marketed: "The caustic truth about

batteries." ~~When/everybody/was~~ While all of our friends were encouraging people to ~~get~~ find

~~themselves~~ x creative ~~hobby~~ hobbies, we wrote "The Hazards of

Hobbies."

~~Every~~ Most magazines feels obliged to ~~do~~ run some seasonal material.

~~And~~ after a few years on the job, editors find Christmas run out of fresh-sounding ideas.

~~and similar editorial holiday issues to be more and more~~

~~depressing as fresh ideas get harder and harder to find.~~

Our newspaper group editor was no exception. One year we

did the coldest spot in the nation, the ~~xx~~ next the snowiest.

What next? Well, there was a northern Wisconsin town

that was red light district from one end to the other all during

summer 's tourist season. What went on there in the depths of winter? We called the article, ____.

"Where are the snows of next ~~x~~ year?" predicted

with help from the federal government's/climate weather and ~~xmx~~

experts, how much colder the U.S. was becoming, and on which states

how fast, and ~~where~~ the big snows would fall, and so on.

Then, too

Editors--and there is readers -- love predictions.

Next year we predicted thanks to the nation's to

#1 weather expert, an M.I.T. professor, that we were about Title:

to have a record cold winter. "It's going to be a red

flannel winter." We even sketched maps, based on the expert's that ed

~~prophs~~ prognostications, showing how much colder various

parts of the country would be and where the heaviest

snows would fall. It was a marvelous story. ~~xkmmx~~

(handwritten left margin, rotated) G We did the prediction bit again

Edited manuscript page. Compare to Ill. 15.4.

Ill. 15.9

++Sometimes the person who's lived the experience gets the entire by-line.

Other times, the actual author is listed second: "As told to...." Rarely, ~~i~~ m

usually only ~~in~~ for articles involving celebrities, ~~does~~ can the author ~~get xxa~~ count on a traditional

by-line.

~~pieking xup xthe xentrant xREADER'S x DIGEST xwe xfind~~

~~personal xexperience xstories~~

How many of us can survive enough falls off 28
near
stor~~ie~~y buildings, or xxxxx recover from enough/fatal

illnesses, to make a living at writing personal experience

do   it a
articles? So, the pros who make ~~at a~~ living ~~at writing~~

~~personal experience stories~~ write about some body else's

triumphs. ⊕ ~~Xxaax~~ The dean of personal
must be magazine writer
experience story tellers ~~is~~ Terry Morris, one-time

president of the American Society of Journalists and

Authors ~~and prolixxprofit~~ ~~prolific magazine writers.~~

Terry abandoned
~~She switched,~~ about 1950, ~~from~~ (writing shortstor~~ies~~y)

in favor   human-interest magazine articles about people

Her genius for
in crisis. ~~But she never abandoned her gift for~~

carried over from fiction to non-fiction and
telling a touching story, ~~so~~ she sold her first two

art~~i~~cles to COSMOPOLITAN and McCALL'S early in 1951. Not a bad
beginning!
Terry's all-time favorite ~~was~~ is "Please don't lose faith
from the viewpoint of
in Me" an as-told-to article ~~by~~ the mother of a
son.
schizophrenic ~~xsaanxthat~~ McCALL'S ran it ~~in~~ July 1953;

we've reprinted the first page nearby~~s~~ so you can

molds
study how a master ~~handles~~ somebody else's personal experience.

Edited manuscript page. Compare to Ill. 15.5.

Ill. 15.10

6.11 The Photo story

to be added to our 10 standard formats.

This is a bonus! ^The photo story ~~was~~ technically

isn't a genre all by itself~~, since~~ it can be ~~used~~

~~as a form of~~ ^a personality piece, a bit of an expose,

a graphic ~~side~~ approach to history, humor ~~...~~ But ^in photo

stories, the writing is often less important than the
          although no editor will object to ~~your~~ good writing. ~~well.~~
photos. ^ ~~But~~ so many writers these days pack a camera

alongside the~~ir~~ typewriter, ~~that~~ we think ~~writers~~ you ought

to keep the photo story in mind as part of ~~their~~ your
          ing
market/armada.
              in a photo themselves
     The photo~~s~~ story, ha~~s~~ to satisfy all of the require~~m~~ments
                                   create
for a good story. ~~xx~~ You must ~~have~~ a lead photo~~s~~, that
              which are detailed in chapter ___.
gets the reader hooked ~~on your photo story~~ and sets a
              of the photos.
tone for the rest. Your pictures have to be organized

~~chronologically~~ or logically. The story has to

have ~~an ending or~~ conclusion. (In a later chapter we'll
                      of submitting photos
discuss te~~h~~chnical aspects such as size, ~~presentation,~~

quality, etc.)

     When we suggested to POPULAR SCIENCE ~~that we do could~~
                 showing that
~~do~~ an article ~~about how~~ home owners ~~can~~ need paint their

palace~~s~~ ~~x~~only once every 10 years, the ~~xix~~ editors liked the

idea. ~~We knew they would!~~ But, they suggested, instead
          supplying
of ~~giving~~ ~~telling~~ the information once in words and ^once again in
                                                  once
pictures, why not do it only once, through pictures with

comprehensive captions. The result was our first pictorial

how-to story.

Edited manuscript page. Compare to Ill. 15.6.

can have a number of separate components and fill a large desk.) We found the following guidelines helpful in making our selection, and pass them on to you.

1. If you buy equipment that's designed only for word processing, you're missing out on the valuable business uses offered by any small computer: bookkeeping, research telecommunications with data banks, and file maintenance of such things as editors' names and addresses.

2. The *software*—the computer program that tells otherwise ignorant circuits to copy down your words and to help you edit them—is as important as the *hardware* you purchase. Unfortunately, you generally can't interchange programs among the many brands of computers. Writers ought to concentrate on selecting the best word processing program rather than the best-priced hardware. No matter how inexpensive or cleverly designed, some manufacturers' computers do not come with easy-to-use word processing software. Some of the programs offered on lower-priced units (and on at least one expensive model) can't perform many of the following functions, which we consider basic to quick and effortless writing:

   transporting chunks of copy quickly from one place to another

   copying text, without destroying the original, onto another computer disk or onto another spot on the same disk

   the following editing modes: *revise,* to make permanent changes in our copy, with the option to store the earlier version or erase it: *view,* to make changes that can be printed out for our consideration without permanently losing our original manuscript copy; *replace,* to change just the few words we want edited; *search,* to go quickly to a selected word or phrase in the manuscript; *append,* to add one set of pages to another and repaginate automatically; and *merge,* to add one piece of manuscript copy to another. And each command that calls up these wonderful operations should require one or two keystrokes on easy-to-use, easy-to-hit keys.

   Good word processor programs add individualized flexibility by permitting the user to insert her own library of commands. Ours permits us to file 52 separate page formats or blocks of text, each up to 1,500 characters long. We can call them up, magically, to appear in our manuscript with just 2 key strokes. When we hit "E," for instance, our pre-programmed machine automatically sets up the correct alignment for Express Mail forms, prints in our name & address, prints $1,000 in the value square, and then prints in the recipient's name & address with just one more command—at 200 words per minute.

Some word processing programs don't leave anything to chance. They flash messages onscreen whenever you need to hit another special button. Having all those prompts and menus is valuable only for beginners. Later on they get in the way of seeing the maximum amount of copy, and that's the most important consideration for most writers. You may want to keep that in mind when you're shopping around.

3. For writers, the computer's printer is the one most important piece of hardware. Editors accept manuscripts printed on the less expensive *dot matrix printers* that are most often sold in computer packages. But for query letters, the more expensive *letter quality printers* are usually *de rigeur*. It's the printers that are most likely to suffer breakdowns, so don't chintz on this item.

4. The computer retailer will be a VIP during your first weeks. He'll hold your hand while you set up your first purchase and learn to use it. If your time is money, pick a retailer you're comfortable with.

Most manuals that come with computers are abominably written. But they're all we have, and they do disgorge valuable tips once the user relaxes at the keyboard. The advice given in many manuals is to fool around with unimportant projects while you learn, but we haven't seen anybody really learn anything that way. Instead, try starting with an actual piece of writing and allow an additional week to complete it. Be extra careful at first to keep backup copies of everything you write—on discs as well as on paper—and plunge right in with the manual close at hand.

Switching to word processing really is easier than most of us used to believe. Frank's equipment arrived by UPS on a Monday. He unboxed it, found outlets for all its plugs, started it working, and wrote his first computerized query letter on Tuesday. On the following Monday he packed away his obsolete electric watchamacallit. Judi's machine arrived on a Thursday. She spent the weekend catching up on her personal correspondence to learn the computer's quirks, and on Monday morning she began the next manuscript, a word-games book, on her NEC. She estimates that it took *one-half* as long as it would have taken had she written it on a typewriter.

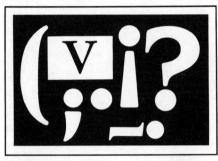

How to Be a Pro

Chapter Sixteen

The Writer and the Law

F ROM THE CLASSES WE'VE TAUGHT, WORKSHOPS we've given, and writers' conferences we've participated in, we know that yearling writers are full of questions about the law. Copyright, libel, taxes, privacy, slander, defamation, contracts—they want to know it all. They think that it's all vital to their careers as writers.

When you get right down to it, though, the law seldom affects writers except in several limited ways:

You should know about libel and privacy laws in order to write defensible articles.

You need to know a smattering of facts about copyright law.

You must live with the tax laws, like it or not.

16·1 Libel

To paraphrase a definition from Harold Nelson and Dwight Teeter's textbook *Law of Mass Communications,* libel is defamation that occurs by written communication which exposes a person to hatred, ridicule, or contempt, lowers him in the esteem of his fellows, causes him to be shunned, or injures him in his business or calling.

The statutes on libel vary from state to state, and judicial precedents waver from decade to decade. Not many years ago, we were able to tell students that they'd almost have to hire a good lawyer as co-author if they wanted to deliberately libel somebody. Now, however, the pendulum has swung against journalists again. We have to be a great deal more cautious when we write about people or institutions in our articles.

Libel is a writer's concern for two reasons: First of all, in almost every libel suit, the publisher is only one of the defendants; another is the author. Secondly, you can't count on publishers to know what is and what is not libelous; you can't even count on them to hire lawyers to read your manuscripts for libel. They may send controversial ones out for legal opinions, but it's not necessarily the controversial manuscripts that give the most problems.

For instance, not long ago we were assigned to do a simple, uncontroversial, bread-and-butter piece. We weren't thinking consciously about libel at any time during the research and writing that went into it. Yet our instincts as serious journalists literally saved the day for us and for the magazine. Without planning it that way, we covered every opening through which a libel action could be pursued.

We researched the manufacturers involved, we researched the public and private agencies that had to pass judgment on the soundness of the product, we researched the opinions of objective outside observers. And among those outside observers was one expert whom we interviewed by telephone. Half a year later, the expert tested our adeptness at handling the legal questions of libel.

The test started just after the issue with our article hit the newsstands. The magazine received a complaint letter from an executive of a company not even mentioned in the story. In essence the builder threatened to sue if not given space in a forthcoming issue to tell that he took serious exception to a quoted statement from the expert.

We paid little attention to the executive's letter because a journalist cannot libel an individual simply by referring to a large group he belongs to. (On the other hand, if we'd said that most magicians in Chicago were perverts, and there were only three magicians in Chicago, then any one of them might be able to sue us for libel because the odds would be two out of three that we were referring to them.)

Now, on to the expert. He, too, wrote a letter to the magazine, and sent it by way of the enraged executive. Judging by *his* letter, he might have had cause for a libel suit if we'd really made the mistakes he claimed we made, and in so doing had damaged his reputation. The most important of his claims was that we'd misquoted him badly. Since the classic defense against most libel actions is the *truth,* if we could establish that what we wrote was reasonably accurate, we'd undercut his claim.

We pulled out the story file. Sure enough, there in our notes was the *exact* quote, so we passed the accuracy test. (Frankly, not every quote in print so closely matches our notes as his did. God smiled on us that day.) But *context* figures in too.

Our notes showed context: they established that we'd been talking to the expert about the very same matters that we later wrote about in that part of the article where he'd been quoted. So we neither misquoted him nor quoted him out of context. Or so we said. If it went to court, so far the case would have been his word against our word along with our notes.

The expert also wrote, in his letter via the executive, that he didn't remember talking to us and, if he had, certainly he hadn't spoken for publication.

Again our scrupulous files saved the day. First, our telephone bill for the proper month established that we'd received a collect phone call from the appropriate city on the very *date* we'd scribbled at the top of our notes—*and always do.* The call lasted twenty-three minutes, so he certainly hadn't called to say, "Leave me alone." Our notes for the previous day showed a phone call to the public relations office at the expert's employer. Alongside the phone number were the names of two experts the public relations department had recommended, one of them our potential plaintiff. We called the public relations office again, and were reassured by them that they'd told the expert why he was to call us—to be quoted in an article.

So far, so good. If we went to trial, we could establish that the conversation took place, that the expert knew why it took place, and that we'd quoted him accurately according to our notes.

At that point we had to face one of the trickier and fastest-changing parts of the libel law: the definition of public figures v. private figures.

If the expert were deemed a public figure, *he'd* not only have to prove that we'd misquoted him, but that we'd done it with malice—a word commonly defined as *reckless disregard of the truth.* If he were a private figure, then *we* might have to prove that we hadn't been negligent: that we had exercised reasonable care in attempting to discover the truth or falsity of what we'd said in print. This could have applied even to the truth or falsity of what we'd quoted the expert as having said.

People are considered private figures if they don't seek publicity, don't do things that affect the public at large, and don't affect the news which reaches the public. However, private figures can become limited public figures under libel law when they intrude or allow themselves to be intruded into newsworthy events. Under that definition, it is entirely possible that our expert would have been called a public figure by the trial judge, getting us off the hook of having to prove that we weren't negligent. The trouble was, a lot of time and money would have been wasted getting to that day in court. And what if the judge had decided the expert was a private figure?

Again our professional instincts backed us up. There seemed to be three facts at possible issue in the quoted statement. Checking our notes, we reassured ourselves and the magazine that, on each of the three points, we'd interviewed two other people besides the expert to establish the accuracy of what he had told us. Our notes had preserved the names, titles, phone numbers, and comments of the six people who verified the information in the expert's quote. No reasonable judge should have said we'd exercised less than reasonable care in attempting to discover the truth. (We don't always triple-check every statement, but our instincts had told us that the expert's statement might be opinion rather than fact, and we wanted to find out for ourselves.)

There was still one nagging matter left, and there wasn't much we could do about it. The expert could still claim that we had damaged his reputation despite all the care and accuracy we'd used. True, he wouldn't have had a strong case, considering how well we'd covered every other aspect of the libel law. But he could have brought in the disgruntled executive, who might have said he thought less of him as a result of our article. So we asked the head of the public relations office at the expert's employer what he thought of the article; he said it was excellent, and volunteered that the quote in question showed high character on the part of the expert and not ill repute. We asked the head of the product's trade association for comment; he said that over 10,000 people had liked the article well enough to write in for more data, and even volunteered to go into court on our side if the matter ever came to that. Breathing a sigh of relief, we passed on to the magazine's lawyers photocopies of everything we'd dug out. The complainers folded up their tents, and that was that.

16·2 Privacy

People have the right to be left alone as long as they keep themselves from becoming public figures. Somebody who is not newsworthy *at the moment,* who is not a government official, and who doesn't comment publicly or for publication about anything of any sort of public concern, has the right not to be quoted, pictured, or named in publications. This has potentially serious ramifications for most writers.

Every time you ask somebody—your neighbor or a total stranger —how she raises her kids, and then quote her in print, you are beyond a doubt invading her privacy unless she's given you permission to (1) interview her, (2) quote her, and (3) use her name in your article. How can you be sure that in six months, when she sees your published story and reads what she said earlier about her lousy brats, she'll remember that she gave you broad consent? The fact is, you can't unless you had her sign a release. Using such a release is not standard operating procedure for journalists at the moment, but it may become common if the privacy pendulum swings further against us.

To date, the most serious privacy cases against magazines to reach the courts have involved people who were once in the news but had faded from the public eye. One, for example, was instituted against *Reader's Digest* by a onetime truck hijacker who said that he'd gone straight for eleven years by the time his name was smeared by a *Digest* article on hijacking. Another was brought by a man who'd been a math prodigy and, at the age of sixteen, had lectured to eminent mathematicians amid great publicity. *The New Yorker* profiled the grown-up math genius twenty-five years later, saying he was living in a seedy flat and was employed at menial labor. In both cases the courts sided with the magazines and authors, saying, in essence, "Once a public figure, always a public figure *to some extent.*" In the latter case, the judge wrote:

> At least we would permit limited scrutiny of the "private" life of any person who has achieved, or has had thrust upon him, the questionable and indefinable status of "public figure."

But in 1971, *Sports Illustrated* profiled a body surfer. He granted the writers long interviews and many photos, which in the court's eyes constituted his consent to the story's being published. Just before publication, however, the surfer learned that there were some aspects of the story that he didn't want published. He withdrew his consent. *Sports Illustrated,* on advice of lawyers, ran the story anyway and lost its day in court. The judge wrote that if consent is withdrawn prior to publication, "the consequent publicity is without consent."

The appeal judge gave *Sports Illustrated* a limited reprieve. It didn't have to pay damages to the body surfer. But the appeal decision haunts journalists, publishers, and constitutional lawyers to this day, since there's no telling when it will be used as precedent to decide another privacy case:

> In determining what is a matter of legitimate public interest, account must be taken of the customs and conventions of the community; and in the last analysis what is proper becomes a matter of the community mores. The line is to be drawn when the publicity ceases to be the giving of information to which the public is entitled, and becomes a morbid and sensational prying into public lives for its own sake, with which a reasonable member of the public, with decent standards, would say that he had no concern. . . . {Virgil v. Time Inc., 527 F. 2nd 1122, 1124; 9th Cir. 1975}

In light of decisions such as the ones just quoted, a noted literary lawyer advised us once at an ASJA meeting to use a simple release form like this one:

> I hereby consent to publication of the interview conducted by . . . . and consent to its publication by . . . . and its subsidiaries throughout the world.

There's no doubt that using a release form for all of our face-to-face interviews would be a fine safeguard. But we haven't started using them. None of our colleagues, that we know of, has either. It must be because, in the past, we enjoyed the giving and receiving of trust that went with being a magazine writer. It's going to take something mighty dramatic to shake us out of that romanticism.

16·3 Copyright

There are at least two reasons for knowing rudimentary copyright law: (1) to know what your rights are so you can maximize your protection and your income from these rights; (2) to know how much of somebody else's copyrighted writing you can incorporate into your own.

As drafted by Congress, the 1976 Copyright Act is quite simple and straightforward. Freely interpreted in the offices of various magazine publishers, the law appears to be complicated and to deal harshly with the rights of writers. So when you are looking for information about provisions of the copyright act, choose your sources carefully.

As Congress drafted it, the 1976 act grants an immediate, automatic, and almost unlimited copyright on your work the instant you write it. You do not have to register your article first with the U.S. Copyright Office; you do not have to type a copyright notice on your manuscript (although it doesn't hurt if you do). When your work is *published,* a copyright notice such as *Copyright © 1984 George Washington* must be printed in the proper location. The general notice that the publisher prints near the front of the magazine protects *your* own copyright in *your* own article.

The copyright law is very protective of creators of artistic works of all sorts—poets, magazine writers, book authors, lyricists, painters, sculptors, and even composers of rock-and-roll music. First of all, in case publication takes place without a copyright notice, the law allows five years for you to correct the error. Second, you don't lose copyright protection if you don't fill out the Copyright Office's forms—although you can't sue for infringement until you do fill them in. Third, the new law, unlike the older version, makes it clear that you may sell bits and pieces of your overall copyright.

Which piece of your copyright should you sell to a magazine? Only a license to publish your article once. You can broaden that a bit by licensing it to publish your article the first time in North America. (U.S. publishers sell enough copies of their magazines in Canada that *first North American serial rights* are sold instead of only *first U.S. serial rights.*)

To protect your interests, as well as to alert publishers that you know the value of what you are protecting, certain formalities are worthwhile. First, at the top of the first page of every manuscript, type *Copyright ©* followed by the year, followed by your name. Example: *Copyright © 1984 George Washington.* Also type *First North American serial rights for sale,* unless you've already sold those rights and are selling a reprint. In that case, type *One-time serial rights for sale.*

The first page of a manuscript has traditionally doubled as something of an invoice between writer and publisher. But it's not a very good medium. The better way for you to alert publishers that you know your rights and expect to have them respected is to submit a formal invoice with every article. This is typical of the language we use on our invoices:

> A *license for first North American serial rights to my Copyright* © 1987 *article* "How I Became a Billionaire" *will be granted to* MadCap *Magazine upon payment of $1,000.*

The principal hitch in the 1976 copyright law is a provision known as "work for hire." It defines the only area in which the author is not the owner of the copyright on his work. In its major use—also its clearest use—"work for hire" applies to staff employees. If you punch a clock at *Time* magazine and write an article for it, Time Inc. owns the copyright.

But the definitions section of the new copyright law includes a second, more controversial meaning for the term "work for hire":

> *a work specially ordered or commissioned for use as a contribution to a collective work . . . if the parties expressly agree in a written instrument signed by them that the work shall be considered a work made for hire.* {17 *U.S.C. 101*}

What's at stake is this: If you write an article and either openly *or* unknowingly let it pass to a publisher as a work made for hire, the publisher will own 100 percent of the copyright. You will not be able to sell or control the sale of reprint rights to other magazines. You will not be able to sell or control the sale of reprint rights to book publishers. You will not be able to sell or control the sale of your article in a film, play, film script, or TV show. You may not even be able to stop your publisher from printing the article on T-shirts.

To prevent transfer of rights without your knowledge, the copyright statute is very explicit about how your work becomes a "work made for hire": First, it has to be specially ordered or commissioned for use as a contribution to a collective work—and most magazine assignments are just that. Second, both you and the publisher—or his representative, the editor—have to agree *in writing* that it is a work made for hire; both of you have to sign the agreement. And third, since the statute uses the word *expressly,* whatever document you and the publisher sign must not beat around the bush; it must state clearly that the purpose of the paper being signed is to transform your article into a work made for hire.

Some publishers send checks with rubber-stamped notations on the backs that say something to the effect that they are buying all rights—which is a term left over from the pre-1976 copyright law. They must believe that if you sign the checks, you endorse the "work made for hire" status. According to both Barbara Ringer, U.S.

Register of Copyright, and eminent UCLA law professor Melville Nimmer, it's not true.

If you receive a check marked "all rights" or "for hire," the most forthright thing to do is to return it and demand a new one without the rubber stamp. We've done that on a number of occasions with steady markets. But when you're dealing with magazines, a check in hand is usually worth two in the mail. Another action you can take is to cross out the rubber-stamped nonsense, endorse the check, and deposit it. We've done this on a number of occasions too. We've also, when whim has overtaken us, simply changed "all rights" into "no rights." Nobody—certainly not the bank—seems to know or care about a check-editing job. Even under the old copyright law—which gave less protection to writers—we collected from one magazine publisher who sold reprint rights for our articles to an encyclopedia. Every one of this publisher's checks had contained the "all rights" rubber stamp; we'd crossed them all out. Since our case never went to trial, we can't tell you what the judge would have said. But we did enjoy depositing the nonrubber-stamped check for several thousand dollars from the offending publisher.

A third recourse you may have is to deposit your check without signing it. Most banks accept such an arrangement, although often you have to remind tellers about bank policy. We're not sure whether this is better or worse than the second method, and lawyers we've asked won't venture an opinion.

So far there have been almost no significant tests of the 1976 copyright law in the courts. The U.S. Copyright Office has been in the forefront in protecting authors' rights under the new law, but we think that's a shame: it's the writers who ought to be in the fore.

16·4 Fair Use

This is the second area under copyright law that is of concern to magazine writers. Fair use does not deal with *your* copyright, but *somebody else's* copyright on words you want to use.

Both the old and new copyright laws allow authors to copy, without having to get permission, parts of copyrighted works—within reason:

> You cannot copy so much of somebody else's work that you diminish its commercial value.
>
> You should not copy somebody else's work without crediting its author.

As you can see, what is *fair* is left pretty much to your discretion—and to the judge's if the original author wants to challenge you after the fact.

Copying one line out of a four-line poem *might be*—but probably would not be—considered more than fair use. Incorporating three paragraphs without permission from another author's eight-page article into your own ten-page article would probably be abusing fair use. On the other hand, if you were writing a book about, let us say, copyright, and you found an eight-page article by the preeminent authority on fair use, you probably could quote three paragraphs of the article in your 300-page book without violating fair use.

In general, if we're writing about a particular subject, and something that is copyrighted by another author definitely figures into the subject, we feel safe using it. But we use it sparingly, with credit, and only if it's the best literary device we know of to make the point we have to make. We don't copy somebody else's words out of laziness, and we never copy surreptitiously.

It's important here to remember that copyright protects words —specific words and the sequence in which they're used. Ideas, conceptions, philosophies, facts, observations, and similar cerebrations are *not* protected by copyright. We always do credit another author whose intellectual observations or conclusions we borrow, but not because of fair use strictures, only out of fair play.

16·5 A Journalist's Code of Ethics

The American Society of Journalists and Authors has, over the years, evolved a realistic code of ethics that is, at the same time, idealistic enough to keep the subject of ethics on the minds of writers and editors. With permission, we copy that code of ethics here in its entirety (Ill. 16.1).

Ill. 16.1 ───────────────────────────

Code of Ethics and Fair Practices
PREAMBLE

Over the years, an unwritten code governing editor-writer relationship has arisen. The American Society of Journalists and Authors has compiled the major principles and practices of that code that are generally recognized as fair and equitable.

The ASJA has also established a Committee on Editor-Writer Relations to investigate and mediate disagreements brought before it, either by members or by editors. In its activity this committee shall rely on the following guidelines.

1. Truthfulness, Accuracy, Editing
The writer shall at all times perform professionally and to the best of his or her ability, assuming primary responsibility for truth and accuracy. No writer shall deliberately write into an article a dishonest, distorted or inaccurate statement.

Editors may correct or delete copy for purposes of style, grammar, conciseness or arrangement, but may not change the intent or sense without the writer's permission.

2. Sources
A writer shall be prepared to support all statements made in his or her manuscripts, if requested. It is understood, however, that the publisher shall respect any and all promises of confidentiality made by the writer in obtaining information.

3. Ideas
An idea shall be defined not as a subject alone but as a subject combined with an approach. A writer shall be considered to have a proprietary right to an idea suggested to an editor and to have priority in the development of it.

4. Acceptance of an Assignment
A request from an editor that the writer proceed with an idea, however worded and whether oral or written, shall be considered an assignment. (The word "assignment" here is understood to mean a definite order for an article.) It shall be the obligation of the writer to proceed as rapidly as possible toward the completion of an assignment, to meet a deadline mutually agreed upon, and not to agree to unreasonable deadlines.

5. Conflict of Interest

The writer shall reveal to the editor, before acceptance of any assignment, any actual or potential conflict of interest, including but not limited to any financial interest in any product, firm, or commercial venture relating to the subject of the article.

6. Report on Assignment
If in the course of research or during the writing of the article, the writer concludes that the assignment will not result in a satisfactory article, he or she shall be obliged to so inform the editor.

7. Withdrawal
Should a disagreement arise between the editor and writer as to the merit or handling of an assignment, the editor may remove the writer on payment of mutually satisfactory compensation for the effort already expended, or the writer may withdraw without compensation and, if the idea for the assignment originated with the writer, may take the idea elsewhere without penalty.

8. Agreements
The practice of written confirmation of all agreements between editors and writers is strongly recommended, and such confirmation may originate with the editor, the writer, or an agent. Such a memorandum of confirmation should list all aspects of the assignment including subject, approach, length, special instructions, payments, deadline, and kill fee (if any). Failing prompt contradictory response to such a memorandum, both parties are entitled to assume that the terms set forth therein are binding.

9. Rewriting
No writer's work shall be rewritten without his or her advance consent. If an editor requests a writer to rewrite a manuscript, the writer shall be obliged to do so but shall alternatively be entitled to withdraw the manuscript and offer it elsewhere.

10. Bylines
Lacking any stipulation to the contrary, a byline is the author's unquestioned right. All advertisements of the article should also carry the author's name. If an author's byline is omitted from a published article, no matter what the cause or reason, the publisher shall be liable to compensate the author financially for the omission.

11. Updating
If delay in publication necessitates extensive updating of an article, such updating shall be done by the author, to whom additional compensation shall be paid.

12. Reversion of Rights
A writer is not paid by money alone. Part of the writer's compensation is the intangible value of timely publication. Consequently, if after six months the publisher has not scheduled an article for publication, or within twelve months has not published an article, the manuscript and all rights therein should revert to the author without penalty or cost to the author.

13. Payment for Assignments
An assignment presumes an obligation upon the publisher to pay for the writer's work upon satisfactory completion of the assignment, according to the agreed terms. Should a manuscript that has been accepted, orally or in writing, by a publisher or any representative or employee of the publisher, later be deemed unacceptable, the publisher shall nevertheless be obliged to pay the writer in full according to the agreed terms.

If an editor withdraws or terminates an assignment, due to no fault of the writer, after work has begun but prior to completion of the manuscript, the writer is entitled to compensation for work already put in; such compensation shall be negotiated between editor and author and shall be commensurate with the amount of work already completed. If a completed assignment is not acceptable, due to no fault of the writer, the writer is nevertheless entitled to payment; such payment, in common practice, has varied from half the agreed-upon price to the full amount of that price.

14. Time of Payments
The writer is entitled to payment for an accepted article within ten days of delivery. No article payment should ever be subject to publication.

15. Expenses
Unless otherwise stipulated by the editor at the time of an assignment, a writer shall assume that normal, out-of-pocket expenses will be reimbursed by the publisher. Any extraordinary expenses anticipated by the writer shall be discussed with the editor prior to incurring them.

16. Insurance
A magazine that gives a writer an assignment involving any extraordinary hazard shall insure the writer against death or disability during the course of travel or the hazard, or, failing that, shall honor the cost of such temporary insurance as an expense account item.

17. Loss of Personal Belongings
If, as a result of circumstances or events directly connected with a perilous assignment and due to no fault of the writer, a writer suffers loss of personal belongings or professional equipment or incurs bodily injury, the publisher shall compensate the writer in full.

18. Copyright, Additional Rights

It shall be understood, unless otherwise stipulated in writing, that sale of an article manuscript entitles the purchaser to first North American publication rights only, and that all other rights are retained by the author. Under no circumstances shall an independent writer be required to sign a so-called "all rights transferred" or "work made for hire" agreement as a condition of assignment, of payment, or of publication.

19. Reprints

All revenues from reprints shall revert to the author exclusively, and it is incumbent upon a publication to refer all requests for reprint to the author. The author has a right to charge for such reprints and must request that the original publication be credited.

20. Agents

According to the Society of Authors' Representatives, the accepted fee for an agent's services has long been ten percent of the writer's receipts, except for foreign rights representation. An agent may not represent editors or publishers. In the absence of any agreement to the contrary, a writer shall not be obliged to pay an agent a fee on work negotiated, accomplished and paid for without the assistance of the agent.

21. TV and Radio Promotion

The writer is entitled to be paid for personal participation in TV or radio programs promoting periodicals in which the writer's work appears.

22. Idemnity

No writer should be obliged to indemnify any magazine or book publisher against any claim, actions, or proceedings arising from an article or book.

23. Proofs

The editor shall submit edited proofs of the author's work to the author for approval, sufficiently in advance of publication that any errors may be brought to the editor's attention. If for any reason a publication is unable to so deliver or transmit proofs to the author, the author is entitled to review the proofs in the publication's office.

16·6 Taxes

It's a lost cause to point out that governments used to support their artists instead of the other way around. Or to add that the free lancer enjoys neither the lobby of big business nor the protective paternalism the government gives to small business. Nonetheless, many provisions of the tax laws have been interpreted to help us in our continuing struggle to keep groceries on the table. But since full-time free lancers are as rare as bald eagles, you may have to teach your local tax auditor how his provisions apply to us.

In the first place, every full-time professional free-lance writer has to accept—and make the doubting tax auditor understand—the principle that everything we do is income-producing. These examples may sound familiar to you.

If you're at a party and somebody says, as they so often do, "Hey, you oughtta do a story about . . .," and the story makes money, you have to pay tax on the money. You are within your rights to deduct the cost of giving and going to parties if you find they lead to article sales.

Likewise, you travel to North Dakota on what you've told the kids is a vacation. But you take pictures of buffalo that end up eventually in a story for a travel magazine, and you meet a crusty old-timer who talks about uranium mining and sell his profile to a company-sponsored magazine. You are within your rights to deduct most of the cost of your trip since you sure are going to be required to pay taxes on the income from the resulting articles and photos.

The principle you must keep in mind, as a full-time free-lance magazine writer, is *intent.* If you can show that you consistently go to parties intending to find article material, that's all the law really asks for. The same for your trips. The fact that you pay taxes on the income resulting from the parties and trips, *before* being audited, helps to document your honest intent. And keeping records of story ideas developed at parties and on trips—or during other forms of research —backs up your serious intent.

Part-time magazine writers can take part-time advantage of deducting expenses. The key philosophical point there again is intent. You have to have offered for sale the stories for which you ran up research and writing expenses. You do not have to have sold, only offered for sale. There are limitations on how many years in a row you can claim to have lost money—spent more than you took in—but rules on this change so often you'll have to research what's applicable when you need to know.

As important as your intent—which you can demonstrate only circumstantially—are your records. You have to prove *where* every penny of your expense money went, *why* it went, *when, how much,* and *to whom.* For expenses below twenty-five-dollars, Uncle Sam used to take your written diary entry as sufficient proof for almost everything. (Check on current regulations for this changing guideline.) In whatever diary you choose to use, make a habit of jotting down stories you're working on, people you're meeting, trips you're taking, money you're spending. You'd be surprised how fuzzy your memory gets about why you went to Hawaii, what you did there, what you wrote about it afterward, and who published (or refused to publish) it.

Writers, like all other professionals, have to hold on to their records until there's no chance the IRS wants to see them. For instance, if you buy a house or condominium apartment to use as your office, and depreciate it over a twenty-year period, you must keep all pertinent records for twenty years plus *at least* the three years during which the IRS can audit your tax returns after the twentieth year. Julian Block, noted tax writer, recommends that you routinely hold on to *all* records for at least three years after you've used them in filing a tax return. That includes letters offering articles for sale. How else do you substantiate that you were in the business of selling the articles for which you claim the expense deductions?

An accountant may be able to help you. However, we've tried a number of different accountants, all highly recommended by lawyers and business friends, and so far haven't found any who could cope with the peculiarities of the business of free-lance writing. Julian warns, "The IRS is one place to get information, but be aware that you can't absolutely rely on them. Even in the IRS's own book, *Your Federal Income Tax,* mistakes are inevitable, and the IRS is not bound by them."

You may have to apply your research skills to your tax questions, as we've done most of the time we've been in doubt. We locate books and articles with tax (and other) advice for businesses, and tailor the tips to our own peculiar craft. Although it's worked for us so far, we're a long way from writing a book called *Tax Tips for Free-Lance Writers.* Maybe you can write that one.

Chapter Seventeen

Economics:
The 3 R's of Writing

I T OUGHT TO BE OBVIOUS THAT IF YOU WANT TO be a professional magazine writer, not a dilettante, economics will have to be on your mind as often as exposition, collecting money as often as quoting experts. But far too many beginners seem to have grown up on Eve Arden and David Niven movies in which debonair authors are wined and dined by fat-cat socialites, or kept by sex-starved debutantes. Alas, when the house lights go up, it isn't that way at all.

Being a professional writer means unflinchingly balancing income against expenditures. Weighing the glamour of a by-line in low-paying *Atlantic* against the comfort of a well-paid but unby-lined piece in *American Hospitals*. Recycling sixteen different excuses that keep the lights turned on until the check comes from the corporation whose million-dollar computer had its monthly breakdown. Telling the kids their bikes will arrive a little late this Christmas because, after paying bonuses to salaried staff, the magazine can't pay until January for the story you turned in last September. If that's the life you're prepared to lead, and if you promise us—*here and now*—that you'll try to go at it with your eyes wide open, we'll share with you the real facts of economic life for the professional writer. We've boiled them down to three Rs: rates, research, and reality.

17·1 Rates, the First R

The income you get from writing is the *assets* side of your writing ledger. Once you've decided to write professionally, you must also decide to maximize that income. There are several ways to accomplish that.

One, of course, is to move as quickly as possible from lower-paying magazine markets into higher-paying ones. But there are limitations to this route. First, you can't count on moving into a higher-paying bracket until you've honed your skills at the lower level. That takes time and perseverance. Second, as you move progressively toward higher and higher-paying magazines, the number of other writers trying to sell to the same markets increases geometrically. That means *your* ideas will have to be more unique, and more uniquely presented, than those of the writers who got there first and know the ropes better than you. But almost every magazine writer who is selling to high-paying markets today started at lower-paying ones.

Another way to earn more money from your writing is to make sure that the magazines you write for steadily raise the rates they pay you. This shouldn't seem controversial in the least, but it is in many circles. Some magazine publishers believe that even if writers do dependable, consistently top-notch jobs, they never deserve raises.

But you do deserve raises. After you've successfully completed several articles for one magazine, you're worth a great deal more money to that editor. First, she probably doesn't have to spend as much of her time editing your articles since by then you've learned the magazine's style. Second, if you've proven you're dependable by delivering articles in publishable shape when you've promised to deliver them, she doesn't need to buy inventory as insurance against missed deadlines or copy that skirts the mark. Isn't that worth a higher rate of pay? We think so, and it's a question you ought to put to any editor who insists on paying you the same rate for your fourth story as your first.

(In addition, as the cost of living goes up—and, along with it, the value of your time and the cost of your overhead—you're entitled to further raises. But in magazine publishing that's such a radical idea that we'd be run out of the editor's office on a rail for even suggesting that writers begin to demand *that*.)

Don't expect to get any raise unless you ask for it, but don't suggest it as if it were outrageous or radical. If you sound unsure of yourself, you're inviting a turndown. In all our years of writing for a living, we've never lost an assignment from one of our regular markets for having asked for more money. We've often won the raise we said we deserved. And when we haven't, often as not we've left the editor feeling he ought to have a talk with the publisher about a bigger editorial budget.

In the area of money, the editor is rarely the ultimate culprit. His free-lance budget is passed down from the publisher's office. It is usually the tiniest slice of the cost of putting out the magazine, coming way behind printing and distribution costs, office overhead, and salaries. Publishers, who often know little about either editing or writing, usually think they could churn out their magazine single-handed if they had the time, and believe every writer is either independently wealthy or a moonlighter knocking out assignments as a break from a high-paying office job. As good businessmen, they raise their advertising rates and cover price to pay for printing hikes, paper hikes, postage hikes, and the office staff's cost-of-living increases. But they don't hike their free-lance budgets because there's little pressure from free lancers to do so. It's as simple as that!

Within the confines of editorial budgets, some editors make it a policy to pay a single set fee for all articles of a certain type. But others have flexible rates, paying more when they're forced to and less to writers who'll work for less. You won't know which policy prevails until you start asking for the additional money you deserve.

17·2 How Do You Find Out a Magazine's Rates?

In considering which markets to try to write for, it helps if you know in advance the approximate rate each of them pays. Of all the reference books we discussed in Chapter 4, only *Writer's Market* includes entries about fees. The less expensive annual, *Writer's Yearbook,* from the same publisher, also lists rates, but for fewer magazines. Information in both volumes is compiled from questionnaires returned by magazine editors, so each entry is as accurate or as misleading as the individual editor wants it to be.

Both *Writer's Digest* and *The Writer* magazines include information in their articles and columns. In general, fees listed there are fairly accurate for first articles published in low-end markets, but may be understated for regular contributors or experienced pros for work published in high-paying magazines.

Most of our own updated information about fees comes from other professional writers. In our get-togethers, we often trade rate information along with other professional tips. Our newsletter from the ASJA devotes several pages each month to an exchange of the latest magazine fees. It's just one important benefit of belonging to that organization of professional writers.

Another benefit of belonging to writers' organizations such as the ASJA, the travel writers' association, the business writers' association, the outdoors writers' association, and local clusters of professional and near-professional writers, is reinforcement: a feeling that you're not in this alone. It helps to hear how others have tackled problems you're facing today; it's encouraging to learn that old pros were greenhorns once; it's bolstering to know that your peers are pushing for more money too. (Names and addresses of writers' organizations are found in *Literary Market Place* and *Writer's Market.*)

In 1974, in a bold step forward, the ASJA developed and published a schedule of recommended minimum rates. It gave younger writers something to shoot for and older pros an established benchmark, and it alerted publishers that writers were becoming more assertive. Unfortunately, the New York State Attorney General's office decided that the schedule represented price fixing. (Don't we wish!) The ASJA agreed to stop recommending minimum rates, and has stopped publishing its recommendations. Fortunately, the schedule appeared once in an uncopyrighted publication so we can personally, without the blessing of the ASJA, share with you what professionals think their time, at bare minimum is worth. (Keep in mind that these minimums were developed in 1974. You need to add an average of 10 percent for every year since to cover cost-of-living increases.)

> *Presented as guidelines, as a basis for negotiating, the following are the minimum rates publishers should expect to pay and writers should expect to receive for professional work.*
>
> RECOMMENDED MINIMUM RATES FOR MAGAZINE ARTICLES
> *1) For trade publications, regional and Sunday magazines outside of the main metropolitan areas, and national magazines of special interest and/or low circulation.*
>
> > *Rate: 20c per word*
> *2) For national consumer magazines of under 3-million circulation. (This category includes national publications like* Harper's, Atlantic Monthly, N.Y. Times Magazine, *and* Family Health.)
>
> > *Rate: 50c per word*
> *3) For national consumer magazines of over 3-million circulation and for prestigious special publications. (This includes the major men's and women's magazines,* TV Guide, Reader's Digest *and other prestigious magazines of special interest, like* The New Yorker *and* National Geographic.)
>
> > *Rate: $1.00 per word*
> *Note: All rates are based on assigned length of article. Standard magazine articles run 2,500–3,000 words; shorts, 1,000–1,500 words. ASJA's policy has always been: payment on acceptance.*
>
> RECOMMENDED MINIMUM RATES ON A TIME BASIS
> *Daily:* $200, *plus expenses.*
> *Weekly:* $750, *plus expenses.*

The ASJA's new Membership Booklet contains a table of prevailing rates for free lance writing. It can be purchased from the American Society of Journalists and Authors, 1501 Broadway, Suite 1907, New York, N.Y. 10036. It is an interesting exercise to compare prevailing rates with the above suggested minimums.

17·3 Collecting Money

On days when we're particularly cynical and a young writer tells us, "I just sold an article to a magazine," we feel like answering, "Don't count on it until you can eat it." Having sold the article is all too often just the first step in a complicated ritual of collecting the money.

A great many young writers don't understand why a magazine that's part of a multibillion-dollar conglomerate should deliberately delay payment of a paltry sum for months and months. We'll explain. If a magazine owes a writer $500 for an article, and holds the money for three months longer in a savings account, it earns about $12.50 interest. That's hardly worthwhile. But multiply the saving by 100 magazine articles, 50 cartoons, 75 photographs, 6 tons of coated paper, 500 pounds of printer's ink, and 10 gross of pencils . . . *then* you start to see some conglomerate-sized earnings from nothing but slowing the outgoing part of the cash flow.

We don't know how U.S. Steel reacts when General Motors owes it several million dollars for months, but we know the frustration we feel when a multibillion-dollar publishing conglomerate owes us a thousand dollars that's long past due. Yet in all our years, we still haven't encountered any surefire magic for prying loose the money owed us any sooner than the company wants to let go of it—other than by constantly nagging the bookkeeper until she wants us off her back. If we nag the editor until *she* wants us off her back, we lose the market. (It actually happened to us with a notoriously slow paying magazine in the health field.)

We try to stay out of situations that threaten to involve delayed payments. When we first do business with a magazine, we inquire about the payment schedule. When we discuss fees, we emphasize that the rate is predicated on prompt payment. If we don't get our check on time—we consider roughly a month time enough—we remind the editor of the promise of quick pay. Sometimes we remind him more emphatically a week or two later. But that takes long-distance phone calls, and time away from our writing.

Before deciding how vigorously to go about collecting what's due you, you must answer two important questions on the magazine's behalf. (1) Did your article, as submitted, really deliver writing that was up to the magazine's standards? (2) Did it deliver what the query promised or the assignment letter demanded? If it didn't do both, it's going to require a rewrite, either by you or by the editor. Barring a formal agreement to the contrary, it's fair of the editor to expect the rewrite to be completed before the check is made out. On the other hand, it's equally fair for the editor to permit *you* the chance at the rewrite, and to get you started on it within a month.

In our experience, the need for a rewrite has been due more often to an editor's faulty communication of what he expects than to our out-and-out failure to deliver what we thought was expected. That's why we try to discuss our assignments with the editors before we begin writing. But even that's not foolproof.

There isn't much you can do, realistically, about collecting money from slow-paying magazines, though writers are sometimes driven to great lengths. One ASJA ex-member once flew all the way from his home in England to Indianapolis to collect a long overdue check. But that was because he was fighting mad and knew he could cover his trip expenses in the New World with other, more easily collected sales. Once, early in December, when half a dozen major publishers owed us altogether a fairly large sum of money—and some had owed it much too long—we designed a pre-Christmas card. We listed the money due, from whom, and for how long. We ended the card, "Merry Christmas?" and mailed copies to each of the editors on the list, all the presidents of their companies, and several publishing trade magazines. Before Christmas we'd collected every penny—and had also been blacklisted by two of the magazines, presumably because their publishers had suffered embarrassment. Interestingly, those were the two who'd held on to our money the longest.

Murray Teigh Bloom, who has headed the ASJA's writer-editor relations committee for many years, helps scores of writers resolve conflicts with editors, mostly over uncollected money. "Most of our complaints," Murray has found, "involve $300 or under pieces. Also, most of these complaints are directed against magazines the writer has not dealt with before. He's gotten a lead, someone may have told him the magazine is buying, and he makes some kind of negotiation." A lot of these assignments are for publishers just starting out or just holding their own at the bottom of the market.

Murray drives home his point by comparing the writing life to a cocktail party. What would you do, he asks, if you found a good listener there to whom you spewed all you knew about Alaska, and after ten minutes your new-found buddy said, "By the way, could you lend me three hundred bucks?" "You'd leave, naturally," Murray says. "But the writer confronted with the $300 assignment from a new magazine doesn't leave. He does the piece even though he really doesn't know anything about the person he's giving the $300 property to."

Having been forewarned, what should you do when *you're* faced with writing for a new publication? As a tenderfoot, it may happen to you often. Murray recommends, "The first time out with a new market, especially when there's $300 or less involved, it would be wise to ask for money up front, half the fee."

It's a rare magazine that has ever given a rookie writer part of the fee at the time an assignment is made. Although it's a logical—and needed—extension of the kill fee (discussed in 11.6), the advance on an article fee, although common in advertising, public relations, music, art, law, and other fields, is catching on only very slowly in writing. When you're just getting started, it's unlikely that you're able to negotiate for a kill fee, let alone money up-front. But you should be conversant with both concepts and begin to expect both kinds of payment just as swiftly as you can.

Early in our careers, we began as a matter of course to submit an invoice for the agreed-upon fee, (plus our expenses, if any) with every manuscript we mailed to an editor. We're in business, and submitting invoices is a businesslike way of showing that there's money due. Editors tell us they appreciate receiving invoices because it saves their having to make out vouchers to start the payment process. (We appreciate that, if it speeds up our checks.)

Our invoices borrow a concept from some merchandisers by offering a small discount for prompt payment and by demanding interest for payment made after thirty days:

2 percent discount ten days;
net thirty days;
1½ percent per month interest added after thirty days.

Only twice have editors complained about the discount and interest provisions, and neither of them was a problem payer anyway. Seldom are publishers well enough organized to get payments through within ten days, but if they do, they're welcome to the 2 percent; it's worth that to us financially and psychologically. After the thirty days expire, if we're the least bit anxious about payment, we photocopy our copy of the invoice, type in the interest that's accumulated, and mail it to the slow payer. It's one of the finest collection tools we've ever found.

If all else fails, you can sue. Sometimes just the threat of suit is sufficient. Most cities now have small-claims courts which writers have successfully used to collect money owed them. But as a rule, an action must be taken in the city where the magazine is published. So if they're in New York, the local Peoria small-claims court probably can't help you.

Unless you have a letter of assignment it's tough, although never impossible, to collect. So get each assignment in writing. If the editor gives it to you over the phone, ask him to confirm it by follow-up letter. If he doesn't, *you* should send the letter. Spell out what you understand the assignment to be, along with payment, deadline, kill fee, etc. End by saying, "Unless I hear otherwise, I'll understand that these are the terms of the assignment."

A number of magazines make collection nearby impossible by promising to pay for first rights on publication. It sounds like a fair arrangement for a publisher with limited resources, but think about the matter from the writer's viewpoint. You agree to offer a publisher your research and writing talents. In addition, since you promise first serial rights, you agree not to offer your article to any other magazine until the first one has published it. In return, that publisher agrees to *nothing,* except that if he should *ever* run the article, he will pay you for it. He may run it immediately, or it may simply sit in the file indefinitely—unprinted, unpaid-for, almost untouchable by you unless you've planned ahead.

We don't deal with publishers who pay on publication for first rights. (We don't even offer them *second* rights, since we feel that publishing a magazine at the writer's expense is unconscionable.) But if you feel you must, at the very least get an understanding in writing of the most distant acceptable publication date. If your work hasn't appeared in print by then, and you haven't been paid, you are free to offer it elsewhere.

"On spec" is another term loosely bandied about by editors. When the term lands in your court, you may be unable to collect what's due you for your work. "Spec" is short for "speculation." Technically, every assignment that doesn't include a kill fee provision is on spec. The editor may like your idea, believe you can write it up suitably, and expect to pay you when the job is done; if it turns out you can't write it up suitably, even after a rewrite, only a rare editor will pay for the useless sheaf of papers you've turned in.

Why, then, do some editors answer a query letter with a letter agreeing to read your suggested article on spec? It seems obvious that they intend to emphasize the degree of speculation. From the experience of young writers who've shared their heartbreaks with us after writing on spec, we conclude that on-spec assignments are made because the editors doubt that your article idea or your article-writing abilities will make it in their market but that, if you want to submit anyway, they'll read it. They may return it without comment, without payment.

Beginning writers often do have to write articles on speculative go-aheads. It's hard to expect financially strapped editors to take chances on unproven authors. On the other hand, while you're proving yourself, find out in advance how much speculation is expected of you. Then realistically assess whether the possible return is worth the probable investment.

17·4 Expenses

Traditionally, the fee agreed on for an article is payment for time spent creating the article. The magazine ought to pay for out-of-pocket expenses you incur doing research. Editors often feel it's a courtesy they should not extend to beginners, but they're more amenable to paying expenses than to promising kill fees.

Allowable expenses can include long-distance phone calls, travel to interviews, books, photocopies, and similar necessities. For big assignments, travel to distant places and hotel expenses are often covered. It's important that you discuss in advance the extent to which a magazine is willing to pay your expenses. Some have monetary limits; others limit the kinds of items they'll reimburse.

When you ask an editor to cover your expenses, you're not asking the magazine for a handout, so don't ever hesitate to raise the matter when talking money at the time you get an assignment. Like all the other terms, get it spelled out in writing in advance.

Once a magazine has agreed to pay for expenses, you are always expected to submit an itemized accounting with the manuscript (or shortly thereafter). Most magazines expect receipts to verify major items. (Send Xerox copies so your originals don't get lost on somebody's desk.)

17·5   Research, the Second R

This is the liability side of the writing ledger. If we could just sit at our typewriters all day and turn out page after page of magazine prose, our standard of living would rise astronomically. However, we must research to find salable ideas, sell them, and then research them more fully. Obviously, it pays to learn how to cut down research time. Chapter 12 suggested ways to make your research time more effective.

There's another economic consideration to keep in mind. Too many beginning writers sell an idea for what seems like a fair price and then discover that they miscalculated: the research time is overwhelming. When you're weighing the pros and cons of a particular idea, you must estimate how much research is demanded. If it seems to be a lot compared to the payment you can expect from its likely markets, you may have to scratch the idea. On the other hand, you may be able to think ahead about how to expand the expensive research into several article sales.

17·6   Recycling Research: Selling Reprints and Spin-offs

Most writers, we have found, think of their files full of research in terms too narrow to derive maximum income. Sometimes they think about selling reprint rights for the original article to lower-paying markets. Sometimes they think about reusing the research for an article with a different focus aimed at a lower-paying market. It's much more profitable to think, more generally, of recycling research.

SELLING REPRINTS

At the end of the recycling spectrum we place the selling of reprint rights. Simply selling the same story more than once is the most obvious, most direct, and often least time-consuming way to make second use of research. Peddling a tangible piece of property to more than one buyer is illegal, of course. But your writing is not tangible property. You're not selling the property, but the *right* for a magazine to *copy* your creation. You can sell that right repeatedly. In the last chapter we discussed at some length how to divide that right into many pieces, which rights you should and should not sell, and what those various rights mean to you under the U.S. copyright statute.

Let's assume that, as a pro, you sell only what is commonly called *first North American serial rights* to the first buyer of your article. This means simply that the magazine that "buys your story" actually buys only the right to be the first magazine (serial) to publish it. As soon as it has enjoyed that right—when your story has appeared between its covers—you can then sell *second publication rights,* often called *reprint rights,* to however many other magazines or newspapers you're lucky enough to interest in your article.

Julian Block, tax lawyer-cum-writer, does this all the time. For example, he recalled for us, "I did a 1,000-word article on how long to keep tax records in case the IRS audits your returns. I've sold that one at least sixteen times for payments ranging from $200 to $15." Julian simply mails a Xerox copy of his original manuscript with a short covering letter offering reprint rights and asking how much the editor will pay for the material. In his covering letter Julian explains that he will not sell reprint rights in his offered article to any competing magazine. So far, the tax records article has appeared in magazines for druggists, undertakers, dairy farmers, electrical contractors, people who manage warehouses, truck drivers, auto repair shop owners.

While it's true that Julian chalks up more reprint sales than anybody we know, many pros count on selling articles more than once. The rate a magazine pays for reprint rights is generally lower than its rate for first serial rights, but it's not always something to sneeze at. Judi sold a reprint of her $600 study-tips article (originally written for *Seventeen*) for $500 to *Nutshell,* for $250 to an Australian magazine, and for $150 for use in a textbook. One of our students sold her story about a new rescue tool to *Milwaukee Journal's Insight* magazine for $50, and sold its reprint to *Elks* for $200.

Magazines are not the only markets for reprints. Newspapers sometimes buy them, and educational book publishers make wide use of them for reading supplements and anthologies. Magazines and newspapers published outside the United States are good reprint markets for many pros. It's tough for United States-based writers to sell to most European, African, South African, and Asian publishers because of prohibitive postage costs. But a number of agencies specialize in marketing foreign rights to articles, and you'll find them listed in *Writer's Market* and *Literary Market Place.* Typically the agency takes up to 50 percent of whatever sales it generates, but since you invest very little of your money and time in a transaction, the split is usually worthwhile.

SELLING SPIN-OFFS

The spin-off relies on your file, crammed full of research notes from a completed story, as the basis of a similar story with a slightly different slant pegged to a magazine that doesn't compete with the first one. You probably don't have to do much, if any, new research for the second story. You do have to sell it and then write it. Both take time, but on stories that have required substantial research, it's time well spent.

How different do spin-off stories have to be? One of the nation's top magazine writers, Norman Lobsenz of Los Angeles, has sold many spin-offs in his long career. "For *Woman's Day,* I did an article on marital happiness: 'What Makes a Marriage Happy?' We were talking about the fact that people who are unhappy can tell you exactly why they're unhappy, and people who are happy rarely can. So by analyzing what unhappy people complain of, we looked into what presumably goes into a happy marriage. For *Modern Bride,* what I did was say, 'How Do You Know That Your Marriage Will Be Happy?' Here are what the experts say are the definitive aspects of marital happiness."

That wasn't much of a shift in emphasis. In fact, Norman adds, "A piece I might do for *Woman's Day* or *McCall's* can often be reslanted for a bridal magazine or for *Modern Maturity.* All I'd be doing is changing the age angle on it."

You may find that some parts of your first article fit neatly into the second article, as is. Can you copy them whole? Legally, the answer is almost always yes; after all, you have the same right to *fair use* of your material as any other writer. (See Chapter 16.) But from a practical perspective, some editors feel cheated if pieces of an article you sold them appear around the same time in an article you've sold to another magazine. The prudent approach, therefore, is to ask editor number one's blessing and to alert editor number two to the prior sale. Norman Lobsenz echoes, "It's not only vital to be scrupulously ethical, it's sensible because you don't want to antagonize a major market by incorrectly using something in a minor market." We've adhered to that policy, haven't been turned down, and find that editors appreciate our openness.

SELLING SIDETRACKS

Unlike some of our friends, we never hire college students to do our research. For one thing, we believe people don't catch all of a story's fine points unless they research it as well as write it. For another, while doing research for one story, we usually find leads to at least two new story angles, and a substantial part of the research we did for the first article fits nicely into the subject areas of stories number two and three. That saves our having to chalk up much research time on our figurative liabilities ledger for the two sidetrack articles. Less time outlay means more profit for us. It may sound crass, but without such down-to-earth considerations, we couldn't make it as free-lancers.

Beginning writers, we've found, hesitate to use any of the research referred to in story number one when preparing stories two and three. They believe that in buying the first article, the publisher has bought the research time and its fruits. This just isn't true. Even if you sold "all rights," all you've sold is the right to publish the *words* in your article. Unused information remains your intellectual property, whether it's in your head or in your file of notes. And published information is in the public domain, there to be used at will by anybody, since *information* cannot be copyrighted, only words.

SELLING EXPERTISE

Our final way of recycling research is a Chinese-restaurant approach. Writers tend to concentrate on one or several areas of interest. In those areas, their continual research eventually makes them experts to some degree. Within the confines of their expertise, each new story sold can draw two pages of notes from column A, three pages of concepts from column B, and, to complete the article, a column C of new research that updates the subject. Such an approach cuts research time substantially.

Some free-lancers make their marks primarily in one or two areas of specialized interest—Julian Block in taxes, Normal Lobsenz in marriage life-styles, Suzanne Loebl in medicine, Hal Higdon in sports, Lee Edson in science, Mark Sosin in the outdoors. Other free-lancers, like us, think of themselves as generalists. Writing about whatever suits our shifting fancies has led to our being considered medical specialists at *McCall's,* education specialists at *Seventeen,* popular psychology specialists at *Playgirl,* obesity specialists at *Weight Watchers,* home improvement specialists at *Popular Science,* and life-styles specialists at *Physician's Management*—although we've written about the law, science, movie stars, government, and how to catch fish.

We find ourselves labeled specialists by serendipity, because fair-paying magazines expect a certain amount of expertise from their writers. If you sell and deliver a well-researched article on any particular subject, you almost immediately acquire a reputation with that magazine—and its competitors—as an expert in that field. There's one subject that, frankly, we're tired of writing about, but because we're considered expert, the assignments keep coming in—and the steady income gives us freedom to investigate new subjects for specialization.

17·7 The *Big* R: Reality

Magazine writing can be as glittery and glamorous as any profession this side of Hollywood. It's a sure ego boost to appear on television sagely discussing the fine points of your latest article. And the head swells measurably every time a trade association bestows its annual gold-plated journalism award on you for, without cost to it, promoting its cause. But glitter sticks to the teeth when you try to ingest it, and glamour doesn't cook up well in a pot with vegetables. Landlords don't take by-lines in lieu of rent. Children have trouble enjoying Mommy on TV with holes in their sneakers. Next year, all those plastic-encapsuled awards will be just more knickknacks to dust.

At the beginning of this book we quoted Alex Haley: "It is at least as difficult to become a writer as a surgeon." By now you're probably convinced of that. But there's a subtler aspect to Alex's comparison. As magazine writers, we take the lives of our readers into our own hands every time we touch our typewriter keys. We advise them about life and love, explain death and health, counsel on diets and exercise, help raise their children, offer comfort to their parents. We teach them to connect homemade lighting fixtures onto potentially deadly wires without harming themselves or the fixtures. We send them into their gardens, onto their roofs, into strange and distant lands. If we've learned our craft, remembered our ethics, adhered to our sense of responsibility, the readers come away happier, healthier, wealthier, and wiser. But if we slip up, we cause mayhem—not only to readers but to magazines that depend on our articles to sell their advertising pages.

Yet publishers who wouldn't think of striking bargains with the white-frocked surgeons about to operate on them, daily invent schemes for bargaining down the demands of writers. We're not sure which is more unconscionable, publishers who train their editors to swivel in their Eames chairs and cry poverty, or writers who swivel in their Salvation Army castoffs and do the same.

The reality of writing as a profession is that you need money to stay alive. You need enough income so you and your kids can lead a middle-class existence like the readers you write for. You need money to cover your own medical plans and your own Social Security. You need cash in the bank to tide you over the months when every expert you need to talk to is out of town and every editor you know has gotten up on the wrong side of the bed. You need *assets* to plunge recklessly into farfetched research (as Betty Freidan did on her own time and money) that may result in not just a magazine story but in a book like *The Feminine Mystique* and maybe an entire movement.

Some people might say we're ending on a soapbox, advocating a writers' revolution. Others, using the pop psychology jargon of the day, might say we're raising consciousness. The way we see it, we're just letting you know that there's more to being a pro than learning your craft. You also have to learn your worth, and then communicate that to the editors with whom you do business.

INDEX

257